# CELEBRATING THE NATION

**Other titles in the Australian Cultural Studies Series**

**Australian Television**
*Programs, pleasure and politics*
Edited by John Tulloch and Graeme Turner

**Dark Side of the Dream**
*Australian literature and the postcolonial mind*
Bob Hodge and Vijay Mishra

**Fashioning the Feminine**
*Girls, popular culture and schooling*
Pam Gilbert and Sandra Taylor

**Featuring Australia**
*The cinema of Charles Chauvel*
Stuart Cunningham

**Framing Culture**
*Criticism and policy in Australia*
Stuart Cunningham

**From Pop to Punk to Postmodernism**
*Popular music and Australian culture from the 1960s to the 1990s*
Edited by Philip Hayward

**Myths of Oz**
*Reading Australian popular culture*
John Fiske, Bob Hodge and Graeme Turner

**National Fictions**
*Literature, film and the construction of Australian narrative*
Graeme Turner

**Resorting to Tourism**
*Cultural policies for tourist development in Australia*
Jennifer Craik

**Australian Cultural Studies**
*Editor: John Tulloch*

# CELEBRATING THE NATION

*A critical study of Australia's Bicentenary*

Edited by Tony Bennett, Pat Buckridge, David Carter and Colin Mercer

Routledge
Taylor & Francis Group
LONDON AND NEW YORK

First published 1992 by Allen & Unwin

Published 2020 by Routledge
2 Park Square, Milton Park, Abingdon, Oxon OX14 4RN
605 Third Avenue, New York, NY 10017

*Routledge is an imprint of the Taylor & Francis Group, an informa business*

National Library of Australia
Cataloguing-in-Publication entry:

Celebrating the nation: a critical study of Australiais bicentenary.

　Bibliography.
　Includes index.
　ISBN 1 86373 213 6.

　1. Australian Bicentary, 1988. 2. AustraliaÛCentennial
　celebrations, etc. I. Bennett, Tony, 1947Û.

　994.063

Set in 10/11pt Times by Docupro, Sydney

ISBN-13: 9781863732130 (pbk)

# General editor's foreword

Nowadays the social and anthropological definition of 'culture' is probably gaining as much public currency as the aesthetic one. Particularly in Australia, politicians are liable to speak of the vital need for a domestic film industry in 'promoting our cultural identity'—and they mean by 'cultural identity' some sense of Australianness, of our nationalism as a distinct form of social organisation. Notably, though, the emphasis tends to be on Australian *film* (not popular television); and not just *any* film, but those of 'quality'. So the aesthetic definition tends to be smuggled back in—on top of the kind of cultural nationalism which assumes that 'Australia' is a unified entity with certain essential features that distinguish it from 'Britain', the 'USA' or any other national entities which threaten us with 'cultural dependency'.

This series is titled 'Australian Cultural Studies', and I should say at the outset that my understanding of 'Australian' is not as an essentially unified category; and further, that my understanding of culture is anthropological rather than aesthetic. By 'culture' I mean the social production of meaning and understanding, whether in the interpersonal and practical organisation of daily routines or in broader institutional and ideological structures. I am *not* thinking of 'culture' as some form of universal 'excellence', based on aesthetic 'discrimination' and embodied in a pantheon of 'great works'. Rather, I take this aesthetic definition of culture itself to be part of the *social mobilisation of discourse* to differentiate a cultural 'élite' from the 'mass' of society.

Unlike the cultural nationalism of our opinion leaders, 'Cultural Studies' focuses not on the essential unity of national cultures, but on the meanings attached to social difference (as in the distinction between 'élite' and 'mass' taste). It analyses the construction and mobilisation of these distinctions to maintain or challenge existing power differentials, such as those of gender, class, age, race and ethnicity. In this analysis, terms designed to socially differentiate people (like 'élite' and 'mass') become categories of discourse, communication and power. Hence our concern in this series is for an analytical understanding of the meanings attached to social difference within the *history* and *politics* of discourse.

It follows that the analysis of 'texts' needs to be set free from a single-minded association with 'high' culture (marked by 'authorship') to include the 'popular' too—since these distinctions of 'high' and 'popular' culture themselves need to be analysed, not assumed.

*Celebrating the Nation*, typifies this cultural studies approach, analysing for instance institutional practices as different as literary criticism and soccer, yet with a similar critical project in these 'high' and 'popular' culture domains. Thus, Pat Buckridge, analysing the Australian literary canon, examines the way that the *Penguin New Literary History of Australia* 'consensualises' Australian culture, with 'social, political and regional oppositions and hierarchies all subsumed in general reconciliation under the sign of the conjunction of high and popular culture.' In particular this effaces an actual dualism in the organisation of the Australian literary canon 'which is secured by its function in the reproduction of class-differentiated skills and knowledge.' Similarly—though dealing with ethnic rather than class difference—Toby Miller describes attempts to efface the markers which profile soccer as 'ethnic' and Other, replacing this with the consensus of 'Australianisation' in a search 'for ultimate signifieds of unity and singularity.' This book examines the various celebratory styles of that search for the cultural consensus of 'Australianness' in the rhetorics of 1988. Yet, as Tony Bennett argues, this consensualising rhetoric was always in tension with other discourses, gesturing externally towards post-nationalism, and internally to the repressed 'deep' time of Australia's Aboriginal peoples.

Culture, as Fiske, Hodge and Turner say in *Myths of Oz*, grows out of the divisions of society, not its unity. 'It has to work to construct any unity that it has, rather than simply celebrate an achieved or natural harmony.' Australian culture is then no more than the temporary, embattled construction of 'unity' at any particular historical moment. The 'readings' in this series of 'Australian Cultural Studies' inevitably (and polemically) form part of the struggle to make and break the boundaries of meaning which, in conflict and collusion, dynamically define our culture.

JOHN TULLOCH

# Contents

# Acknowledgements

Much of the work for this study was made possible through the support of a Griffith University Research Grant. The editors and the contributors who benefited from this support would therefore like to thank the University for its generous assistance in this matter. Our thanks, too, to the Research Assistants who, at different times, assisted us in the collection, collation and interpretation of the considerable archive of research materials this project has drawn upon. Barbara Ramadge Ross, Joy Doherty, Barbara Johnstone and Bronwyn Hammond all served the project excellently in those ways. Our work also benefited from the administrative support of the Institute for Cultural Policy Studies. Our thanks, therefore, to Sharon Clifford, Glenda Donovan, Bev Jeppeson and Robyn Pratten. Without the expert stenographic services of Olwen Schubert, Karen Yarrow and Janice Mitchell our ideas would never have seen the light of day. Critical studies, finally, need cooperative objects of analysis. Our thanks, therefore, to the Australian Bicentennial Authority and other Bicentennial organisations and events which lent us their assistance.

Most of the chapters comprising this book are published here for the first time. Two, however, were first published elsewhere. Tony Bennett's 'The Shaping of Things to Come: Expo 88' was first published in *Cultural Studies* 5 (1), 1991. Peter Cochrane's and David Goodman's 'The Great Australian Journey: Cultural Logic and Nationalism in the Postmodern Era' is excerpted from a longer study first published, under the same title, in *Australian Historical Studies* 23 (91), October 1988. We are grateful to the editors of both journals for their permission to reprint these articles here.

# Acronyms

| | |
|---|---|
| ABA | Australian Bicentennial Authority |
| ABC | Australian Broadcasting Corporation |
| ABE | Australian Bicentennial Exhibition |
| ARBA | American Revolution Bicentennial Authority |
| ARBC | American Revolution Bicentennial Commission |
| ASA | Australian Society of Authors |
| ASF | Australian Soccer Federation |
| *ASW* | *Australian Soccer Weekly* |
| BESBRA | Brisbane Exposition South Bank Redevelopment Authority |
| BIE | Bureau International des Expositions |
| CBD | central business district |
| CCC | Canadian Centenary Commission |
| EEC | European Economic Community |
| IPA | Institute of Public Affairs |
| NSL | National Soccer League |
| SBC | South Bank Corporation (Queensland) |
| WASP | white Anglo-Saxon Protestant |
| WEP | World Expo Park (Queensland) |

# Notes on contributors

**Tony Bennett** is presently Dean of the Division of Humanities at Griffith University. His publications include *Formalism and Marxism, Bond and Beyond: The Political Career of a Popular Hero* (with Janet Woollacott) and *Outside Literature.* He is at present compiling a study of museums to be published under the title *Show and Tell: The Museum, the Fair and the Exhibition.*

**Pat Buckridge** teaches in the School of Australian and Comparative Studies at Griffith University. He has written on the politics of Australian literature and literary studies.

**David Carter** teaches in the School of Australian and Comparative Studies at Griffith University. He is the editor of *Outside the Book: Contemporary Essays on Literary Periodicals* and *Images of Australia: An Introductory Reader in Australian Studies.*

**Peter Cochrane** teaches History at Sydney University. He has published in numerous areas including economics and labour history, political economy, military history and social history. He writes occasional features for the *Age, Sydney Morning Herald* and the *Canberra Times.* His forthcoming book is *The Legend of the Man with the Donkey: A Little Epic.*

**Jennifer Craik** teaches Media and Cultural Policy in the Division of Humanities at Griffith University. She has published *Resorting to Tourism* and is writing a book on fashion.

**Jane Crisp** has teaching and research interests, and publications in the areas of film and media studies, and popular fiction. She is currently a lecturer in the Division of Humanities at Griffith University.

**David Goodman** teaches Australian Studies at the University of Melbourne, and is interested in the cultural history of colonial Australia.

**John Hutchinson** teaches in the Division of Humanities at Griffith University. His publications include *The Dynamics of Cultural Nation-*

*alism* (Allen and Unwin, 1987), and he is currently completing a short study, *Modern Nationalism.*

**Colin Mercer** teaches in the School of Cultural and Historical Studies at Griffith University. He is the Director of the Institute for Cultural Policy Studies.

**Toby Miller** teaches Communication Studies at Murdoch University and is a weekly commentator on popular culture for ABC Radio in Perth. He has previously worked at Griffith University and the University of New South Wales as well as in the service of the government.

**Robin Trotter** is a postgraduate student at Griffith University researching in the area of museums.

# Introduction: national times

*Tony Bennett*

Few passages in the *Bulletin* have proved more enduringly citable than that from the editorial of 26 January 1888 in which New South Wales is castigated for hollering 'with an empty and artificial glee in honour of the hundredth anniversary of the day she was lagged'. James Edmond's anti-imperialist intent is made clear enough when he goes on to remark that 'the occasion for which we are called upon to rejoice with an exceeding great joy' is 'the day when the festering vileness of England was first cast ashore to putrefy upon the coasts of New South Wales' and proposes, as a more appropriate occasion for national celebration, the anniversary of the Eureka rebellion: 'the day that Australia set her teeth in the face of the British Lion'.

Yet it is equally important to note that, for the *Bulletin*, 1888 seemed premature for *any* kind of national celebration. As the editorial unfolds it is less the maladroitness of the symbolism of 26 January that engages Edmond than the perception that the century since settlement had been, from a nationalist point of view, empty time—time not yet marked by any deeds or events judged worthy of national commemoration. Taking the recently concluded centenary of American independence as his point of comparison—celebrations, he argues, held 'not on account of an empty flight of years, which pass alike for man and beast, for the noble and the ignoble, the slave and the freeman, but in honour of the triumph of liberty over grasping tyranny'—Edmond sees the celebrations of 1888 as celebrating nothing but the passage of time itself:

> And yet the childish, frothy, boastful celebration so carefully worked up by the pitiable politicians of New South Wales is based almost entirely on the fact that a hundred summers have shone on the new community planted in the great lone continent—that Time has rolled onward with all nations since the world was young; and the banners wave and the fireworks blaze because the sun and moon have not stood still for PARKES as they did for JOSHUA.

The centennial editorials of the major state and regional papers struck a different note, of course, yet one which confirmed this aspect of the *Bulletin's* diagnosis. For, in summarising the eventfulness of the past one hundred years, it was their place within a colonial, imperial or racial time that was emphasised rather than any sense of their forming part of a specifically Australian temporality. As a consequence, the nation was placed curiously outside of time. Neither marking, nor marked by, time's passage, Australia was consequently exiled from the centre of the discourses in which, ostensibly, it was celebrated. While the *Newcastle Morning Herald and Miners' Advocate* thus had no doubt that the time of the nation was destined soon to arrive, it was equally adamant that such a time had not yet come and, urging that 'it is vain to strain the mental vision in an attempt to look beyond the horizon which is the limit of a man's life,' saw no point in trying to anticipate the form the nation might assume when it arrived at its beckoning rendezvous with itself. The *Age*, disclaiming any full title to participate in the celebrations ('because, in point of fact, we are not a hundred years old, and do not enjoy the privilege of tracing our *genus et proavos* [birth and ancestry] to the sturdy thieves and beggars who were landed on the shores of Sydney Cove when George the Third was King'), proposed spatial and temporal horizons for the celebrations that were metropolitan and imperialist in their associations. Projecting a distant future in which Melbourne would attain the contemporary status of Thebes—the site of a glorious past of interest only to archaeologists—the interim period is envisaged as one in which the colonies will combine to form a United States of Australia. The conception of this federation as 'the Greater Britain of the South', however, is clearly imperialist rather than nationalist, and it is certainly not republican!

The *Argus*, similarly, was in no doubt that: 'In 1988 the Empire will be, and it will be Peace'. It was equally in no doubt that it would be white, and offered an account of the continent's development in which progress was measured by a projected increase in the whiteness of the population. 'A glance at the leading daily papers of the capitals,' it thus opined, 'is an easy way of realising the stage now reached by the Australia which a hundred years ago was the home of a few prowling blacks.' As to the future, this was predicted in unusually confident terms:

> The social future also has no wavering or misty prospects. The fiat has gone forth that Australia is to be a 'white man's' country. The troubles brought upon America by the introduction of an inferior race are not to occur here.

This was not, however, an early anticipation of the White Australia policy. The future which beckoned was not that of an autonomous national people but that of a race whose constitution and mission were transnational in their conception:

> We have the spectacle now of the world being largely governed and influenced by the British race from two little islands in the German Ocean; but in Australia we have an island continent—little less in area than the whole of Europe—reserved for this active, indomitable and ruling people.

In brief, whether their tone was celebratory or anti-celebratory,

Australia was scarcely visible within the rhetorics which organised the major newspaper editorials on Anniversary Day 1888. Ambiguously installed between competing times, the moment marked by 26 January 1888 was one characterised by the tension between a fledgling national time that had not yet properly begun to run its own course and a racial–imperial time that had not yet passed. Australia could not, in Benedict Anderson's terms, be imagined as a community moving through a homogeneous time nationalised by its own passage because of the countervailing weight of both sub-national (state) and supra-national (racial and imperial) imagined communities.[1]

Much the same was true of the manner in which the celebrations were conceived, conducted and participated in—or not. This is not merely a matter of observing that, outside coastal New South Wales, participation in the celebrations was thin and sporadic or, in the case of Adelaide, non-existent. Nor is it simply to observe the extent to which rivalries between states undid any putative pretensions to national unity, as was the case with Melbourne's upstaging of Sydney in holding the International Exhibition the New South Wales government had publicly rejected as too costly. Rather, and overshadowing these considerations, the very conception of the celebrations, of their purpose and what they were to be celebrations of, lent to them a texture and density that was only thinly nationalised.

Under the influence of Parkes's conception, the celebrations were thus limited to a week and organised to commemorate the establishment of British rule in Australia rather than to mark the foundation of a nation.[2] Their historical tilt, accordingly, led back beyond the embarrassment of convict origins to locate the continent within a British-centred project of discovery, settlement and development. One consequence of this was the emergence of Cook and not Phillip as the central hero of the celebrations, but Cook conceived as an *English*, not an Australian, hero.[3] Perhaps more important, however, the imposition of this thematic constraint on the celebrations prevented post-settlement history being linked to a moment of foundation so as to construct the rudiments of a narrative for a nation developing through time. True, the theme of 'how far we have come since then' was repeated endlessly, but the 'we' here was British not Australian and the measures of its advance were typically offered in the form of nationally neutral indicators of capitalist development: the number of acres under plough, the amount of wool and coal exported—Australia playing its role in the imperial scheme of things.

It would, then, be a mistake to view the celebrations which took place in January 1888 as a national centenary. The conditions of existence for such an event were not then sufficiently developed. The emergence of a nation as a thinkable entity, Nicos Poulantzas has suggested, requires the establishment of the 'historicity of a territory and the territorialisation of a history'—and not just the one and then the other but the two, simultaneously and in relation to one another.[4] In allowing a territory to become nationalised by imbuing it with a particular history while also allowing that history, through its anchorage to that territory, to itself be nationalised, these interacting processes jointly construct the image of a people–nation, a territorially bounded subject seemingly fashioned by a common history. That such a people–nation was not, on the whole, envisaged or addressed in 1888 was because the time of the post-settlement/invasion period and the space comprised by the different colonies occupying the continent of Australia were mapped onto one another within another set of time–space coordinates supplied by the history of the 'British race' and the near global reach of its imperial dominion.

Whether or not the same can be said of the 1938 sesquicentenary celebrations is a moot point. The balance of opinion, however, suggests that these were still proto-nationalist in both organisation and conception. The program of events was determined by a Celebrations Council established by the New South Wales government with little attempt to involve other states in that program or to coordinate activities with them. There was, accordingly, little participation in the celebrations outside New South Wales and, even there, not too much participation outside Sydney. Moreover, many aspects of the celebrations were, it seems, arranged with interstate rivalries primarily in mind. The centrality accorded to Phillip in an Australia Day re-enactment of the landing at Sydney Cove was thus intended very much as one in the eye for Melbourne which, in celebration of its own centenary in 1934, had constructed Cook's childhood home in the Fitzroy Gardens.[5]

More important, perhaps, was the fact that Phillip was scripted to retread the boards of history more as an emissary Englishman than as an incoming Australian. Arriving, it would seem, virtually unaccompanied—for at both the re-enactment and the subsequent March to Nationhood through Sydney, the convict portion of the First Fleet was officially deemed to have been absent from the moment of the penal colony's foundation—the historical record was adjusted to allow him to claim Australia as 'the most valuable acquisition Great Britain had ever made'. In this respect, as Julian Thomas has convincingly argued, the central, coordinating celebratory rhetoric of 1938, governing the conception of films such as *A Nation is Built*, was one which, in telling the story of Australia's subsequent development as the realisation of the vision of a founding patriarch, yoked the nation back to its pre-national origins in an imperialist project.[6]

By contrast, there can be little doubt that 1988 was, as the jingle had it, the Celebration of a Nation, thus comprising perhaps the first such occasion when Australia, as nation, was rhetorically present at its own celebration. Conceived, like all such celebrations, as a moment for compiling an inventory of the nation's accomplishments, the main accent was placed on displaying the Australian people to themselves in all their multicultural diversity. Informal, participatory and inclusive, the atmospherics the Bicentennial organisers sought to produce were those of the festival. For Jim Kirk, Chairman of the Australian Bicentennial Authority, the aim was 'to host a year-long national party for every man, woman and child' so as to exhibit to ourselves 'the richness, freedom and diversity of a cosmopolitan country composed of the peoples of more than 100 societies, from Aborigines to immigrants'.[7] *Australia Live*, the multimedia extravaganza which kicked off the year, was similarly described as 'a multi-network command performance by an entire population at work, rest and play, a live, spontaneous celebration of the national spirit showing the unpretentious way we are'.[8]

Yet if the celebrations of 1988 were thus more clearly nationalist than their precursors, they were not unequivocally so. Indeed, it seemed, in the judgement of some, that Australia's arrival at a point of national celebratory possession of itself had come almost too late. Australia's beckoning insertion into the wider geopolitical community of the Asia–Pacific region combined with the putatively post-nationalist flavour of much postmodernist culture and criticism was thus interpreted as representing new international horizons of time and space which made the very conception of a festival intended to mark the passage of national time appear outmoded.[9] While this is probably putting the point too strongly, the celebratory styles and rhetorics of 1988 were undoubtedly marked by a tension between, on the one hand, the need to fashion a distinctively national time, and, on the other, the equally pressing imperative—if that national time were not to seem already outmoded—to dovetail it with the transnational time of the postmodern.

Nor was this the only source of discursive tension that had to be negotiated in claiming 1988 for the nation. In his influential study of the origins and development of nationalism, Benedict Anderson refers to the struggles of the indigenous populations of colonised territories as 'the last wave' of nationalism. Yet this overlooks the case of 'settler societies' like Australia and Canada where nationalist discourse is more typically obliged to override the conflicting prior loyalties and bonds of imaginary solidarity of different immigrant populations, as well as the conflict between all these and the claims to autonomy of the indigenous population, in order to establish a ground for its own operation. Indeed, it is in the discursive eddies and cross-currents produced by its attempts to negotiate these different tensions that 1988 throws into relief some of the conditions nationalist discourses require and the ways in which they meet them. For, long before the year arrived, it was clear that its celebratory rhetorics would be caught in a pincer between an external time that gestured beyond nationalism and an internal time, the ancient 'deep time' of Australia's Aboriginal peoples, that preceded and resisted incorporation within the particular version of national time that the Bicentenary constructed.

Our concern in this study is precisely with these eddies and cross-currents, and with what they have to tell us about where Australia and its representations are heading. We have thus not attempted to write the history of the Bicentenary. Nor have we sought to deal comprehensively with Bicentennial events and programs. Rather, and in line with a concept that was in vogue at the time, we have opted for a 'slice of life' approach in that each of the chapters deals with a specific aspect of the Bicentenary (sometimes in comparison with other national celebrations) with a view to highlighting some of the distinctive qualities—of style, rhetoric and politics—that marked the passage of 1988.

While our interests focus mainly on official views about what the Bicentenary was or should have been about, this should not be taken to imply that these were the only voices of 1988. In her study of the genesis of modern national festivals in (where else?) revolutionary France, Mona Ozouf diagnoses the central contradiction of such celebrations. Conceived, ideally, as a means of rebaptising individuals as citizens and so strengthening the bonds of empathy through which a sense of common national belonging is organised, the national festival was envisaged—again, ideally—as a spontaneous event which would result in 'the mingling of citizens delighting in the spectacle of one another and the perfect accord of their hearts'.[10] Yet, as Ozouf argues, while the purpose of such festivals 'was to bring together the entire community . . . they never ceased to exclude some people and to engender pariahs'.[11]

In marked contrast to the celebrations of 1888 and 1938, the Bicentennial conception of the nation was one that included, or desperately sought to include, Australia's Aboriginal peoples. This invitation, however, was refused in a year-long program of non-participation and protest that proved by far and away the most significant source of opposition to the Bicentenary which, at the same time, transformed 1988 into an occasion for something else: the celebration of survival against the odds. In his classic essay, written more than a century ago, Ernest Renan drew attention to the role of forgetting in organising a sense of shared nationhood:

> Yet the essence of a nation is that all individuals have many things in common, and also that they have forgotten many things. No French citizen knows whether he is a Burgundian, an Alan, a Taifale, or a Visigoth, yet every French citizen has to have forgotten the massacre of Saint Bartholomew, or the massacres that took place in the Midi, in the thirteenth century.[12]

In their stance toward 1988—40 000 years don't make a bicentenary—the organisers of the Aboriginal Bicentennial boycott displayed a commitment to a form of political remembering which, in its demonstration that white Australia has a black history, ought not to be forgotten.

# PART I

# A time and a place

# 1

# State festivals, foundation myths and cultural politics in immigrant nations

*John Hutchinson*

During the early critical years of the French Revolution, republicans inspired by examples from ancient Greece and Rome instituted a series of commemorative festivals to arouse 'a love of the fatherland' and of popular liberty by, in the words of Chénier, 'sowing great memories throughout the year and [making] all our civic festivals an annual and commemorative history of the French Revolution'.[1] Thus was the state festival invented as a rite of national regeneration. Since then most states have periodically sponsored such festivals, either of a 'spontaneous' or organised character.

In this chapter I examine the commemorative festivals of three countries which in the last 25 years have celebrated their birth as national communities: Canada in 1967, the centenary of its establishment of a federal state; the United States (US) in 1976, the Bicentenary of the Declaration of Independence; and Australia in 1988, the Bicentenary of its settlement by Europeans. Although there were important differences between these societies, they have three striking features in common. Firstly, although there had been earlier commemorations of the national founding in both Australia and the US, they were the first officially organised, territory-wide commemorations of the nation's founding staged by these countries. Secondly, they were products of liberal–democratic federal societies established by European colonists and shaped largely by a British heritage. Thirdly, they were festivals of settler societies which had become (in Anthony Smith's schema) 'immigrant nations'. By this term Smith refers to 'new world' societies, founded by colonists from (in most cases) a single ethnic core who, dispossessing the indigenous inhabitants, establish an independent state and later admit waves of migrants from many ethnic backgrounds, seeking to absorb them through equal citizenship rights. Thereby, an ethnic is transformed into a multicultural territorial political community.[2]

As I shall show, these official festivals represented ambitious and selfconscious experiments in nation-building, extending over a year and involving a considerable public investment, both in terms of money and planning time over several years, in countries whose federal character and multi-ethnic population created analogous problems of securing cohesion.[3] To resolve these problems the festival planners constructed roughly similar formats and themes but, despite this, they generated distinctive sets of controversies which extended several years beyond their initial planning stage to the commemorative year itself.

The study of such festivals reveals three things. Firstly, governments in such societies possess only limited capacities to engage in explicit programs of nation-building. Secondly, even in 'immigrant nations', supposedly more tolerant of multicultural diversity, ethnicity underpins foundation myths and the distribution of power and poses major problems for social cohesion. Thirdly, such nations, as new world societies, are marked by distinctive 'status anxieties', formulated in a language of maturation, that require them to assess periodically their progress through time and to construct landmarks as galvanisers of future action.

### Common aspects of the three festivals

*Communitarian structure*

Despite their status as state events, the festivals had a similar communitarian ethos and structure that derived from the liberal–democratic and federal characteristics of their societies. This was exemplified in several ways. Firstly, the drive to have celebrations came from outside the federal government. In Canada, businesspeople influenced the decision of the government in 1959 to stage official celebrations. In the US, long before the government's commitment in 1966, Philadelphian municipal representatives developed plans in 1956 for an International Exposition and lobbied President Kennedy as early as 1963; Bicentenary commissions were established in Massachusetts (1964) and Virginia (1966), two of the original thirteen colonies.[4] In Australia, the government's announcement in 1978 was preceded by the agenda of social visionaries such as Donald Horne.

Secondly, the planning agencies themselves—the Canadian Centennial Commission (CCC), the American Revolution Bicentennial Commission (ARBC), and the Australian Bicentennial Authority (ABA) —were established by the government in a bipartisan spirit, given quasi-autonomous status (although appointments were made by the President or Prime Minister), and organised on a federal basis. These agencies each emphasised that the occasion was not 'a party put on by the government' but a celebration of the people, and they articulated their role as catalysts rather than definers of the event. In order to achieve maximum participation at the community level, they presented a 'horizontal' view of group status: all had equal rights in the celebrations.

Thirdly, in keeping with this communitarian ethos, the agencies confined their role as project initiators of a few central events, especially those based on the nation's 'birthday'. They relied heavily on state/provincial and municipal energies and also on private initiatives, for example coordination with voluntary organisations, notably in Canada with the Canadian Centenary Council, a body of business and professional people. Similarly, there was an emphasis on obtaining sponsorship from the business community, as is evident from the key appointments to the agencies and their funding. Fisher, Chief Commissioner of the CCC, had been Executive Director of the Canadian Tourist Association; Daniel J. Mahoney, Chairman of the ARBC (1970–74), had been Chief Executive Officer of Norton Simon Inc.; John Reid, Chair of the ABA (1979–85), had been Chairman of the James Hardie group.

Fourthly, although the agencies sponsored 'high culture' initiatives of a permanent and temporary character, including national archives, cultural centres, historical and science museums and so forth, there was a special effort to ensure popular interest in the commemorative year by the inclusion of mass sporting events (e.g. in Canada, the Winter Olympics and the first Pan-American games), the provision of leisure and sporting facilities, popular concerts and spectacles.

*Common themes: new world experiment, ethnic diversity, conquest of distance*

Although the content of founding myths of the countries varied, each festival celebrated three major themes: the nation as unique new world experiment as yet unfinished and oriented to the future; as exemplary multi-ethnic collaboration; as representing the triumph of human will (through politics and technology) over continental nature. Political symbols and ceremonies celebrating the 'success' of the liberal–democratic federation were central. In the US, the Declaration of Independence, the Constitution, and the Liberty Bell were highlighted; in Canada, the historic voyage of the Fathers of Confederation from Quebec to Charlottetown of 1864 was re-enacted; and in Australia, a new Parliament House was opened by the Queen. But perhaps the major theme of the commemorative year was that of the nation as heroic journey undertaken by different waves of pioneers. In particular the role of technology and communications in creating a nation, uniting territories and peoples was central: the Tall Ships parades in both the US and Australian Bicentenaries, celebrating multi-ethnic origins; the Canadian Confederation Train Exhibition, travelling on the Canadian Pacific Railway which, by linking western and eastern provinces on its completion in 1871, helped make federation practical; the Conestoga wagons and prairie schooners re-enacting in reverse the conquest of the western frontier in a two-year journey across all 48 states of continental USA; the Australian Travelling Exhibition, which portrayed the theme of Australia as the product of three migrations.

In their mobility, these exhibitions embodied the theme of the nation as a continuing voyage of discovery and triumph over distance. President Ford's address on 4 July 1976 to the Conestoga wagons at Valley Forge linked futurist and transethnic themes to those of the frontier in referring to his country as: '. . . at the beginning of a continuing adventure [the] US remains today the most successful realisation of humanity's universal hope. The world may or may not follow, but we lead because our whole history says we must.'[5]

*Controversies and receptions*

A third distinctive feature is that from their early planning stage, in spite of their communitarian–participatory format, the celebrations generated a series of prolonged controversies over several years that went far beyond a discussion of the commemorative moment to engage in prolonged critical reflections on the entire past, present and future of the national community. These debates were at first intermittent, confined to the elite (opinion-forming) level, and usually obscured by the 'foreground' of 'normal' politics; but they grew in resonance as public interest rose with the approaching year and largely shaped the final definition of the occasion and its reception.

Although different views of the occasion were canvassed even before the official launches, controversy began only after the planning agencies began to formulate themes. This provoked four sets of overlapping controversies: the financial and technical competences of the agencies; the respective weight given the states or provinces; the ideological agenda promoted; and the national vision presented, including the place given within it to non-dominant ethnic and indigenous peoples. In all three countries there were recurring anxieties expressed by governments and the public about the pace of planning and its financial management. This led in the US to the replacement in 1974 of the ARBC and its members by a streamlined American Revolution Bicentennial Authority (ARBA), and in Australia to the resignations of its two chief officers in 1985.

The second controversy was the degree to which the festival should have a central focus and the weight given to particular regions in it. In Canada there were resentments expressed at the dominance of the 'central' provinces of Ontario and Quebec (notably the large sums given to the latter for the Montreal International Expo). In the US controversies erupted, firstly, about the choice in 1970 of Philadelphia as the site of an International Exposition against the claims of other cities and states, and then because of its abandonment in 1972 which elicited claims that the Bicentenary had lost a unifying focus. In Australia, several states protested that the national festival was, in terms of attention and prestigious events, a New South Wales affair. The third controversy centred around political biases of the agencies.

In the US there were protests at President Nixon's rejection of the original liberal objectives of extending the democratic vision of the revolution by a federally funded renovation of the urban environment in favour of a celebratory populist ethos, dubbed the 'Buycentennial' by the left because of its emphasis on business sponsorship and consumerism. In Australia the ABA was criticised by conservative British monarchists for undermining core Australian values and promoting alien Labor republican (and multicultural) ideals pandering to anti-capitalist minorities.

Finally, the agencies provoked a storm of ethnic grievances. In Canada these were largely fought out within the CCC or at inter-provincial level by Anglophone and Francophone factions, the latter, resentful of English hegemony, insisting on the commemoration being renamed as one of confederation rather than of Canadian nationality (the existence of which they denied).[6] In the US, the ARBC was rocked by attacks on its alleged WASP character that was reflected in a lack of attention to ethnic minorities, including blacks and indigenous peoples. In Australia 'British' Australian critics denounced the ABA's multiculturalist biases in favour of the 'new European' postwar migrants, whereas many Aborigines rejected the idea of commemorating the European invasion of their country.

The celebrations themselves (extending to a year in Australia and Canada and 1½ years in the US) were marked by mass attendance (in the millions) at the central events (Op Sail in New York Harbour on 4 July 1976; the arrival of the Tall Ships and the First Fleet Re-enactment in Sydney Harbour on Australia Day; the Canadian Centennial Train and Caravan exhibitions) as well as by vigorous participation at the grassroots levels.[7] Nevertheless, participation was patchy: some groups and states showed little enthusiasm and, in some cases, hostility to the whole occasion. In Canada, the absence of an official celebration on 1 January in Quebec province 'sounded a chilling note', and demonstrations in support of Quebec separatism dogged the year, climaxing with the visit of President de Gaulle.[8] In the US, blacks and many Indians were apathetic, and New Left groups and Puerto Rican and other activists staged noisy demonstrations. In Australia, the Aboriginal Northern Land Council declared 'a national year of mourning' and Aborigines organised vigorous protest meetings and marches on Australia Day and thereafter.

This brief overview of the festivals raises four questions to be explored in the rest of this chapter. Firstly, why did countries imbued with an anti-centralist ethos decide to institute such elaborate official festivals for the first time? Secondly, why should festivals organised according to a 'horizontal' and communitarian format stir intense controversies? Thirdly, what, if any, were the effects of such festivals? Fourthly, what can they tell us about the problems of building cohesion in immigrant nations?

## Why were the festivals staged?

Since these festivals were the first of their kind, there was no inevitability about their staging. Why then did these countries decide to commemorate their founding as a state occasion and in such an elaborate and extended fashion?

There are several reasons: the rise of the federal state as embodiment of the nation; the need for cohesion; economics; the status anxieties of 'new' nations. It is probable that the first two reasons were dominant, but what weight these factors had, and at what times, in determining the unfolding design of the festival can only be answered by further detailed empirical research. The first ensured that it would be an official occasion, given the financial and administrative backing of government, and be promoted internationally; the second that it would have a special intensity and moral character; the third that it would contain 'spectacular' events; the fourth that it would be highly elaborate, encouraging not only an extensive reflection of the national experience, but also a preoccupation with creating permanent memorials in order to mark the progress of the nation in space and time.

### The federal state and the nation

The fact that these festivals were staged as official events with the expected participation of the citizenry reflects, in the perception of political elites themselves, the growing identification of the federal state in communities initially imbued with a strong anti-centralist ethos. In the early stages of planning, it is true, there was little likelihood of the governments presiding over the ceremonies, and they showed only a casual interest in the event. But as the year approached, it became perceived as a means of making an important statement about the international status of the political community among the nation states of the world. The year itself was marked by a procession of heads of state to these countries.

We can observe these patterns most obviously with respect to the US, where there was a shift in importance over its history from communitarian to statist symbols, focusing on the figure of the President and the Constitution.[9] Giving impetus to these trends had been the New Deal of the 1930s, two World Wars and, above all, the Cold War which had given the US state a world role as the leader of the Western democracies against Soviet communism. The Bicentenary became a form of international cultural politics, reinforcing American credentials to Western leadership by celebrating, in the words of the ARBA, the '200th anniversary of the oldest continuously surviving democratic republic in the world'. One quarter of the Bicentenary was predicted to take place internationally.[10]

By comparison, the federal state of Canada was much weaker, beset by mounting challenges from the provinces, especially Quebec, and with its economy increasingly penetrated by American capital. Nevertheless, by the late 1950s and the 1960s there was a growing anti-American nationalism, as expressed in Canada's independent stand on the Vietnam war and its sympathetic stance to the developing world. Thus in October 1963, Prime Minister Lester Pearson, in seeking to cement this international identity, announced as a central component of the Centenary, the International Development Programme to promote development in the Third World and give a dynamic outward and international dimension to the celebrations.[11]

In Australia, although the states still enjoyed considerable power, the federal government was growing in authority with the increasing economic integration of the country. Australian governments from Fraser to Hawke deliberately defined a foreign policy independent of a Britain oriented increasingly to the European Economic Community (EEC), that made Australia a leading supporter in the Commonwealth of Black Africa's campaign against South Africa and linked it to its Asian neighbours. One of the five major goals of the Bicentenary was 'to achieve international participation and to strengthen relationships with neighbouring countries'.[12]

*National cohesion*

A second important motive in all three countries was the need for national cohesion. Each festival was long preceded by a historical and cultural search for roots and authenticity. In the US this was indicated by marked rise in 'pilgrimages' to historic sites and parks from the early 1960s, one of the peak years being 1976; in Australia, it showed in the revival of interest in vernacular styles in building and landscapes and in the restoration of historic 'goldrush' towns; in Canada it was evidenced by the return of artists from abroad to make their careers in Canada.[13] A recurring theme was that the occasion be used to formulate adequate symbols of national identity and construct a new set of agendas for societies beset by deep-seated differences about the meaning of the national experience for the conduct of foreign policy, the operation of key constitutional and political institutions, and the power and status of ethnic and other groups. This theme was stressed more heavily as the year approached.

Canada's Centenary was sponsored at a time of rising tensions between French and English Canadians over Quebec's claims that the original federal compact between the two 'founding peoples' had been betrayed by federal governments. John Fisher, for many years before, appealed to Canadians in his radio broadcasts to seize the opportunity of the year to strengthen Canadian unity. In 1963 he stated: 'I know something is wrong somewhere. One of our prime jobs during the centennial will be to promote Canadian unity . . . If we were not having a centennial, we would have to invent one.'[14]

The quest for national cohesion intensified during the 1960s as Quebec–Canada tensions worsened over the issue of bilingualism, and as English Canada was convulsed by the divisive flag debate which saw the replacement of the red ensign by the maple leaf on the national flag. Not surprisingly, this drive was reflected in the bicultural structure of the festival and in the orientation to youth, the 'coming generation'. One of the major projects was to promote interprovincial visits of young Canadians across Canada, which the planners claimed was 'extremely important at a time in which the country is in need of inter-group and inter-regional understanding'.[15] There were others: the formation of ethnic councils and events to give recognition to the multicultural dimension of Canada.

In the US the establishment of the Bicentenary was preceded by the assassination of President Kennedy and disorders engendered by black demands for civil rights and demonstrations about the Vietnam war, and accompanied by conflicts between largely Democratic supporters of federal activism in social affairs and largely Republican defenders of the states' rights and the market. Many of the initiators of the Bicentenary, such as Senator Matthias, advocated that the occasion be used to promote new federal programs, that recasting the democratic and egalitarian vision of the revolution would integrate embittered disadvantaged minorities such as the blacks into American society by, for example, the reconstruction of the inner cities. This desire for unity strengthened as the year approached, reinforced by continuing Vietnam demonstrations and the humiliations and divisions of Watergate.[16]

The initiation of the Australian Bicentenary had been preceded by the bitter constitutional battles between Liberal and Labor parties after the dismissal by the Governor-General of the Whitlam government in 1975. In discussing the establishment of official machinery for planning the event in 1978, both the Prime Minister (Malcolm Fraser) and the Leader of the Opposition emphasised the unifying and positive aspects of the occasion. They were not alone: from 1977 onwards various pressure groups suggested that the event be used to end the embarrassing alienation of Aborigines from Australian society by being the setting for the promulgation of a treaty meeting Aboriginal grievances over such burning issues as land rights.[17] As the year approached, the theme of unity became more insistent, even as conflicts accelerated between Aboriginal and white Australia over land rights and between 'Anglo-Celtic' and the 'European' Australians over multiculturalism and immigration. Thus John Reid claimed in 1985, 'the people have made it known that they are sick of divisions'.[18]

*Economic motives*

Economic motives, too, were a factor in the planning of the festivals, two of which had expositions attached, and business representatives played a very prominent part in the planning. In part this was to ensure the financial viability of the projects; corporate sponsorship, to varying degrees (notably in the US where the private sector funded well over half the activities), was regarded as an important funding source.[19] But, in addition, all three countries viewed the events as a means of boosting tourism and the leisure industries, increasingly important in postwar societies. Thus in Canada, the Commissioner of the Centenary Commission, John Fisher, was prominent in the promotion of Canadian tourism. It was hoped to attract a record influx of visitors, particularly from the US and from new areas, which would result in a tourist expenditure of $1 billion. Similarly, James Kirk, head of the ABA, looked to use the occasion to reinforce Australia's rising visibility as a tourist destination and to gain new tourist markets, which would also boost the building and communication industries. One of the three major themes of the US Bicentenary was Festival USA, designed to encourage foreign visitors and, indeed, Americans to travel extensively to experience the ethnic and cultural diversity of the US.[20]

This rationale was reflected in the design of the festivals: major international sporting events, military spectacles and, of course, international expositions. Heritage projects such as the Australian Longreach Stockman's Hall of Fame were financed to provide alternative industries in tourism for otherwise depressed areas. Furthermore, in the US and Australia as the approach to the year coincided with a depression of economic activity, the festival was regarded as a counter-recessionary instrument.

*A maturation rite*

Once the state had decided to mark the occasion, the festivals were likely to take on a reflective character, induced by the status anxieties of the intellectuals of new world countries who lacked the depth of an extensive past as a basis of their worth. Claiming instead a unique but (necessarily) unfulfilled future identity, they felt compelled periodically to reassess the entire experience of the collectivity to determine how far they had come in their cultural voyage.

Central to this anxiety was a deep-seated cultural ambivalence vis a vis the metropolitan culture from which they came and from which they had, to varying degrees, broken away. Thus on the one hand, they differentiated their societies as dynamic youthful nations from an exhausted old world borne down by its past. On the other, they felt an inferiority complex before the cultural 'maturity' and depth of the 'parental' culture from which so many of their social institutions and modes of consciousness derived. The marking of the first or second centenary by an extended festival of self-assessment was, in the eyes of some of its prominent advocates (notably the planners), to function as an important rite of passage of—*maturation*—creating some formative experience that would resolve these tensions and inspire the nation for the challenges to come.

This theme of maturation could be conceptualised in different ways. In Canada, it was framed as the process of nation-building itself: the Canadian planners sought to propel Canadians into a distinctive selfconsciousness, claiming that, 'without fully realising it', Canadians were participants in a unique human experience that had resulted in colonies achieving 'the status of a modern industrial power' which was 'recognised for its contribution to human welfare and the cause of peace in the world'.[21] In concrete terms Canadians built permanent landmarks in the form of cultural centres: the brash former colony was to show its maturity by its entry into the world of 'high' culture. Expo '67 was also intended to demonstrate Canada as a sophisticated modern industrial society.

In Australia, David Armstrong, inspired by the Canadian 'coming of age' in 1967, promoted the Bicentenary as 'a unique, once-in-a lifetime opportunity . . . the focus for nothing less than a massive national programme of social and community development, a chance to complete unfinished business'.[22] Similarly, ABA chairman Reid suggested, in a striking phrase, that the people wanted the occasion to leave 'monuments to the future', but ideas about this varied.[23] Many saw the Bicentenary as a historic opportunity to seize national autonomy from Britain by announcing a republic (thereby ending constitutional dependence represented by such institutions as the Governor-Generalship), and a new national anthem and flag. Thus John Warhurst argued that the Australia–Britain relationship was 'not a mature one . . . it was the relationship of a child to its mother'.[24] Others, in addition, enjoined their fellow citizens to show their maturity as a nation by their willingness to engage in critical reflection as well as celebration, and acknowledge the need to give decisive redress for the evils done to the Aborigines during colonisation through a constitutional treaty enshrining land rights.

Even in the US, which had achieved auto-emancipation from Britain in the War of Independence, influential figures such as James Michener, who wrote the final report of the first ARBC, explicitly defined the occasion as 'a rite of passage' and 'as a coming of age'.[25] Here, too, conceptions varied, with conservatives and radicals stressing the need either to face up to world responsibilities or to tackle poverty and historic wrongs (to black Americans) at home.

## Controversies and cleavages in immigrant nations

The festivals were organised by non-governmental agencies, with a mandate to unify the nation and offer, supposedly, equal participation to all. Why then were they almost immediately embroiled in controversies which continued largely to the end, some of which evoked fundamental questions about the legitimacy of the nation state? There were several reasons.

Firstly, with regard to criticisms of the managerial performance of the agencies, the problem was that, although in theory non-partisan bodies, the agencies were open to considerable pressure from the federal governments, which controlled appointments and finance, and which were heavily influenced by the electoral cycle. At first the agencies were paralysed by the inertia of governments unlikely to preside over the occasion; then changes of government led to changes of theme and personnel; and, as the respective years approached, there was further disruptive interference by governments concerned about their image in the eyes of the international community and of their own population. These problems were multiplied by the need to work through state (or provincial) governments.

A second problem for the agencies was that, because these were novel events, they had no precedents, as they repeatedly complained, for devising such an elaborate year of activities. Planners had no obvious guidelines to follow or bank of expertise on which to draw at a national level, and this was the more onerous because the organisers were obliged to combine several different and potentially antipathetic purposes. For similar reasons, there were inchoate expectations of the events, leading to complaints, particularly in the US and Australia, of the failure of the planners to create appropriate national rituals or forms of celebration for the occasion.

A third reason for the intense controversies was that mounting a successful *national* festival was always going to be difficult in countries with only a comparatively recent history from which to construct a rich and inspiring occasion. This was compounded by the fact that much of this history was attached to states or provinces many of which had preceded the formation of the federal state and remained powerful units of political and economic power, jealous not only of the centre but also of each other. There were attendant 'siting' problems: whereas in old centralised states such as Britain or France, the capital cities, as historical, political, cultural and financial centres, were 'natural' sites of national ceremonies, Washington, Canberra, and Ottawa, built as 'compromise' capitals, were regarded by the citizenry as artificial politico-administrative constructs detached from the 'real' life of the country.

The agencies tried to get around this problem by mounting or sponsoring travelling exhibitions. Embodying the idea of the nation as the conquest of space, these sought to link the central experiences and symbols of the nation to locality by providing room within the exhibitions for the distinctive celebrations of the many small towns in which they stopped. Nevertheless, many of the founding events had specific territorial linkages which were jealously guarded, and so had the potential to be divisive as much as unifying.

These problems were most visible in the cases of the newer states of Canada and Australia which lacked a war of national liberation to serve as a founding myth. As the Canadian Centenary Commission admitted, Confederation did not generate the dynamism of a revolution, and there were 'few events to fire the imagination of Canadians everywhere in the country'.[26] In Australia, neither 1788 nor 26 January (the national day) had great national resonance: throughout the preparations of the festival, there had been arguments between the advocates of 26 January, Federation Day and Anzac Day as the most appropriate national day. Both countries had to borrow rituals and significance from Britain by having the Queen and the royal family preside over some of the major ceremonies.

A problem for Canada was that only four of the ten provinces (Ontario, Quebec, New Brunswick, and Nova Scotia) had federated in 1867. There were worries about the level of participation in some of the later arrivals, despite the decentralised format which guaranteed each provincial capital funding for building a major cultural centre.[27] In fact, the festival had an Ontario and Quebec thrust, though as we shall see, they had different perceptions of the event.

The planners in Australia had a different difficulty: how to transform an official (New South Wales) state occasion into a national event. Of course, '1788'—the landing of the First Fleet at Botany Bay, Sydney—had been commemorated Australia-wide in 1888 and 1938, and 26 January (the day of the landing) had long been the national day, but because the state of New South Wales had also appropriated the moment as the founding of the 'premier' state of Australia, this had excited interstate jealousies, especially between Victoria and New South Wales.

In trying to nationalise a festival associated with a particular state, the ABA was handicapped by the weakness of Canberra as a centre (although important ceremonies such as the opening by the Queen of the new Parliament House were held there): indeed, it felt compelled to set up its headquarters in Sydney, which reinforced complaints in the rest of Australia about the privileging of New South Wales. The ABA sought initially to detach the occasion from its Sydney moorings by downplaying the events of the year 1788, notably the landing of the First Fleet, but it could never fully succeed because of the activism of the New South Wales government which, with its own priority claims to make, alone of the states gave generously to its State Bicentennial Council ($70 million compared with Fraser's $166 million for the entire Bicentenary). The resulting proliferation of New South Wales projects reinforced the sense of exclusion felt by the other states, three of which—Western Australia (1979), Victoria (1985) and South Australia (1986)—were distracted in this period by the prospect of commemorating their sesquicentenaries.[28]

By contrast, the US had a powerful myth of auto-emancipation uniting the people and based on a large common store of symbols, legendary events and heroes of the revolutionary period, and most of its states had entered the union under the tutelage of the federal government. Moreover, the capital, Washington, had acquired, since World War II, more of a national status as the stage on which the US strutted as leader of the Western world. Many of the major ceremonies were based there, including the 4 July weekend celebration of the sacred document of the US, the Constitution. Regional groupings of states formed to cooperate in the design of Bicentennial projects. Nevertheless, the commemoration of the birth of the nation state inevitably focused attention on the historically significant sites in the original thirteen states, between which there were strong rivalries.

The first ARBC (1967–69), which had a strong Virginian member-ship, was perceived to have an eastern bias when it adopted plans to base major activities in Boston, Washington, Philadelphia and Miami. Although Nixon, in replacing its members in 1969, declared that the celebrations 'belong not only to the thirteen original states, but equally to the newest', in 1970 he selected Philadelphia as the site for an International Exposition to serve as a national focus (as in 1876).[29] This was criticised by other cities and states, and the ARBC eventually had to abandon these ideas for an ad hoc decentralised format that pushed the responsibility for projects onto the states and municipalities.

There was, however, a fourth serious barrier to creating a suitable unifying national experience in these societies: Interpretations of the foundation myths and core symbols of the nation were tied to concep-tions of group status and had implications for the current series of overlapping conflicts in these societies about the distribution of power between different political parties and movements; between (and, in Canada, within) the 'old' core settler population and 'newer' ethnic minorities; and between European and indigenous peoples.

In Canada the idea of Confederation between two nations was invoked differently by Liberals anxious to create a neutral Canadian identity with a new flag and biculturalist policies and Conservatives determined to retain traditional British symbols; by English- and French-Canadians, the latter regarding the practice of Confederation, which had resulted in English economic and cultural hegemony, as a betrayal of the original compact; and by newer ethnic groups who demanded a multicultural rather than a bicultural ethos.

In the US the 1776 revolution and the Constitution meant different things to different people. Democrat President Johnson justified federal activism in advancing social reform by referring to the original ideals of the Constitution. Republican strict constructionists resisted Johnson's reforms in the name of states' and individual rights guaranteed by the Constitution. Black civil rights leaders made a contrast between the original egalitarian ideals and their history of discrimination; as did Indians, until the 1960s excluded from the terms of the Constitution, which they regarded as 'blind' to the expropriation of their lands.

Likewise, the 1788 settlement symbolised for Liberals the centrality of Britain and the Crown in Australia whereas, for Labor, it meant the founding of a new democratic culture which had yet to achieve true autonomy. For Australians of 'Anglo-Celtic' stock, it symbolised their priority over the postwar European migrants who, in the name of multiculturalism, sought to change the national flag, anthem, language and immigration policies. For Aborigines, now struggling for land rights, the settlement symbolised their conquest and near 'genocide'.

Since interpretations of founding events implied hierarchies of power, the planning agencies faced an impossible task in creating an official consensus on national symbols. Various expedients were tried, notably a horizontal approach to groups, dubbed 'tactical pluralism', that included an extension of the celebration to cover not just the founding events but the full range of the country's history in an attempt to incorporate the experiences of indigenous peoples and later arrivals (both states/provinces and peoples). But such approaches were either perceived as hypocritical by the marginalised, or, if seriously pursued, rejected by the dominant groups. There were no neutral national symbols, and, indeed, given the political resonance of the occasion, governments in Australia and the US were unable to resist the temptation to enforce on the agencies their ideological agenda, which in turn provoked criticisms.

After his election in 1968, Nixon gave the planning a conservative Republican thrust by pushing the ARBC to a states-centred mode that celebrated 'middle' America and was funded by private enterprise. He rejected, as redolent of the Democrat 'big government' ethos, the original conception of a federally funded renovation of the inner cities and the environment that would extend the democratic vision of the revolution by opening opportunities for black and other poor ethnic minorities. This left the ARBC exposed to ideological and ethnic criticism. The first was effectively articulated by a New Left group, the People's Bicentennial Committee, who, mobilising popular disillusionment with Nixonian republicanism over Watergate and Vietnam, dubbed the festival 'the Buycentennial'. They argued that the lack of interest in the revolutionary nature of 1776 and the commercialisation of the event exemplified the betrayal of the original American democratic vision at home and abroad by governments tied to multinational capitalism.[30] The second attack was on the exclusive composition of the ARBC, when, in 1972, it was disrupted by resignations from youth and other representatives, who complained of the dominance of white middle-aged conservative business interests and the lack of interest in the concerns of the young, ethnic minorities and women.[31] Indeed, radical blacks and Indians argued for a boycott of or counter demonstrations against an event with little relevance for them.

Gathering criticisms and fears that the Watergate scandal would torpedo the whole enterprise led, in 1974, to the replacement of the cumbersome and discredited ARBC by a streamlined ARBA, to desperate efforts to secure participation by women and ethnic minorities, and to the promotion of an 'American Issues Forum' that would involve Americans in the evaluation of their historical experience, in order to defuse criticism that the Bicentenary was degenerating into a fiesta of commercialised trivia. But this opened the ARBA to attack from 'libertarian' Republicans. Concerned about the failure of the Nixon counter-revolution, they objected to a perceived leftist tone to the Forum, and, more fundamentally, to an agency which they characterised as yet another incompetent arm of Big Government, smothering by paternalist central direction what should have been a joyful celebration by and of the people.[32]

In Australia in 1983 the election of Hawke's Labor government on a republican platform (including support for a new national flag and national anthem) led to a return to the ABA's original conception, vetoed by Fraser, of a multicultural nation that would make amends for past mistreatment of the Aborigines. This entailed a future-oriented festival that downplayed the Imperial and British aspects of 1788. Thus the ABA planned to substitute for a re-enactment of the landing of the First Fleet on Australia Day 1988, a parade of Tall Ships from different countries to symbolise Australia's multinational heritage, and proposed that the Australian Travelling Exhibition be organised around the concept of 'one nation from three (equal) waves of migrations' (Aboriginal, British and European).[33]

But, for many, this cultural egalitarianism devalued the British contribution to the making of Australia by equating it with the brief postwar experience of European migrants and met the response from Aborigines that '40 000 years don't make a Bicentennial'. It led to a critique from conservatives, already strongly mobilising in 1984 against high rates of Asian migration and Aboriginal land rights campaigns, that the ABA was subverting the core values of traditional Australia (the British heritage of monarchy, parliamentary democracy, free enterprise, the Anzac traditions) and presenting Australia as a land of incoherent diversity without unifying traditions and values.[34] At the same time, Aborigines, increasingly blocked in their campaigns for a treaty recognising their prior possession as the *original* inhabitants, rejected the Bicentenary and its conception of them as migrants as a hypocritical farce. Alarmed at the prospect of these controversies sabotaging the Bicentenary, Hawke and the new officers of the ABA backtracked. Increasingly they promoted spectacles such as an international naval review that, by highlighting the armed services, gave comfort to the conservative lobby, and gave grudging support, under pressure from public campaigns, in 1987 to the ailing First Fleet Re-enactment consortium.

The Canadian case was distinctive. Because of the estrangement of the two dominant language cultures, territorially separated in large part, most of the debates took place within intergovernmental forums or the CCC rather than in the public domain. In effect, the planners 'solved' the problem of integration by bilingual fudging (saying different things to each language community) and permitting two different celebrations, one for English Canada, the other for Quebec and heavily oriented to Expo. This 'solution', as we shall see, proved to be illusory.

**The consequences of the festivals**

I argued before that there was no inherent necessity for states to commemorate their national birth and in such an extended fashion. But once they decided, at times of deep-seated social conflict, to give an official status and elaborate attention to these (literally) extraordinary commemorations of such moments, they focused attention on those *transcendent* questions—about the identity of the nation and the status of various groups within it—that are normally submerged beneath day-to-day issues, and they created expectations of their decisive resolution. As we noted, governments and their agencies engaged in a series of expensive initiatives to achieve certain goals, and the official nature of the festival galvanised, in turn, responses from a range of elites who sought to coopt the occasion to advance the claims of their respective groups.

As we will see, neither governments nor, with one major exception, non-dominant groups were successful in their aims. Nevertheless, one of the major consequences of these festivals was to stimulate a wide-ranging debate about the meaning and direction of the nation among the intellectuals and elite groups who found themselves propelled into the public spotlight by the moment. Increasingly, the commemoration itself became perceived by opinion-makers not just as a means to ends but rather as *the* gauge of the national 'will'. Failure to live up to such heady hopes brought with it consequences unintended by the initiators of these festivals.

*Realisation of official goals*

How far were the official goals of state legitimation, tourist promotion, national integration and landmark achievements realised? With respect to the first goal, all states, in securing large-scale foreign participation, boosted their self-images and prestige, reinforced links with British roots and with the homeland states of their later migrants, although the effects were uneven.

The greatest beneficiary was the US, which, demoralised by the slur of Watergate on its primary political institution, the Presidency, recovered some degree of self-belief in its democratic world mission as a result of the active participation in its celebrations by more than 100 countries through visits by heads of state and through festivities organised on their territories. The *New York Times* editorial of 4 July 1976 remarked on the extraordinary outpouring of esteem from so many nations. After Watergate and Vietnam, the friends who were ashamed of the US 'seem to be saying now that they see America's better values surviving. The oldest written constitution still in effect . . . assures this nation a solid place in the hearts that cherish the world's receding zone of freedom.'

Canada highlighted its credentials as an international actor with the visits of 60 heads of state. But the festival nearly led to a breakdown in relations with France as a result of De Gaulle's decision to stir up Quebec separatist sentiments during a truncated visit, and tensions with the US over Canada's criticisms of the Vietnam war were exposed in President Johnson's surly visit. Although the Australian Bicentenary was used to emphasise the country's recently acquired status as a distinctive multicultural nation through visits from heads of state from the newer migrant countries, the year probably reinforced its reliance on British symbols, given the centrality of the royal family in the major ceremonies.

Although the second goal, tourist promotion, was achieved in the short term, the long-term effects, as Jenni Craik indicates in chapter 8, were questionable. As regards the third objective, the official festival failed to achieve national cohesion in the sense it intended. As we have seen, the conceptions of national unity were politically driven, evoked bitter controversies among elites, and had an uneven appeal to the various social groups. True there was mass attendance at the central spectacles, and, in Canada and the US, strong local participation by many municipalities who tied their local centenaries to the national event. But this outbreak of sentiment in the US was as much a communitarian assertion of nationality independent of the federal office holders, or a product of contingency in the case of Canada.

Thus the US Bicentennial year had a cathartic, grassroots and nostalgic character that resulted from its following the resolution of the agonising constitutional crisis of the Nixon Presidency, during which there was an unprecedented collapse of confidence in official institutions and a sense of helplessness before the crises of the cities and social disorders. This was expressed by the emphasis on local, small-town heritages and a return in the eastern states to the nation's 'youthful' vigour through local re-enactments of the revolutionary past.[35]

In Canada, the Centenary functioned initially as an accidental outlet for English Canadians imbued with an inferiority complex vis-a-vis their domineering southern neighbour, the US, to express national pride. Enjoying an economic boom and basking in international attention and praise (of the Montreal Expo), to their own surprise they had the unusual opportunity of being able to favourably compare their country's economic well-being, peace and apparent social harmony with the discomforture of the US, wracked by recession and mired in social discord over civil rights issues and the Vietnam war. But as we see below, the early sense of Canadian harmony was illusory, and the festival later revealed the existence of two mutually unintelligible nations and generated, during the visit of De Gaulle, a full-scale national crisis.

In Australia the attempt to create a new multicultural nation, reconciled with the Aborigines, collapsed, and fudging reached the level of bathos when Australia Day was celebrated by a procession into Sydney Harbour both of Tall Ships (symbolising multiculturalism) and of a re-enactment of the First Fleet (symbolising British origins).

*Cultural politics and the status order*

If, then, the official nation could claim only partial success and certainly no landmark achievements, what impact did the festivals have on the intense competition for symbolic and material power in these periods? To what extent were groups able to advance their goals by participating in, coopting or resisting the occasion? In concrete terms, how far were groups able to extract concessions from the federal state? Successes of groups were very uneven, and here I wish to examine briefly two ethnic groups, alienated from the official state, whose cultural politics throw light on the problems of identity and cohesion of the immigrant nation: the Quebecois of Canada, and the Australian Aborigines.

The success of the French Canadians in Quebec is interesting because it shows the divisive implications of such occasions for states when faced with an alienated ethnic minority that is strong in terms of its numbers, territorial concentration, political resources (a provincial government) and international allies (France). Thus as a price for its participation, the Quebec government won several major symbolic and material concessions: the commitment and financial support of the federal government for Montreal's bid to obtain an International Exposition in 1967; a redefinition of the Centenary as the commemoration of confederation rather than of nation; the obtaining of the largest sum of all the provinces for heritage projects which it channelled into a celebration of a specific Quebec heritage (predating that of confederation), distinct from that of English Canada; the use of Expo—identified as a provincial achievement—to pose as a quasi-independent state with its own foreign policy by effectively controlling the access by distinguished visitors such as President De Gaulle to the Expo.[36] These achievements, together with the controversy of De Gaulle's visit, served to intensify a sense of Quebec's identity and autonomy vis-a-vis English Canada.

Most poignant was the position of indigenous peoples, in all three countries, alienated from a nation state built on the expropriation of their lands, which excluded them from citizenship until the 1960s and viewed with relative indifference their demoralised and impoverished status. However, the festivals were preceded in Australia (and the US) by a politicisation of these peoples, focused on rights to traditional lands and self-management. This was made possible by the emergence of an indigenous intelligentsia of lawyers and civil servants and the creation by the Whitlam Labor government of independent power bases in the form of the Northern Lands Council, the Department of Aboriginal Affairs and legal aid centres. The festivals stimulated this radicalised indigenous intelligentsia to use the commemoration to strengthen their campaigns for land rights and the redress of other grievances.

Although otherwise weak in terms of numbers, organisation and access to resources (e.g. the media), these peoples possessed a symbolic power in their capacity as *natives* endowed with an ancient and distinctive iconography and culture. This could be used as a lever against states, trying to distance themselves from their European imperial origins and active in pursuing ties with post-colonial Third World societies, for two reasons. First, native grievances, if articulated, would subvert, in international eyes, the celebrations of these countries as new world and multi-ethnic societies by highlighting their origins and continued basis in European racist conquest. Secondly, these grievances made it more difficult for these political communities, searching for emblems of distinctiveness vis-a-vis the 'old world', to appropriate aspects of the indigenous culture in order to give a spurious historical depth and cultural romance to societies otherwise noted for a pragmatic materialism. In all three countries some attempt was made to fuse a sense of the primordial (the timeless land) with a futuristic ethos (e.g. the Eskimo Katimak design of the Canadian Pavilion at Expo; the use of Ayers Rock, a sacred Aboriginal site, as a symbol of Australian uniqueness).

To gain their participation or, at least, acquiescence, the states felt compelled to make gestures (e.g. the handing over to Aborigines of the management of Ayers Rock) and offer financial incentives. On their part, the indigenous peoples could use the unusual world spotlight directed at the nation state to exert collective pressure on the governments through adverse publicity, threats of demonstrations and even violence in order to extract funding for projects specific to their needs (better water, health, and housing facilities on their reservations). The Australian Bicentenary, in particular, was significant for the employment by Aborigines of a new transnational politics, made possible by the development of links with radical anti-colonialist forums and United Nations agencies which compelled a reluctant Australian government, at that time vociferous in the anti-apartheid campaign, to concede very reluctantly in 1987 a Royal Commission into Aboriginal deaths in custody.

The achievements of such groups, however, were limited by internal weaknesses (geographical dispersal, 'tribal' divisions, lack of Western education and organisational skills, poverty) and the larger constraints on governments (faced in Australia with a conservative backlash over the issue of land rights). The major effect of the occasions may have been to accelerate the politicisation of these groups.

*The nationalisation of public discourse*

Obviously an event that foregrounds issues of national identity and future directions privileges cultural producers and national intellectuals, propelled from querulous obscurity into the limelight by public expectations of their capacity to evaluate the import of the commemoration for a general audience and to affirm the distinctive creativity of the nation. Thus the occasion serves as a catalyst to emergent forces, enabling the realisation of long-term cultural initiatives, previously frustrated by indifference, which now gain recognition and finance.

On the individual level, projects such as the Longreach Stockman's Hall of Fame were completed because of Bicentennial funding. In all three countries a permanent and concrete legacy was left in the huge range of heritage and cultural projects in the centres and localities that added significantly to the patrimony of the nation, financed by central, state (or provincial) and local governments and by private sponsorship. Such celebrations might have a still more dramatic impact where they were preceded by a collective build-up of cultural energies. In Canada, because of the provision of commissions and exposures in the public media, an emerging national orientation among artists crystallised into a major cultural revival. This sustained itself beyond the year by forming permanent trade and professional associations that in turn helped establish the Federal Cultural Policy Review Committee to promote the development of a Canadian national culture.[37]

The major cultural effect, however, of the festivals was to reinforce among elites and, to a lesser extent, the educated public the discourse of nationality as the proper idiom of political identity, by engendering over several years a series of overlapping debates about the proper forms of the festival and the historical significance of the occasion. For, by investing the commemorative year as a decisive moment for assessing the international status of the community, the continued relevance of its political legacy, and the prestige and rights of its constituent groups, they encouraged citizens to consider the problems and dilemmas of the present in terms of their relationship to the founding moment, and thereby accept the teleologies of nationalism.

Various intellectuals might agonise over the proper form of festivals, the thinness of the national cultural traditions and the lack of a genuine interest in history in comparison with other societies. But this itself encouraged comparisons between the values and practices of their community and older societies and between past and present. Contrasts might be made, as in one polemical history, *A Nation At Last?*, aimed at the Australian popular market, between the rhetoric of authenticity and autonomy used in the Bicentenary and the realities of multinational capitalist control of the economy.[38] Such critiques, however, based on assumptions about Australian exceptionalism and the need for Australian economic autonomy, merely mirrored nationalist tenets. This process recreated and generalised the familiar conceptualisations of their society as a new world society and tendencies to analyse the problems of the present in terms of a quasi-personification of the nation as young and in need of 'maturity'.

Hence, one of the recurring themes of commentators was the representation of the occasion as a rite of passage, as an index of the 'maturity' of the young nation which was on the verge of 'coming of age' (or becoming 'a nation at last'). For example, in the US a range of crises in the areas of the environment, education, the constitution and foreign policy were attributed both by left and right (though in different terms) to 'arrested' development: to the unwillingness to sully the imagined innocence of youth by facing the responsibilities and complexities of modernity. Or, alternatively, others complained that the current demoralisation had occurred because the US had sacrificed its new world revolutionary mission to become a cynical great power just like the corrupt old world imperialisms.[39] In all three countries the anniversary year itself, therefore, was to be judged by its ability to propose decisive solutions to fundamental problems.

The very expectations of social regeneration aroused by festivals led to varying degrees of public disillusion. Commentators in the US increasingly looked back nostalgically to the model 1876 Centenary, which fell at an equivalent time of political corruption, economic recession and discord in the aftermath of the civil war. With its unifying focus on the Philadelphia International Exhibition, this had allegedly rallied the nation by its triumphant demonstration of American technological prowess to achieve world economic leadership in the twentieth century.

Since these were state festivals, this sense of failure had consequences in the political arena. In Canada, the shocking eruption of English–French divisions ushered in the era of French-Canadian Pierre

Trudeau who, elected in 1968 as leader of the Liberal Party and Prime Minister on a platform of national reconciliation, sought to accommodate French grievances by removing British symbols from and by promoting bilingualism in Canadian public life. In the US, the Bicentenary intensified a growing reaction against the failures of 'Big Government' and the social ills of the cities in favour of a nostalgic return to a mythic nation of small-town certainties and innocence. This communitarian nationalism had long-term effects, for it was exploited successfully against the Presidential incumbent in the election of 1976 by the populist Jimmy Carter, in presenting himself as the charismatic outsider who would clean out the Washington stables. Carter's Presidency reinforced a suspicion of social engineering and a revival of conservative religious values. In Australia, the divisive experience of 1988 may have created the groundswell to change the foundation myth itself, from one of ethnic settlement to the (more neutral) political establishment of Australia as a federal state in 1901.

### Conclusions

Three main conclusions follow from the above analysis. The first is that, although the holding of these festivals indicates a measure of integration of the federal state with civil society, the state faces considerable limitations on its attempts at nation-building for three reasons. Firstly, in a federal system it is not able to control the actions of states or provinces, which have their own agenda and make decisions which can shape the occasion. Secondly, such elaborate events, with their extended planning time, offer hostages to fortune (including political disasters such as Watergate, economic recessions, or immigration debates), which change the popular perceptions of these festivals in unpredictable ways. Fortune can favour the planners: the Canadian Centenary, in occurring at a time of increasing Canada–US tensions, was able to unite English Canadians against a significant 'other'; but then came another random factor: De Gaulle. Thirdly, there are inbuilt contradictions between the desires of official elites to impose a national definition and the needs of a democratic state to be able to legitimate itself to its citizenry and to the international order by claiming a broadly based participation. As we saw, the US and Australian planners initially promoted a partisan vision which they had to jettison, and, in desperation, turned to anodyne public spectacles to achieve the appearance of popular consensus.

A second lesson is that there is a gap between the official self-image of such multi-ethnic societies as egalitarian, and the existence of ethnically based status hierarchies. Even in new world societies with a relatively weak historical sense and without mythic claims to 'primordial' homelands, foundation myths are associated with a specific ethnic core population and with patterns of power and exclusion, and cannot easily be manipulated. This was demonstrated when Australian planners cut against the symbolic grain of an ethnic settlement myth, identified with British Australia, by trying to convert the occasion into a festival of multiculturalism. Of course, this may show the need for a more neutral civic or political foundation myth, but the experience of Canada and the US suggests that such myths are essentially contested in multi-ethnic societies, increasingly so as an indigenous intelligentsia develops, capable of making transnational links with the 'fourth world'.

Finally, such festivals reveal, both in their idioms and ambitions, the status anxieties of these countries, formulated in a language of maturation. The fact that such nations still conceptualise themselves so has its absurd side, since the US has claims to be the oldest modern state in possessing a continuous democratic constitution since 1788. Moreover, there is a deep ambivalence within national intellectuals imbued with a 'Peter Pan' complex, for to 'come of age' is to lose one's 'youth'.[40] Yet this ambivalence is not simply rooted in historical peculiarity but is the local expression of twin and competing impulses felt by all national elites: for their countries to be acknowledged, on the one hand, as *distinctive* (based in this case on their *new* world origins and subsequent multi-ethnic migrant character); and, on the other, to be recognised as *normal* members of the established international political and economic community (as, in this case, they become world actors and as industrial development detaches them from their pioneer roots).

There is no final resolution to these competing drives, and the concept of 'maturity' that emerges out of their interplay has no objective referent: 'maturity' entails not a surrender of distinctiveness by becoming like the old European nation states but simply the will to face the future by overcoming the problems and illusions of the past. The continued use of this idiom, however, reveals the insecurity of societies without the dignity of an immemorial lineage which, in defining themselves in futuristic terms, feel the need of a periodic stocktaking of their achievements and weaknesses as a platform for action.

For this very reason, such state festivals became the focus of existential and social anxieties, and of expectations that these anxieties would be resolved in a decisive way. But because 'maturity' is subjectively defined, and means different things to left and right, the festivals generated conflict as groups, in the absence of a significant 'other', indulged their different expectations of the occasion. They therefore failed to function formatively *in the sense intended* as galvanisers of a once-and-forever transition. They became landmarks, however, in another sense: because of the very conflicts they engendered. For these conflicts elaborated options in a common idiom and, by highlighting the intensity of divisions, inspired fresh initiatives of national reconciliation.

# 2
## Regular imaginings: the newspaper and the nation
*Colin Mercer*

### The nation as *habitus*

The daily newspaper is an ephemeral form. The 'ephemera', in one of its meanings, is a zoological term designating a low and indeterminate form of life which, 'lives for one day only: it is transitory, short-lived, poorly differentiated'.[1] But newspapers know about the quotidian. Newspaper technique historically has defined, classified and constituted the quotidian and its coordinates as both a firm foundation and a representative stylistic form. Representative, that is, of a certain texture of the ordinary, the daily: banal and prosaic qualities which, as any traveller knows, are just those that define *this* culture rather than *that*. Here, for example, from Australia in 1988 is a 'Day in the Life' feature which links the daily, the banal, the historical, the topographical and the ethnographic in a logic of comparative nationhood:

> A peerless Kangaroo Island day. A powder blue sky, a sapphire sea.
> John Lavers couldn't think of a reason not to go looking for crayfish and abalone and scallops for his Australia Day barbecue off one of the great diving coastlines of the world.
> Yesterday, back in the country of Lavers's birth, the sky off England's Brighton beach was an undivided grey, the same spiritless view Captain Matthew Flinders escaped 180 years ago to chart the unknown, unending shores of southern Australia.
> Lavers could have been a trade union official back there yesterday. He might have slipped on the ice as he was leaving the factory, and broken his leg, as a workmate did once, only to find that the foreman had clocked him off before he was treated.[2]

Daily, banal, prosaic but with a texture that offers it as definitely circumscribed and peculiar; that is, as national. This is the syntax of a temporally and spatially defined 'way of life', the nation as *habitus* and the daily as the genre which will provide some of its major forms of classification.

The *habitus* is, in Pierre Bourdieu's definition, a 'system of acquired schema functioning in the practical state as categories of perception and appreciation or as principles of classification. At the same time these categories are organising principles for action'.[3] Put more simply, the *habitus* might be described as the techniques, practices and 'environment' in which it is possible to be and feel 'at home'. The *habitus* also figures in the work of Marcel Mauss, Erwin Panofsky and Norbert Elias to designate, variously, 'habit forming forces', 'mental habits' and the forces which will determine the 'structure of the personality and the psychic economy of the individual'.[4] Elias, for example, explains 'national character' as the historical outcome of a particular arrangement of codes of conduct, constraint and manners which are the result of long contests of power between established and ascendant classes and groups. Commenting on what have been dubbed elsewhere the 'peculiarities of the English', Elias suggests that:

> . . . when, in the course of the nineteenth century, most of the aristocratic privileges were abolished, and England with the rise of the industrial working classes became a nation state, the English national code of conduct and affect-control showed very clearly the gradualness of the resolution of conflicts between upper and middle classes in the form, to put it briefly, of a peculiar blend between a code of good manners and a code of morals.[5]

Class struggle and reconciliation, as we might put it, at the breakfast table. At this site and occasion of reading, of course, there is one regular and important mannering technology—the newspaper.

Elias's analysis of the relationship between 'civilising techniques' and state formation stops more or less at the end of the eighteenth century with the demise of court societies, but it is possible to follow some of the paths flagged by him in the relationship between a regular material cultural form like the newspaper and the elaboration of techniques for forming and mannering populations and citizens in the much more complex, extended and diverse national societies which emerged in the nineteenth century. Following this route, we can propose a concept of the nation itself not as a static structure, a container of dominant ideologies, a simple 'invention' or, indeed, a 'myth', but rather in terms of the rituals, daily practices, techniques, institutions, manners and customs which enable the nation to be thinkable, inhabitable, communicable and thereby governable. This is the nation as *habitus* and there are implications for the ways in which the cultural history of the newspaper is to be approached. The newspaper and related ephemeral print forms perform for national populations some of the functions that conduct manuals of various types performed for the exemplary elites of the court societies preceding nation states:

repertoires of conduct, systems of distinction and classification and modes of affiliation and identity.

The newspaper and other ephemera enable three transactions to be carried out: an operation of classification and delineation of diverse phenomena; an operation enabling forms of social identity and affiliation—a 'specific way of being in the world'—to be established; and an operation which establishes in tangible forms the existence and arrangement of groups, classes and communities.[6] In 1988 the newspaper and other ephemera performed these operations in highly visible and concentrated forms. The various techniques and sub-genres included the photo-essay and historical narrative, politico-moral commentary and the 'literary witness', the diarised re-enactments of 1788 in newspaper and magazine, and the 'characterologies' of true, ordinary, dinki-di or exemplary Australian persons or families. This distinctive repertoire of images and phrases produced and deployed four dominant and contiguous categories through which the nation could regularly be imagined.

### The peopled nation

This offers a territory which is 'full', 'diverse' and 'sliceable' by journalistic technique to reveal its rich complexity and *ethnos* (that is, its loosely articulated but sovereign identity as a historical people *in* and *of* a territory) in a demarcated time and place. This is an ethnography of Australia which concentrates on characters, communities and lifestyles but, above all, on how they relate. The technique here constantly relates 'people' to 'places' with a distinctive logic of 'belonging' or 'affiliation'. In various inflections, which would constantly relate the tropes of character, land and history, this was a major and popular form in presenting 1988 and could be seen from tabloid to broadsheet, from local to national and in the monthly magazines. This mode overlaps with the next which was slightly more rarified and, because of the special role of the land in the literary repertoire produced by the resilient historical tryst of romanticism and nationalism, often required the special techniques of 'literary witness'.

### The topographical nation

This is the territory, from suburb to Uluru, mobilised in two distinctive ways: as an icon of ordinariness (the suburb, the outback town, the racecourse, the inner city street) and as an icon of tactical ancientness (Uluru, the Bogong High Plains, the Western Desert, Kakadu). The ordinariness of suburban gardens, the Victa lawnmower and daily tasks constantly remind us of a present ethnographic texture while the ancientness attempts, in various ways, to elaborate a mystical genealogy back to the mists of time. These needed to hang together somehow and during 1988 there were multiple versions of this collage, patterns for which the newspaper is ideally suited through its modes of address, writing and pictorial techniques and a mixed-genre page format. This mode, in turn, allows access to the next.

*The historical nation*

On Australia Day 1988 (26 January), the *Sydney Morning Herald* ran a souvenir lift-out with a full colour front page. Beneath an emblazoned scroll announcing 'Australia 1788–1988', there are nine or so hearty eighteenth century tars in row boats from HMS *Sirius* heading towards Sydney Cove. We know that it is Sydney Cove because on the left is the Sydney Opera House, on the right the Harbour Bridge and straight ahead Circular Quay with the CBD prominent in the background: back to the future in the visual analogy to so many modes of historical narrative, recollections, diarisations and genealogies prominent during the Bicentenary and which offered forms of lineage and continuity. The emblem of one such attenuated form of Anglo-Saxon continuity, the *Magna Carta*, was on show at Expo 88 in Brisbane and its technology of display was described in terms which might stand as a useful metaphor for a dominant form of historical narrative: ' . . . a tunnel of history through rooms which will eventually lead viewers to a darkened module'.[7] This mode will try to negotiate and establish an uneasy relationship with the features of the final category which has many darkened modules reached through tunnel vision.

*The contested nation*

History became a problem in 1988. The 'stuff' of history—events, processes, people—was offered a variety of narrative forms but dominant among these was the 'daily slice' in diarised, first person or commented mode: an operational ethnographic history which occurred in forms from the daily *Australian* to the sepia pull-out of the *Australian Women's Weekly* to the Bicentennial diaries available at ever-decreasing cost throughout the year. The *Official Bicentenary Diary* 'was created to fulfil the objective of lifting the normally dull, everyday diary to something truly appropriate to the year 1988'; while the *Personal Bicentennial Diary* (same publishers, different format), 'allows for an entry for each day, an area for photos and a section where you can list your forebears'. To complete the correspondence you could fill in your own daily entries against those for each day, two hundred years ago, by Captain Phillip, Lieutenant Bradley, Private John Easty, Major Ross, Chief Surgeon White or Judge Advocate Collins. The diaries stood as metaphors for the role of the recorded daily regime in the procedures of commemoration which the print media foregrounded so prominently and where the newspaper would operate as the collective diary of a nation. But these forms and techniques of nationhood also stand as a reminder of the major component of Australian culture which cannot, in any of these terms, material or conceptual, be 'commemorated': aboriginality. Since all of this depends on a certain idea of personhood and social identity, on a certain concept of the land and an inherited mode of history, and, above all, on the plausibility of the narrative and photographic techniques of the newspaper in representing and connecting these forms, it is, of course, incommensurable with those ideas and practices of the person, the land and the connective logic of events which are operational in Aboriginal communities and cultures. Aboriginal culture was represented in the 'rich diversity of life' mode:

> Aboriginal demonstrators who had hoisted land-rights flags on poles around La Perouse [Sydney], dropped the flags to half-mast as the ship entered the bay and started chanting 'shame, shame'.
> However, their protest was accepted with such good humour, respect and understanding by the crowds that the chanting quickly died away.
> Even the most ardent activist obviously found it hard to be outraged when no-one would take offence.
> It was a true family day in a rather old-fashioned and delightful way. Rugs, picnic hampers and ice chests were spread on the grass . . . a deckchair for granny and an umbrella over the baby's cot.[8]

The articulation of the problematic to the rich texture of the ordinary was a favoured mode during 1988.

These four categories have as their condition of intelligibility the regularity and style of the newspaper genre itself and the evolution of its particular historical relationships to 'peoples', the land as territory and the domain of governability which traces their relationship. Let me now relate these categories to the newspaper in more specific terms.

As a condition of its emergence and intelligibility, the newspaper must consolidate a delimited range of publics and reading capacities. The transactions enabled by the newspaper allow a substance and texture to be traced and forms of familiarity and intimate relations to be established between the politico-cultural borders and 'content' of a community and those persons who have been trained and formed to recognise themselves as members of that community. The following passage is taken from one of a series of reports on how Australia celebrated Australia Day and delineates the simultaneously official and cultural borders at the moment when they are crossed:

> Nothing could be more typically Australian than a bring-your-own naturalisation ceremony.
> In uncomfortable 8am heat at the Perth beachside suburb of Cottesloe, ice chests and picnic hampers were just as indicative of Australia Day as the cardboard certificates clutched proudly by the newest Australians.
> The 26 would-be Australians and their friends were told to bring their own breakfast—and booze—to help them ease into their new identity.

Barbecue facilities, a bush band and even a glass of champagne were provided by three local councils.

Like Australia, it was not a polished affair. But the distinctively Aussie touch—the 30°C heat, flyspray, snags, Vegemite, spilt champagne—all had a heart-warming feel.[9]

The newspaper—the use of the form, its techniques and genres and characteristic popular idioms, its ability to handle heterogeneity—is a primary technology of affiliation. It is one of those devices which secures, in Edward Said's definition, 'the range of meanings and ideas conveyed by the phrases *belonging to* or *in a place*, being *at home in a place*'.[10] What is at issue here is not a question simply of represen-tation, but a daily regular form of reading and training in knowing where you are and how best to do things there. Doing things, that is, from offering an opinion on a matter of import, to mowing your lawn, fixing your car, knowing where to be and what to do, or regulating your domestic relationships through a horoscope, agony column or entertainments page. The newspaper is a key technology in the forma-tion of those plural but demarcated arts of living and doing, the capacities and dispositions of the 'everyday', the coordination of which, in a saturated network of identifications, classifications and lifestyles—the *habitus*—has been one of the preconditions for the solidity of modern polities.

The newspaper is an active cultural technology for elaborating and consolidating what actually *counts* as society and how 'what counts' gets incorporated and individuated in modes of behaviour and forms of identification and affiliation.[11] Here I am concerned with what counts and has counted as a *national* society since that is precisely the form in which this entity named 'society' has been thought of since at least the end of the eighteenth century. So, how does the newspaper fit and what role does it play, to use Said's words again, in securing '. . . the nuances, principally of reassurance, fitness, belonging, asso-ciation, and community, entailed in the phrase *at home* or *in a place*'[12] which, in the context of the argument developed here, count as historicised ideas of both culture and nation?

## The thick and the thin: some protocols for analysis

The newspaper is, like the zoological ephemera, short-lived and poorly differentiated. Neither of these qualities will commend it to the purview of cultural analysis, which requires long lives and clear differentiation: the thick rather than the thin. As Meaghan Morris has put it: '[m]odern institutionalised criticism . . . has for over a century relaunched and revised its project not only by "bordering", or differentiating its objects, but by progressively taking a "distance" from previous read-ings of texts that somehow survive through *time*'.[13]

Needless to say, something literally as ephemeral as the newspaper which does not allow differentiation and 'bordering' in these terms doesn't stand a chance. But the newspaper can voraciously assimilate all major genres—the portrait or character sketch, the literary and political essay, the psychoanalytic consultation, poetry and, during the nineteenth century, the novel itself—and requires a much more particularising and historicist mode of enquiry. Criticism has been happier with thick books which are durable than with thin newspapers which are disposable. The problem is that criticism, when it gingerly ventures into the domain of the quotidian claiming a form of street credibility, has often used the methodology which it applies to the thick book on the thin newspaper and found it wanting on all sorts of grounds—political, moral, ethical and aesthetic. The newspaper could not be recognised for what it is: a material, daily technology of the nation as *habitus*. There are also crucial differences in the object itself which relate to quite distinct practices of reading and daily usage which a critical–aesthetic methodology has not been able to address:

> . . . the book is composed on the understanding that it will be read attentively . . . The newspaper must be set-up on the understanding that it will be read inattentively. Moreover, a book is composed for consecutive, a newspaper for inconsecutive, reading; the nature of the book-page is homogeneous, of the newspaper, heterogeneous. It follows that news-para-graphs relating occurrences of the most diverse character demand a different setting from the consecutive paragraphs of a book.[14]

The etymology of the 'ephemera' exists outside of the zoological domain in the form of the word *ephemeris*; an astrological almanac or table, a record of daily occurrences, a diary or an order of religious services. This is appropriate in so far as all of these have an enhanced role to play in the repertoire of national celebrations where the regular, the quotidian and the ordinary assume a representative significance with regard to the nation's ethnographic texture. This representativeness is secured both through technique—the panoramic photo-essay, the montages of 'people and places'—and through generic styles of report-age which will narrate 'the people'—both 'storying' them and giving them stories—in terms something like the following:

> . . . those millions of ordinary, average, run-of-the-mill Australians who live and work, laugh and play, love and dream and die without ever becoming a famous face or a household name. They are the salt of the earth and the core of the land, these people, and we owe them all a salute and a thank you for their contribution . . . the strength of the nation lies with its people, and, for that matter, the places they live—the ordinary paved and sewered suburbs and the hot little country towns that snooze away the summer by the river.[15]

The newspaper, from the headline and the leader through essays, features, commentary and correspondence columns to the weather and the horoscope, performs these tasks of registering, forming and tabulating the texture of the daily in ephemeral ways which have enormous significance in cultural histories of nationhood. The newspaper offers, within the history of nations, modular and transposable techniques for figuring what A. D. Smith has called their *ethnies*, meaning their ethnographic 'substance'. The ephemerality of the newspaper form—which has now assimilated the major functions of the almanac—does not make it amenable to those traditions of cultural theory and analysis which go seeking within or beneath the textured tableau of representation for something else—value, meaning, ideology: that is to say, something worthy and, more importantly, demonstrable through a form of evidence which is textually substantial. The day and the daily would hardly bear thinking about here: they exist below this threshold of visibility and intelligibility. One of the issues to which my argument is addressed is, then, how to restore this threshold of intelligibility. To the thin form of the newspaper, we would need to restore something like what Clifford Geertz, in an argument against the search for deep structures which he calls 'sociological aestheticism', has called 'thick description'.[16] Thin as a commodity and as an aesthetic object, the newspaper is thick in cultural history. Let me now trace the argument back from 1988.

### A time and a place: one day, one nation

Consider the following uses of the daily as metaphor for the national *habitus*:

> It is early morning on a Melbourne tram. The changing face of Australia is there to see. Where do we come from? We come from everywhere, including here, and therein lies just one of our strengths.[17]

> An image of urban Australia. It is 5.07 on a weekday afternoon and weary office workers are sharing an experience that more than half Australia's predominantly urban population goes through daily: the commuter ride home from office to suburbia. These commuters are riding the Sydney rail network from the city to the outer suburb of Campbelltown, a one hour trip that symbolises their commitment to the great Australian dream—a home of one's own—however far from work that might have to be.[18]

> **This ancient, untamed land still waits and watches**
>
> Dawn came to the Bogong High Plains like a soaring kestrel.
>     The first, faint flickers of pink were engulfed by vivid layers of red, rose and gold, splashed high in the sky as White Australia's 200th birthday was celebrated on the roof of a continent by a show 100 million years old . . .
>     The stage for the show is old beyond imagination, furtive beyond penetration.[19]

> It is 7.40pm and the tourists gather to photograph Ayers Rock at sunset. This sandstone monolith rising from the flat, red earth symbolises Australia

to people of the world wherever they live. The rock has sacred significance to our original inhabitants and injects a mystical aura into the minds of those who came late to a very ancient, fascinating continent.[20]

Daily rituals: historically clocked moments in the life of a community on the one hand (dawn, early morning, 5.07 pm, 7.40 pm) and an 'un-clockable' timelessness on the other (Ayers Rock, the Bogong High Plains—'old beyond imagination'). Old, certainly, but equally certainly 'imaginable' as integral to Australianness and, in this configuration, *to this only*. The prosaic and the quasi-poetic are contiguous in these forms of journalism and the photo-images to which they correspond. Together they support Benedict Anderson's proposition that techniques for elaborating both a sociologically solid 'community in anonymity' with a clocked daily existence and a sense of 'an immemorial past' are necessary in order for nations to be, in the strong sense intended by Anderson, 'imagined'.[21]

A 'strong sense' of imagining entails an attention to the technologies and mental tools[22] which enable it: to techniques of reportage and presentation as well as to techniques and practices of reading and the forms of representation of groups, communities and nations. The meaning invested in the concept of 'imagining' here is therefore quite distinct from any romantic connotations. Indeed, it is strictly at variance with that 'esemplastic power' advocated by Coleridge in his commentary on Wordsworth's poetry. Whereas this power consists in ' . . . awakening the mind's attention from the lethargy of custom'[23], the 'imagining' involved in the argument developed here does precisely the opposite: turns us back to the 'lethargy of custom' and the techniques of its representation, among which the newspaper may be counted as primary, both historically and contemporaneously.

The newspaper in its historical development is a cultural technology which will enable things to be thought and new 'mental tools' to appear over a long period. Among these things which get thought—notated, regularised, pictured and, above all, *related* to the whole of which they are represented as parts—are 'customs and manners'. The relationship between this subject matter, previously the domain of gentlemen antiquarians, and the newspaper developed an increasing momentum in the nineteenth century with the advent of forms of production and new journalistic techniques which would ensure the wide and rapid circulation of these types of writing and the development of new practices of reading. These tools or techniques, including the important development of a serialised *feuilleton* journalism concerned with lifestyles, manners and customs and regularising the forms and coverage of popular 'diversions' and entertainment and, later, the uses of photography and photo-journalism, will enable a community of a particular type to be thought, imaged, imagined in very strong, repetitive, cheap and accessible forms. The newspaper *as genre* will provide an array of technologies which enable a national imagining to be transacted.

This genre will enable the nation to be understood as, in A.D. Smith's expression, 'ethnically full'[24] and therefore amenable to a certain technique of slicing—through individuals, families, communities, places and the land—to reveal their substance or *ethnos*.

There is a certain relationship, then, between the 'daily' and the 'national' which enables the circulation and coordination of references to work, travelling, to the land, its timelessness and 'secrets' (the 'daily' in its repetitive and prosaic mode simply confirms this), the character-istic activities and behaviours of peoples: travelling, working, buying homes, photographing. The 'time' of the day and the 'space' of the nation, when coordinated in this way, amount to something quite dense which is produced by the historical convergence of a 'politics of daily life' and the consolidation of a national domain of governance. This long-term historical convergence provides a context for my argument and analysis which enables the tracing of pertinent connections between the newspaper and the *ethnographic imperative* which has determined and shaped the forms of modern governance since the seventeenth century.[25]

This is a longer duration than is customary for the formation of what we now know as nations and the major historians and theorists have tended to focus on the period from the mid to late eighteenth century with regard to national*ism*. For the nation as such, however, there are good reasons for looking further back in history to some of the enabling conditions of its emergence. Included among these conditions are ' . . . the overlapping but often conflicting techniques for equipping individ-uals with discrete ethical capacities and statuses'[26] among which we must certainly count some of the new forms, technologies and practices of reading of ephemera. These techniques would include, from the very earliest stages, forms of correspondence and ethical advice on matters marital, financial and political between editors and an increasingly defined but necessarily anonymous bourgeois public. These forms of correspondence and advice were, of course, early versions of the 'Agony Aunt'[27] who maintains a powerful presence today along with other 'advisory' and 'correspondence' components of the newspaper which can lay claim to certain powers of ethico-moral reconciliation and persuasion designed to be exemplary for publics and populations. What better way to reform manners than to establish a conduit through which they could be regularly and publicly represented and glossed by 'men of letters' with dispersed and anonymous but definitely national audiences with whom they could, via this new form, 'correspond'? This glossing of manners and customs continues. Here are some specimens of commentary from 'men of letters' of one sort or another in Australia in 1988:

> The Bicentenary has been, so far, an uncomfortable exercise in moral quandaries rather than an occasion of unconfined joy, or a considered

assessment of how far we have come from what we were to what we are as an identifiable nation-State and as a civilised contributor to the human condition of the global village to which we belong.

If we put the Aboriginal factor aside momentarily, in order to see what we are celebrating, then an unwelcome truth becomes grotesquely self-evident.

We are acclaiming the tyranny of mediocrity. We are demonstrating the tyranny of mediocrity. We are vociferously championing the virtues of a society which exemplifies the rule of mediocrity.[28]

This Australia Day marked the triumph of the people and their quiet sense of national pride over all those politicians and bureaucrats who had earlier done all they could to turn it into a very different day.

Originally, the Hawke Government and the Australian Bicentennial Authority (ABA) had agreed to make 1988 more a time of contrition than a festival of restrained pride and thanksgiving. All the propaganda resources of the nation were to be devoted to wagging the official finger at the Australian people.

They were to be told to repent and to accept the new future that pushy minorities hoped to impose on them.[29]

Recently I tried to convince the Immigration Review Committee that despite our apparent wide differences in ways of living, our urbanisation, our sophistication and the ethnic diversity of Australia, the Bushman or a variant of the Bushman was still the emblematic 'Australian' or the personification of Australia . . .

The Bushman was perhaps inescapable because of the legendary pioneer experience and the inescapable Bloody Bush . . .

These would mould our emblematic perception of ourselves for a long time because our culture would return and be returned to it for the foreseeable future. There seems to be a continuous transfer of this legendary experience both to later generations and to new arrivals, by humor, use of language, customs, playground lore and so on.[30]

People, their manners, customs, moral qualities and environment: the newspaper is the only printed cultural form which is able to 'collect', notate, tabulate and physically format these heterogeneous factors and simultaneously offer politico-moral commentary on them in a way that does not cause any problems of internal incoherence, disunity of form, and so on. The newspaper form historically enables genealogies to salamander their ways, tracing the shapes of a domain—the nation— and the features of its internal texture and character—its *ethnos*—and tracing the filaments of governance.

*Newspapers and the governable: a brief history*

The 1988 celebrations—the 'Celebration of a Nation', as the theme was—neither commemorated the whole of territorial Australia, being only the anniversary of the founding of the colony of New South Wales, nor of politico-administrative Australia, since that was not established until 1901 and then with the exclusion of its indigenous inhabitants from citizen rights. Notwithstanding historical accuracy, the event may serve to remind us of a specific relationship between print culture, historically new and broad forms of identity, affiliation, and government which, as Elizabeth Eisenstein argues in the following passage, has definite conditions of emergence within material print culture:

> Printed materials encouraged silent adherence to causes whose advocates could not be found in any one parish and who addressed an invisible public from afar. New forms of group identity began to compete with an older, more localized nexus of loyalties . . . The exchange of goods and services, real estate transactions, the provision of charity were all eventually affected. Personal attendance was increasingly supplemented by vicarious participation in civic functions and municipal affairs. Cheap versions of the magnificent prints which commemorated civic ceremonies, such as royal entries, enabled some stay-at-homes to experience 'public' festivals.[31]

Where would you look these days for information about real estate, goods and services, municipal affairs, civic ceremonies, royal entries and public festivals? The answer is obvious and we can sharpen Eisenstein's argument with regard to one of the most important products of print culture which would progressively be able to fulfil *by itself* all of the conditions listed by her under the general heading of 'printed materials': the newspaper. It is surely relevant to the history of governance that the newspaper is the first genre in which format, audience and orientation will enable the co-presence of the voice and body of the sovereign, whether vested in an individual monarch or a deliberative body, and the voice and body of 'the people', however narrowly or expansively defined.

There are, then, specific conditions of emergence for the newspaper form. These conditions are, of course, print culture, the consolidation of national languages, the establishment of an infrastructure of regular and repeatable supply of information and communication and the emergence of an erastian domain of governance. Necessary but not yet sufficient conditions: what begins to make them sufficient is when they are able to offer the reader a position, an identification, a place of informal knowledge and an expectation of a commodity form, albeit ephemeral, from which things can be understood on a regularised and daily basis.

The newspaper inaugurated this regularised mode of communication and the varied techniques for its consumption which would shift the imperatives of conduct formation, advice on exemplary modes of governance, civility and 'manners' from the private, individualised genres of conduct manuals, Governours, books of etiquette and other devices of conscience—and conduct—formation in the post-Renaissance period into the more strategic but much less 'transparent' domain of the 'ordinary moral education of the people'.[32] The people would be addressed and narrated via an increasingly popular mode of writing on the customs, manners and petty pleasures of the nation. The slow and uneven but definite emergence and consolidation of national vernacular cultures which we can trace through cultural technologies like dictionaries, grammars, anthologies of national literature and vernacular pocket edition bibles to politico-administrative technologies like chanceries, road systems, educational apparatuses, currencies and insurance schemes offer a genealogy for an embryonic national domain. Further, it is possible to know this national domain, that you are in it and part of it, through the demarcated domains of both 'home' and 'overseas', which will have the effect of securing that comparative distinction and allowing its internalisation through the practice of private reading.

Elizabeth Eisenstein notes the complaints ' . . . about the "sullen silence" of newspaper readers in seventeenth-century coffeehouses [which] point to the intrusive effects of printed materials on some forms of sociability'.[33] Benedict Anderson registers this tendency as having a particularly important role to play in imagining the nation when he argues that the newspaper or, more precisely, the 'ceremony' of its consumption, is a ' . . . vivid figure for the secular, historically clocked, imagined community'. This ceremony of consumption transacts and secures a relationship between a mode of reading, 'in the lair of the skull' and a 'community in anonymity which is the hallmark of modern nations'.[34] This the beginning of a relationship between news and governmentality in its broadest sense of a strategic network of communications.

Théophraste Renaudot, under the guidance of a cleric well aware of the relationship between the press and government, Cardinal de Richelieu, was the first to combine a quite specific type of advertising and the publication of news with explicit objectives of social amelioration. A threshold had been crossed in which communication, well-being and governance could easily coexist within a genre or, rather, within a form of communication which would produce its own distinctive sub-genres of advertising, diversions, news, commentary, the essay and so on.

> It seemed to Renaudot that one of the causes of poverty in the society around him was the fact that those with goods and services to supply often failed to make contact with those who needed them . . . Renaudot moved . . . to Paris and set up . . . the 'Bureau d'Addresses et de Rencontre' . . . and provided a convenient brokerage between rich and poor. Renaudot's handbills explained that the Bureau provided the means whereby 'anyone may give and receive information on all the necessities and commodities of human life and society'. The aim was to reduce beggary in the streets of Paris by helping the workless to find employment, masters to find apprentices, borrowers to find lenders, the homeless to find shelter, the sick to discover medicaments.[35]

The exchange of information, regularised and institutionalised in this way, with a benign belief in—or optimism for—the transparency of the social domain offers a logic of assistance and a logic of surveillance at the same time. What combines the indigent, the working, the sick, the credit-worthy and the purchaser of commodities here is a logic of communication within demarcated domains traversed by roads and the filaments of governance and increasingly replete with an *ethnos*.

It is in relation to precisely this period that Michel Foucault has charted the conditions of emergence of a concept central to new modes of governance—police (*la police*)—which, he argues:

> . . . includes everything . . . But from an extremely particular point of view. Men and things are envisioned as to their relationships: men's coexistence on a territory; their relationships as to property; what they produce; what is exchanged on the market. It also considers how they live, the diseases and accidents which can befall them. What the police sees to [*surveille*] is a live, active, productive man . . . the police must ensure 'communication' among men in the broad sense of the word . . . As a form of rational intervention wielding political power over men, the role of the police is to supply them with a little extra strength. This is done by controlling 'communication', i.e., the common activities of individuals (work, production, exchange, accommodation).[36]

Of course this doesn't really include everything: it includes everything which is thought to be governable and communicable. It signals a threshold which has been passed after which these entities and imperatives could be thought *together and strategically* as within the domain of the governable and communicable. This is the condition of emergence of 'news' as an integral rather than contingent form of communication. And there could, in fact, be no better genre to accommodate and distribute these techniques of governmentality than the emergent form of the newspaper containing news, information and— since another function of police is to survey 'everything pertaining to men's happiness'[37]—diversions and amusements.

The newspaper form, assimilating some prior techniques of correspondence, literary commentary and early forms of advertising, provides some of the mental equipment and techniques by means of which these new coordinates could be navigated on a systematic and regular basis. As such it is a crucial device and cultural technology through which a certain sense of the national community may be inscribed. A nation can increasingly be 'imagined' which is peopled, traversed, delimited by roads and frontiers, narratable in terms of politics, business, military affairs, commodity circulation and exchange and, not least, petty pleasures, diversions and amusements. These were of course the objectives of those writers who maintained a constant though ambivalent relation to the new mode of writing known as 'journalism' from Defoe, through Swift, Addison, Steele and Johnson through the eighteenth century. In fact, without the emergence of the journalistic ethnographic imperative, that wholesale representation and glossing of manners and customs that started in the mid eighteenth century and reached a zenith with the 'folklore' obsessions of the early nineteenth century, it is impossible to explain the role of those spectatorial literary devices known as *Spectator*, *Tatler*, *Idler* and *Rambler*, concerned as they were with traversing the native country and narrating its manners and customs, the petty pleasures and divers amusements of its newly discovered peoples. Impossible also to explain the shifting threshold between what constituted *belles lettres*—what Johnson called the 'dignity of writing'—and the imperative to talk about, narrate, excoriate the everyday manners and customs of the peoples upon whom the narrative gaze was obsessively, albeit sometimes reluctantly, fixed.

### The lethargy of custom

We need to know more about what the newspaper as a cultural form actually *does*, as a technology for forming persons and citizens *in* national populations. That is to say, we need to elaborate a cultural history of the newspaper in terms both of its distinctive patterns of presentation, its forms of daily usage and its modes of addressing and forming audiences and publics: let me take an example from 1988. 'A Day in the life of Australia is a combined effort by writers and photographers on News Limited newspapers around Australia. It looks at Australia Day, 1988, through the eyes of Australians right round this country.'[38]

This is the 'slice of life' genre, a genre which is, of course, only imaginable if it is accepted that a certain idea of life as a nationally and ethnographically specific type of life is, indeed, *sliceable* and intelligible to an audience when sliced. For this purpose certain types of photograph and the 'heterogeneous page' are ideally suited—the group portrait, for example: 'Residents of Moola Grove, Ashgrove [Brisbane, Queensland], celebrate Australia Day with a street party on a cul-de-sac adjoining their street'[39]; or the close-up cameo: 'George Albert Warneke, Order of Australia, outside his opportunity shop in Paddington, Sydney'[40] or the character in working-environment medium close-up (to allow the image of the artesian well in the background): 'The backbone of Australia, the men who work the land. Ashley Severin does daily battle with the elements to carve out a living on his cattle station at Curtin Springs, in the Northern Territory'.[41]

The key strategy which is obvious but not necessarily easy to implement is that these images and captions will *hang together*: that, like all good rhetorics, they will persuade particular audiences located, reading and browsing, in specific times and places. This is not a universal mode of address—a slice of life in this mode would be unintelligible in cultures not trained in the techniques of 'slicing', or unfamiliar with what counts as 'life' represented in this way—but located, read and browsed in a particular time and place which will, indeed, allow us to confirm that this is, indeed, 'One Day, One Nation' and is legible as such to an audience who will know how the texture and 'feel' of the daily will correspond to the 'feel' of the nation. The precise nature of the relationship between, say, a Hills Hoist[42], an artesian well and an Akubra hat[43] and the peoples, histories and topographies which accompany them will be determined by a specific national rhetoric and not a universal logic of the signifier. As one of the official songs for the celebrations put it: 'It's a feeling . . . just like you and me'. That is all that has to be said because the 'you', the 'me' and the 'feeling' have long been established in the historical circulation of classifications, identities and affiliations enabled by, among other things, the newspaper as a national genre.

## Slicing: geography, history and the communication of the living

Readers of the daily and weekly press as well as the weekly and monthly magazines in Australia in 1988 will have gained some sense of the close relationship between the newspaper form, the nation as a politico-cultural entity and, in particular, the nature of its *ethnos*. They will have acquired a sort of daily, tactical, cross-sectional knowledge of the peopled, topographical, historical and contested nation.

'One Day, One Nation' was the banner for the *Australian*'s four-page pull-out photographic supplement for Australia Day 1988. Time and space and, most importantly, a way of configuring them around the central coordinates of 'people' figured largely in this supplement. The feature opened:

> Time has always had an elusive, equalising quality in the land they despairingly called 'timeless'. Aborigines were locked into the Dreamtime and convicts, in a dazzling new light, were imprisoned more by the timespan that separated them from Old England than balls and chains.
>
> Time was to become not merely the measure of distance from the fledgling colony at Port Jackson but, as the essence of tyrannous distance, a unifying force itself . . .
>
> As modern [camera] shutters blink across the ancient continent a surprising harmony appears. The railway lines like streamers in the wind of the Western Desert carry passengers across time zones and along the steps of the explorers to liaisons in the east. The road train, rattling down from the north, brings sustenance to the south.
>
> Above all, here are the people, Australians old and young, rich and poor, at work and play, paradoxically united in spirit by the enormous distances which separate them. By time.[44]

The major picture on the front page of the supplement is an aerial shot of a road train creating a 'shroud' of dust in the sparsely vegetated outback, marked only by some tracks and an unsealed road on which the truck travels near Quilpie in the Queensland southern interior. This will be the truck bringing sustenance to the south. There are two smaller pictures at the bottom of the page: the first is of a crew of railroad gangers near Kalgoorlie in Western Australia; the second of the 'legendary bushman R. M. Williams and his blue heeler Nipper' sitting by a campfire at midnight allegedly listening to yarns. The moon is enormous in the background. At the top left of the page are six small, cameo photos of an elderly man, two young Aboriginal kids, a worker in a hard hat and goggles, a young bearded man wearing an Akubra, a young smiling Western Australian policewoman and an elderly woman with definite connotations of ethnicity.

Roads, railways, tracks, map coordinates, the circulation of commodities and ordinary people: the random but necessary coordinates of a territory. What is it that might link these entities? What is the logic of their connection and of those elsewhere in the portfolio—a lighthouse, a dam, a soldier, a cleaner, an oil platform worker, Parliament House, an artesian well, a party in a pub, a shopkeeper, a cemetery caretaker, tourists, lovers on a park bench, a tatooist and so on? Ordinariness, certainly. The technique of the panorama as well: ' . . . a tolerant form, infinitely indulgent of lapses of attention, momentary or lengthy distraction, shifts of mood, and variations of intensity in involvement'.[45] But, much more importantly, *the conditions of emergence and acceptability* of the public figuration of ordinariness and the technique of the panorama: the possibility of representing a nation through the coordinates of time, space and ethnos.

It is not impossible to see here a connection with that initial bringing together of disparate domains and entities, their coordination and 'communication' into the potential domain of government—or the domain of the potentially governable—which occurred in the early eighteenth century and which Foucault has commented on by way of the *Compendium* of the French administrator Delamare. Delamare lists eleven areas in which 'government' can be operative. These range from religion and morals through roads and buildings to the liberal arts, labour and the poor. 'What', Foucault asks, 'is the logic behind intervention in cultural rites, small-scale production techniques, intellectual life, and the road network?'.[46] Foucault's answer, through commentary on Delamare, takes the following form:

> [Delamare] makes the following remarks as to the police's eleven objects. The police deals with religion, not, of course, from the point of view of dogmatic truth, but from that of the moral quality of life. In seeing to health and supplies, it deals with the preservation of life; concerning trade, factories, workers, the poor and public order, it deals with the conveniences of life. In seeing to the theatre, literature, entertainment, its object is life's pleasures. In short, life is the object of the police: the indispensable and the superfluous.[47]

This is a logic which we can also interrogate with regard to the newspaper panorama and, indeed, the newspaper genre as a whole because here again we have a line to be traced from roads and dams to the provision of forms of religious, ethical and moral life in their diverse locations. The newspaper 'fits' this emergent logic of governmentality. By the nineteenth century a certain style and format of writing—the *feuilleton*—had emerged as a deliberate and indissociable counterpoint to the 'serious'. This style and format addressed

> . . . theatre, art, literature; experiences of town life and travel and all kinds of news coming from behind the scenes; the immediate environment and day-to-day life which were not always important but nonetheless worthwhile, for some readers even significant; all attractively written. Because in most cases its content differed considerably in style from the loud and pathetic manner in which political affairs were reported, and often purposely conveyed a personal note, light, lively, friendly and human, the whole genre, which was more than just a stylistic form and incorporated a way of looking at things, was given the name *feuilleton* (light reading matter).[48]

The day-to-day, the lively, the friendly and the human. It is not possible to ignore the connections which can be established between the historically evolved components of the newspaper *as genre* and this new threshold beyond which things hitherto disparate could be brought together spatially, if not thematically, within the heterogeneous newspaper format, imagined as communicable and therefore as governable.

There is another condition, however, which is fundamental to coordinating that domain of governability: its spatial limits or, properly speaking, its 'cultural territory'. That there may be, beyond the asylum, the hospital, the prison and the factory, a discipline and domain of knowledge which deal with classification and social identity in terms of frontiers, territories and the production of *national* geographical knowledge—'geography being together with history constitutive of the national discourse'—is something which occurs to Foucault very late in his work but which is absolutely central to the formulation of a domain of governmentality where the 'inmate' is the 'national man' in a 'space of confinement which is both infinitely vaster and less hermetic'.[49]

The circle of the frontier is produced by widely disseminated forms of geographical knowledge historically developed in diverse genres. Roads and highways and the ethnographically distinctive things that happen on them in picaresque and epistolary novels, travel writing and other genres from the late seventeenth century, traverse, record and frame *nations* in the first instance. Among other things, they delineate the manners and customs which can be observed and recorded along these circumscribed tracks. The newspaper, its techniques and, in particular, the practices of reading which it engenders, are an important part of this 'spatial history' because these will enable regular and accessible procedures of 'internalisation', the formation of certain 'mental habits', the 'incorporated and thereby individuated social' of the *habitus* which will delineate the way of being and living in the cultural territory.

Writing of photographic expeditions in nineteenth century Australia, Paul Carter notes that it was in their nature to choose ' . . . certain kinds of expedition scenery [to favour] certain viewpoints, certain *tableaux vivants*, and not others'.[50] Whereas journeys of exploration tended to exclude the use of photography because their primary objective was the 'constitution of a track', in the photographic expeditions, the track was taken for granted; 'it was a road where other events and activities could occur'.[51] This is the mode which has been inherited by photojournalism of the sort which was prominent in 1988 and which produces what Carter calls elsewhere 'diorama history—history where the past has been settled even more effectively than the country'.[52] It is this truncated section of the juncture of history and geography that the newspaper is so effectively able to slice through to reveal a texture which national citizen-readers can understand.

Journeys and voyages across the native land and even small segments of it, from suburb to CBD, get saturated with modes of affiliation. The journey itself is to somewhere—work—but is also about, for example, the 'great Australian dream' as with the passages with which this chapter opened: it has a *telos*. It also has a visible substance of community, an *ethnos*—the changing face for all to see—and offers a mode of address which is not at odds with the contents of the photo-essay: where do we come from? Collective existentialism is a popular mode in the newspaper form, phrased commonly in terms of origins, journeys and destinations. Roads, trucks, public transport, the Tall Ships and forms of identity, temporal and spatial, are etched across a peopled land which, through the etching, acquires a nomenclature and texture of nationhood. As A.D. Smith argues:

> If it is true that those units stand the best chance of forming nations which are constructed around an ancient ethnic core, then both 'history' and 'landscape' become essential vehicles and moulds for nation-building. But their greatest influence is indirect; through the myths and symbols of community which they evoke.[53]

It is patently obvious, of course, that white Australia has no such 'ancient ethnic core' and in order to claim something like this must have recourse, predominantly through the use of images of the land and time, to its indigenous populations which may be represented as having such a core but are not interested in using it for these purposes. Hence the metaphysical tropes of land, time, frontiers and journeys and the existential discourses of 'who are we, where do we come from?'

But the metaphysical and the existential, aesthetically interesting—and useful to editorial writers—as they may be, are components, techniques and devices for representing the *ethnos* rather than ways of analysing it. The national, and not only nationalism, has frequently had to make its pasts metaphysical and to represent relationships to that past as existential, as explanatory of a specific mode of 'being in the world'.[54] The limits of this explanation were clearly on display in Australia in 1988 and the historian, writer and critic Humphrey McQueen, in the now defunct *Times on Sunday* (10 January 1988), was the first white commentator to shoot down the nonsense of the 'timeless harmony' attributed to Aboriginal populations on the two counts of 'timelessness' as assessed against European historical time and 'harmony' with the land. Different concepts of time, certainly; different techniques for distributing and operationalising what counts as time also, but the popular idea of timeless harmony, shared by the most well-intentioned commentators, is the result, intentional or not, of a longstanding historical attempt to extend the dark tunnel of national time and to 'graft' indigenous cultures tactically onto the more precise and historically clocked—1788–1988—time scale of nation-building in a logic of continuity: the construction of an immemorial past come what may.

This was one of the ways, down the scale of time, that a problematic indigenous population got handled in the print media in 1988. Another way was across the display of space marked out by a putative equality of 'lifestyles' and the complementary narratives of migration which would add up to the rich texture of 'One Day, One Nation'. In Paul Carter's formulation, this 'turns space into place' not simply by visual technique but by anchoring those spaces with a diverse national char-acterology. Little Percy Bates is an Aboriginal boy pictured in front of a dilapidated corrugated iron shed 'on the bed where his father nor-mally sleeps out under the stars at Wilcannia' but becomes simply a part of the panorama's 'tolerant' vision and thereby semantically equiv-alent to, for example, Able Seaman William Goddard, lead labourer Terence Benson, caretaker Jeff Ridgwell or workman Antonio Santos in the heterogeneous page of the photo-essay which was the *Australian*'s Australia Day feature commented on above.

Australia in 1988 offered particularly condensed examples of the relationship between the newspaper form and the nation as a complex politico-cultural domain. The historical development of the newspaper form in offering and consolidating ways of imagining, in the strong sense, the overlapping 'spheres' of the peopled, topographical and historical nations, their modes of communication and governance, was clearly on display, as were the limitations of this form of imagining in a situation where ' . . . through policies of cultural pluralism the state is now actively supporting forms of cultural identity whose defining boundaries are not those of the nation state itself'.[55]

Arguably, this has always been the case in an Australia which, in spite of early efforts, could never quite 'fit' the models and procedures of the nationally 'normative' European polity. But in any case it is clear that the techniques, devices and genres produced by the newspa-per form—techniques which have historically played a crucial role in forming individuals, citizens and populations—are not easily able to handle that which does not fit the national. In this case the indigenous and the multicultural do not fit these devices of national orchestration except by the traditional theme of 'unity in diversity' and it therefore seems important to do some serious thinking about what cultural techniques and resources, including the daily material culture and technologies of the newspaper, are appropriate to a situation where ways of imagining are dislocated historically and politically from the actual configuration of social forces. This would be one way of displacing those metaphysical concepts of culture which have always been so useful to an impoverished nationalism.

# 3

## Past history, present concerns: the bicentenary of the French revolution

*Jane Crisp*

For younger settler societies like Australia or America, a bicentenary year asserts the very fact of having a past history to authenticate one's claim to a national identity. For an older nation like France, however, the events of 200 years ago that were being commemorated in 1989 form part of a very much longer historical identity. One thousand years of nationhood had already been celebrated two years previously in the anniversary of the beginning of the reign of Hugues Capet, under whom much of what we now know as France was originally unified. The 1989 edition of the booklet 'Celebrations Nationales', published annually by the Ministry of Culture, could devote 110 of its 149 pages to commemorations not associated with the bicentenary of the French revolution, and going back as far as the year 989. Such an incontestable possession and representation of an ancient past means that an older nation is likely to be free of anxieties about whether it has a genuinely distinctive and internationally recognised national culture which cannot be written off as a degraded version of some overseas parent culture. Nor does one need official ceremonies to prove the existence of a national past stretching back centuries when one lives amongst buildings and places that bear tangible witness to this fact, and when such daily rituals as buying French bread and preparing and eating French food proclaim a national identity that the citizen can be proud of and yet take for granted.

Notwithstanding the degree of confidence in national identity provided by an incontestably ancient history and distinctive culture, older nations are not immune from present anxieties and needs which celebrations of the safely distant past may help assuage. In the case of France, there were defeats suffered in two World Wars, the German occupation, the loss of empire and of influence in Indochina and Africa, and, more recently, the unrest in one of its few remaining colonies, New Caledonia. Moreover, 1989 was actually the 75th anniversary of the outbreak of World War I, and the 50th of the outbreak of World War II: both these anniversaries were already scheduled to receive their share of attention, and gain added impact from the opening up later that year of the postwar frontier between East and West Germany. The French celebrations of the more distant past, therefore, centring on such highly symbolic achievements of 1789 as the taking of the Bastille and the declaration of human rights, helped proclaim at home and abroad that France had an enduring importance capable of transcending any recent setbacks that might still haunt the national consciousness. Indeed, in the absence of definitive victories to celebrate, the theme of leadership in the struggle for freedom from oppression can become a vital means of affirming the integrity of nation and people.

Perhaps even more significant to the bicentenary than the recent past, however, was a date that was still to come: 1992 and the united, frontierless Europe. The 1989 celebrations of the French revolution asserted France's central role in the ideas and actions that had produced modern Europe; hence they reinforced its claims to leadership in the Europe of the future, as well as providing a reassuring affirmation of national identity before the forthcoming removal of national bound-aries. Significantly, it was this future and its opportunities, rather than any achievements of the past, on which President Mitterrand dwelt in the speeches that began and ended the bicentenary year, and this future which implicitly underlined the major official celebrations during 1989.

Any national celebrations which have a past event or date as their ostensible excuse will obviously focus to a considerable extent on recalling that past; they will also, however, involve ways of using the celebrations and the images of the past that they circulate and celebrate for marking the present and for preparing the future. The French bicentenary can be conveniently considered, therefore, in terms of these three interlocking themes: recalling the past, marking the present, and preparing the future.

### Recalling the past

The revolutionary past was recalled in a whole range of standard ways—commemorations, re-enactments, exhibitions, theatrical produc-tions, films, television programs, books and special issues of news-papers and magazines. In broad terms these tended to function in two complementary ways, both providing a year-long narrative of the historical sequence of past events and also recreating or evoking the past in its materiality as something that could be relived in the present.

The events of the revolutionary past were woven into a complex present narrative. The key events of 1789 were recalled in sequence: the meeting of the Estates General (a pre-parliamentary group of regional representatives) with Louis XVI at Versailles on 5 May 1789, for example, recreated in a costume parade; and the foundation of the National Assembly on 17 June, celebrated through illuminations of the facade of the Assembly building. These celebrations served as a build-up to the taking of the Bastille on 14 July and to the major official celebrations which were scheduled for the 200th anniversary of this symbolic event. The daily events of 1789 were also narrated in considerable detail throughout 1989. *Figaro*, a right-wing daily, made a regular feature in its weekend magazine of the 'News of 1789' compiled from newspapers of the period. The highly respectable *Le Monde* each month issued a 32-page French revolution special covering that month's events in 1789 and including essays on key figures and issues from the larger revolutionary period around such appropriate themes as 'Legitimate violence?' and the 'Right to insurrection' for July and the taking of the Bastille.

Also being recalled were events from the larger period of revolutionary history between 1789, the decisive year of rupture with the old order, and the definitive establishment of the French republic in the 1870s. One such event was the execution of Louis XVI on 21 January 1793, commemorated by royalists as an anti-bicentenary protest; another was the French victory at Valmy on 20 September 1792 over the invading Prussian supporters of the royalist cause, celebrated with extra pomp this year by the present-day government to boost army morale in the anniversary year of more recent defeats. Finally, these more recent anniversaries, together with the way the bicentenary was being used to make a statement about France's current political standing and its role in the 1990s, provided a sense of an even larger narrative linking the revolutionary past with 'history in the making' in the present.

This sense of narrative and of a historical perspective on events was complemented by the range of opportunities on offer to travel back in time and experience that past revolutionary world. You could walk down 'a Paris street during the revolution' at the children's amusement park in the Bois de Boulogne, or 'relive the greatest moments of the revolution' at the 'exhibition–spectacle' in the Tuileries Gardens, or thrill to the words of Danton and Robespierre at Robert Hossein's production, *La Liberté ou la Mort* ('liberty or death'). French children were encouraged to dress up in period costume and even parade in the streets as part of their school projects and commemorations related to the bicentenary. In mid July 8 out of the 74 theatrical presentations in Paris evoked the revolution. Special film and television productions also recreated the period, notably the documentary dramas *Les Années Lumière* and *Les Années Terribles* ('the years of light' and 'of terror') directed by Robert Enrico, on cinematic release in the second half of 1989, and two popular television mini-series, the wildly romantic 'La Comtesse de Charny' directed by Marion Saurraut and based on a Dumas novel, and the more upmarket 'La Grande Cabriole' by director Nina Companeez, screened earlier in the year. To these could be added any number of rescreenings. The prestigious *Danton*, the 1982 film directed by Andreij Wajda and starring Gérard Depardieu, for instance, was the prime attraction of a major television channel on the weekend before 14 July; the city of Paris put on a whole series of free open-air film showings, including Abel Gance's *Napoleon Bonaparte* (1935), Jean Renoir's *La Marseillaise* (1937) and Ettore Scola's *La Nuit de Varennes* (1981).

Films and spectacles on revolutionary themes could be, and were, presented elsewhere to commemorate the bicentenary. A striking feature of the local recalling of the past, however, was that the places where the revolution 'happened', and the material objects that have survived from that time, were available to be exploited. Sites and buildings associated with the period were heavily promoted. You could follow the itinerary in one of the guidebooks to revolutionary Paris, and even though the Bastille no longer exists, you could stand where it once stood and trace its outline marked in darker coloured paving stones. At the Conciergerie, where many prisoners, including the royal family, were held, a freshly constructed exhibit showed you the royal cell, as it was then. The Procopé, a café–restaurant which habitually advertises itself as being the oldest in Paris, capitalised on its revolutionary links right down to the names of the dishes on its 1989 menus. Many of the Paris museums and libraries had items that could be promoted for their connection with the period. There was a noticeable build-up during the year from 9 out of the 91 exhibitions in late March having some connection with the revolution, to 25 out of 125 in July, when the celebrations peaked. Some of these exhibitions were fairly tangential, representing little more than the adoption of an obvious theme. The Museum of Technology's 'technology in revolution', for instance, required little alteration to its standard displays of eighteenth- and nineteenth-century machines, beyond a few fresh placards. Others, such as the one on caricature and political cartoons put on by the National Library, or on 'the birth of national sovereignty' put on by the National Archives, were specially mounted for the occasion.

### The past as object—exhibit and souvenir

The fascination of the material object as witness to the past, which such historical exhibitions as these both exploit and foster, was perhaps most evident in the Museum of Costume display, which was especially popular with parties of schoolchildren. Here you could see garments once worn by Marie Antoinette and the Empress Josephine, as well as the red bonnets adopted as their insignia by the revolutionaries. These last were elongated caps very unlike those on sale in the tourist shops, which took as their model the Phrygian bonnet worn by the allegorical figure of Liberty. The exhibition also served to remind one that the term 'sans-culotte' used of the urban lower classes did not literally mean the 'without-trousers' it so readily became in caricature, cartoon and today's naughty postcard, but simply those without the culottes (kneebreeches) worn by the nobles and clergy. Both cases exemplify the tendency of symbolic forms to take over from their more prosaic originals.

The appeal of the material object was also exploited by the souvenirs available for purchase during the bicentenary year. Indeed, the sale of revolutionary and bicentenary memorabilia was an obvious example of how much celebrating past events has to do with present profits. The commercial exploitation to which the present occasion lent itself was neatly summed up by a modern work displayed outside the exhibition of revolutionary caricature: a red Liberty bonnet in a display case, with the label '1789' marked down to 'sale price 1989' and beneath it the caption 'The revolution—profit from it'. Among the souvenirs proper (objects made primarily to be sold as souvenirs of the bicentenary as distinct from programs and newspaper supplements which could also serve this purpose) were revolutionary caps, bonnets and cocardes (tricolour rosettes); reproductions of the text of *The Rights of Man and of the Citizen*; kits for making cardboard models of the Bastille; copies of commemorative plates issued during the revolutionary period itself; and, inevitably, T-shirts bearing various revolutionary icons. Selling the past, however, and in particular the revolutionary past, is a standard tourist line in Paris, so it was more a question of the proliferation of such souvenirs, and giving prominence to the date, rather than of there being anything new offered for sale.

Although there were plenty of souvenirs that did capitalise on recalling the revolutionary past, there were just as many which were specifically designed to mark the present anniversary itself. These included special issues of stamps, coins and medals; and, for the more affluent, a limited signed edition of a Bernard Buffet lithograph of Marianne (the French republic) for 18 500 francs (A$3700) and promoted as a good investment. At the other end of the scale there were T-shirts with the official bicentenary logo of three stylised tricolour birds (liberty, equality, fraternity) for 48–120 francs (A$9.50–$24); or, simply, a one-franc postcard with revolutionary emblems and the date printed over a standard view of Paris. Or, for a less than permanent souvenir, some sweets in tricolour packaging, or a bottle of bicentenary champagne. Even goods that were not associated in any way with the bicentenary could still be so promoted: Cartier's ran full-page advertisements for its luxury items using a slogan appropriated from the declaration of rights: 'Men are born free and equal in rights (but nothing prevents them from being different). Cartier, the art of being unique'.

*Competing versions of the past*

As well as serving commercial interests, the past can also be enlisted on behalf of present-day political interests. The needs of the present help determine which events are recalled and what significances these are given; and, in the process, certain past events (as the taking of the Bastille demonstrates) may well acquire a symbolic power far exceeding their original substance.

Given the length and complexity of the revolutionary period and the political and social interests at work during it, there was plenty of scope for competing interpretations of its significance. The events themselves, however, have been well documented and their frequent violence never really in doubt, so the situation was rather different from that in Australia, for instance, where previous silences and ignorances about, not least, the level of violence, have only recently begun to be redressed and official versions of colonial history contested. But even when the historical events are well known, there is still the matter of which of these events are given prominence and what sort of value is attributed to them. The effect of present biases was evident even in the most straightforward museum exhibitions put on for the bicentenary. The forgery of 'assignats' (a form of paper money introduced by the revolutionary government) was presented variously as a clever counter-revolutionary strategy to undermine the economy, an evil foreign plot, and a valuable stimulus to technological development.

Conflict over the interpretation of past events was also occurring at the highest academic level. Throughout the year a running public debate was carried on between the traditionalist Marxist historian Michel Vovelle and the 'revisionist' Francois Furet over whether the events of 1789 had opened up a range of possibilities or had predetermined what the outcome of the revolution would be; indeed, the final issue of *Le Monde*'s series on the revolution made a feature of the summing-up comments by these 'two protagonists of the bicentenary'. Both historians were in agreement, however, in criticising the tidying up of the complex revolutionary period into a 'classic' revolutionary cycle from absolutism to autocracy via the collapse of an old regime, idealistic hopes and the initiation of a virtuous republic, followed by a period of anarchy and bloodshed, and ending in a dictatorship. This model, Vovelle for one suggests, needs to be seen as very much a retrospective one strongly influenced by the revolutions that have occurred during our own century.[1] Interestingly, the way such constructions of the past may function in making sense of the present was being amply demonstrated in the use being made of the French revolution as a reference point in reporting the various 'people's revolutions' that were changing the political face of much of Eastern Europe towards the end of 1989. Similarly, the present-day political value to be gained from association with past revolutionary initiatives was manifest in the issuing of competing claims by the British and the Americans during 1989 to have achieved earlier and better revolutions than the French. Margaret Thatcher's 'we do things more peacefully here' was widely quoted; detractors, though, were quick to point out her convenient disregarding of the violent English suppression of Irish supporters of the French revolutionary cause. Significantly, Furet and Vovelle were both concerned to distinguish the French revolution as being different in kind from, and more genuinely revolutionary than, the earlier American and British ones which might otherwise be seen to steal some of its credit.

## Popularising the past

The simplified models of the revolutionary period to which Vovelle and Furet were objecting tended to be reduced even further in more popular representations such as cartoons and comic postcards. In these the conflict becomes a straightforward opposition between two monolithic groups—decadent aristocrats versus an oppressed people or, conversely, aristocratic culture versus a brutish mob. This suppresses the diversity of the commoners, who become 'ordinary people' instead of a range of distinct and often competing groups, from propertied upper bourgeoisie to small business folk, artisans, manual workers and peasants (many of whom had to wait until considerably later, as did women and blacks, for political representation and social justice). Such oppositions also ignore the clergy, the second of the three 'estates' or orders into which pre-revolutionary society was divided. Evidence of their involvement could be seen in early caricatures of bloated clerics being forced to vomit or defecate their wealth; many religious establishments were destroyed or secularised during the revolution—Notre Dame, even, became a warehouse for a time.

The fictionalised accounts of the period on television were likewise subject to simplifications and omissions. In both 'La Comtesse de Charny' and 'La Grande Cabriole', invented characters supposedly representative of their epoch, mixed with figures from history. Despite the directors' professed intention to cover the period, the aristocrats tended to get the limelight, and history was, typically, reduced to the lives and loves of individuals, with a decided preference for 'the clash of feelings rather than of ideologies'[2]—a preference all the more noticeable in the case of a period so marked by precisely the clash of political and philosophical ideas. Interestingly, though, the possibility of history being open to competing interpretation was canvassed elsewhere on television in the form of modern 'retrials' of Louis XVI and of Marie Antoinette.

## Constructing the past—the symbolic moment

When the choices of historical interpretation and emphasis were being made by government or local authorities, the interests at work were particularly visible. The events the French government chose to highlight were, naturally enough, those usually seen as being positive achievements—the taking of the Bastille, the declaration of rights, and the victory at Valmy. As we shall see, though, these were celebrated not through historical reconstructions but through selfconsciously modern ceremonies in line with the government's emphasis throughout the bicentenary on marking the present and on preparing for France's future role in a united Europe. The conservative town council of Versailles, however, chose as their major celebration the re-enactment of the convocation of the Estates General to Versailles by Louis XVI, thus giving prominence to what could be interpreted as the king's attempt to respond to the widespread demand for constitutional change by initiating a 'royal revolution' that might have led to France becoming a constitutional monarchy like Britain.[3] Commercial considerations, however, were probably at least as important here as any point-scoring against the socialist government since. Versailles derives much of its income from exploiting the city's royal associations, and had plenty to gain from promoting these in a year when more tourists than ever were expected to visit the country.

Jacques Chirac, the right-wing mayor of Paris and former Prime Minister, while not openly opposing the bicentenary arrangements nonetheless made the centenary of the Eiffel Tower the city's major contribution to festivities. Nantes, the provincial capital of La Vendée region, which had been a major centre for counter-revolutionary activity and had consequently suffered brutal suppression, chose to recall these events rather than the more positive ones selected for official celebration. However, this area is noted as a leader of conservative, agrarian opposition to the central government, and habitually cites its past whenever a protest against some perceived neglect of regional interests is needed; the enduring rhetorical usefulness of the Vendéen massacres has probably helped keep them alive in local memory.

The politics of choice seemed evident, too, in Margaret Thatcher's gift of an early edition of Charles Dickens' novel about the Terror, *A Tale of Two Cities*, as the bicentenary tribute from the British conservative government to their chief adversary within the European community. Few commentators saw the choice as coincidental; even the newsreader who reported this gift on France's Channel One permitted himself the wry observation that the book seemed to be principally about how pleasant London was then and how horrid Paris!

No account of choosing moments from the revolutionary past to commemorate would be complete without some comment on the prominence given to the taking of the Bastille, the event generally seen as the official start of the revolution and the date of which was to become the French national day. The birth date of the National Assembly, which constituted the first step towards full representative government, might have seemed a more logical choice for this honour, but it lacked the symbolic power of the taking of the Bastille. An impressively medieval fortress situated in the heart of Paris, the Bastille had lent itself readily to all sorts of horror stories, even though records of the time suggest it was used for holding only a few well-to-do prisoners, and for short terms and in comfortable circumstances at that—judging by the accounts they ran up with local restaurants.[4] Moreover, it was already destined to be pulled down, and held only seven prisoners when it was taken. But in the popular imagination the Bastille was the prime emblem of arbitrary royal power and, by extension, all feudal, unjust power; this 'minor' victory therefore had an immediate emotional and propaganda significance, expressed at the time in mythic evocations of long-term prisoners freed at last from their chains into the light of a new day, as, it was believed, the whole of France was soon to be.

The event was also one that seemed to bear out contemporary optimism about the possibility of all classes and walks of life working together for the common good—an optimism visible in cartoons from the period showing the Bastille's taking and later demolition as moments of united endeavour. The subsequent blood-letting during the Terror, followed by the return to absolutist rule under Napoleon, added to the significance of this early achievement. The impact of this event at the time is evident in the popularity of commemorative medals claiming to be made from the very metal of the liberated prisoners' chains and models of the Bastille carved from its stone.

Indeed, the birth of modern France and the coming triumph of private enterprise capitalism were probably exemplified not so much in the taking of the Bastille as in the success of Pierre-Francois Pally, the upwardly mobile son of Parisian bistro owners, who made a great deal of money out of the demolition of the Bastille—and whose table models of the fortress were such a profitable line. In fact he was built up as one of the principal heroes of 1789 by the modern media. The mythic significance of the taking of the Bastille was to have a modern counterpart in the opening and demolition of the Berlin Wall—another tangible, readily grasped symbol of liberation that captured the popular imagination later in the bicentenary year. The two events were frequently linked in French newscasts at the time; in the words of one news-presenter, 200 years earlier, the walls of the Bastille—another symbol of absolute power—were falling . . . '. Pieces of concrete purportedly from this later wall also rapidly entered the souvenir market.

*Using the past in present protest*

Despite events from the revolutionary period being inevitably very much to the fore during the bicentenary, no one aspect of this distant past ever really became a serious issue in itself. Royalist protest was routine and fairly minor—a ceremony marking the date of Louis XVI's execution, the occasional 'Vive le Roi' scrawled on bicentenary publicity posters. It received little media attention: the royalist disruption of a concert of revolutionary songs got no more than a short paragraph in the social/gossip/small items section of *Le Monde*. Although the French revolution was unquestionably a bloody civil conflict, the descendants of the groups who were in conflict and suffered historically are none of them still significantly disadvantaged or discriminated against in France today. Nor has there been any international groundswell of support for royalist or catholic causes to match that for black, colonised peoples which gave added force to protests by and on behalf of the still disadvantaged Aborigines in Australia. Indeed, there was little sign of any French group capitalising on the heightened media attention on their country to activate international awareness, as pro-Aboriginal activists had done during the Bicentenary and the Brisbane Expo in Australia.

The French bicentenary celebrations themselves, however, did provide an opportunity for the local airing of present-day issues. The right-wing parties and dissenting factions on the left accused Mitterrand and the socialist government of spending too much on the bicentenary (although there was also widespread acknowledgement that whatever party was in power, some such celebration and considerable funding for it would have been seen as necessary). Mitterrand was presented as predominantly motivated by self-aggrandisement: seeing himself as God or as King (the choice of Versailles as location for one of his bicentenary speeches was much cited here);[5] and wishing his presidency to be remembered by four impressive buildings to Pompidou's more modest one.

The key dates of the bicentenary celebrations also lent themselves to use by protest groups. The Renault workers, on strike over the sacking of ten of their members, exploited the significance of 14 July to give added punch to a public demonstration, as did *L'Humanité* in articles on that day supporting their cause. The Goude spectacular on the Champs Elysées provided inspiration for many newspaper cartoons at this time: a declaiming Mitterrand is personally fitted for a rooster outfit by Goude on the front page of the satirical weekly *Le Canard Enchaîné* of 12 July; four barefooted blacks pant under a huge sack labelled 'Third-World debt' while Bush roars with laughter—'That Goude, what wit, what talent'. 'Um, no—the Goude parade is later,' hisses an embarrassed Mitterrand on the front page of *Le Monde* of 15 July.

A prominent subject of criticism and debate in Paris around 14 July was whether this year's celebrations were for the people or for the benefit of visiting dignitaries. A page-two headline in *Le Monde* on the 15th declared: 'The Bastille has been stolen'; *L'Humanité*, also on page two, noted the irony of relegating ordinary citizens to mere spectators behind steel barriers at the celebrations of their once active role in history. Similar criticisms were also being expressed in the cafés and marketplaces. As Bette, who runs a cheese stall in the Place Monge, put it, 'normally the 14th is more or less for us, the ordinary people, but not this year, oh no, this year it's for the heads of state'. Comments like hers were evidence of a street-level awareness of the extent to which major national celebrations may be aimed at the outside world and serve to make a statement about your country to it. They also point to the possible alienation of ordinary citizens from what are supposed to be *their* festivals, an alienation often exacerbated by inconveniences caused by such special arrangements as streets being closed to all except official vehicles (one of the regular Monge markets, for example, had to be cancelled because stallholders could not get their vans to it).

## *Local indifference*

Any account of the celebrations and their commercial or political exploitation, however, like many of the foreign newspaper articles about Paris during this period, tends to give a misleading impression of the extent of local interest or involvement in the bicentenary and even of its local visibility. Claims of the all-pervasiveness of commemorative souvenirs and of celebratory window displays, for instance, held good for very limited areas of the city, most notably those promoted heavily with overseas visitors. On 11 July I surveyed a cluster of popular shopping streets only a short walk away from Notre Dame and the Pantheon. Out of 180 commercial premises, only two gift shops had a prominent display of bicentenary wares; six other shops had made a noticeable attempt at some sort of purely decorative display, although the red bonnets among the tricolour ribbons at a jeweller's and the model of the Bastille in a hairdresser's window were the only ones with a specific bicentenary reference. A further two shops were simply exploiting the date through slogans that few sales promotions could resist: 'a revolution in prices' and 'prices decapitated'.

A check on the 14th revealed little change, beyond additional tables outside restaurants to cope with the obligatory feasting that marks this day, although there were two new displays worthy of note. The butchers at the bottom of the Rue Mouffetard were now wearing tricolour hats and ribbons, and a nearby bar had Mitterrand's 'head' displayed on a pike outside. This low visibility of bicentenary display had particular significance in light of the fact that the Rue Mouffetard, which is the busiest section of the area surveyed, actually celebrates its local identity each December with a lively week of dressing-up and street activities in which almost all the small businesses participate.

Further evidence of local indifference towards the bicentenary was the high percentage of respondents to a survey of popular knowledge about the revolution, made early in 1989, who had no opinion to offer about the significance of people or events from the period.[6] Indicative, too, was the absence of protest T-shirts. I saw only one in Paris, probably homemade: on it 'the bicentenary, my arse' was painted over the official birds logo parodied as vultures dripping blood. There was also a noticeable dearth of bicentenary references in the regular television news or in the different channels' signature clips during late December 1988 and early January 1989, suggesting the relative unimportance of the advent of even this national anniversary year beside such international news items as the Armenian earthquake and the Lockerbie air disaster, or the regular seasonal preoccupation with the price of caviar.

*The recent past—the valorising of resistance*

Although there may have been no significant grievances left over from revolutionary times for the bicentenary to bring to the fore, more recent history may have left a legacy of anxieties which a major national celebration could serve to address. As the 75th anniversary of the outbreak of World War I and the 50th of World War II, 1989 recalled military defeats and enemy occupation that there are still people alive in France to remember. Four-and-a-half thousand members of the resistance were executed at Mount Valerian on the outskirts of Paris between 1940 and 1944—more than twice the number guillotined in the capital during the revolution. These more recent anniversaries were extensively commemorated during 1989, and the events that were to follow recalled in television documentaries, special issues of newspapers and magazines (such as *Le Monde*'s '1939–1940: The Terrible Year'), and in newly released feature films, including Bernard Tavernier's elegiac evocation of the period of cleaning up and painful resumption of normal life after World War I, *La Vie et Rien D'autre* ('life and nothing else'). This film was publicised as 'a monument', playing on its dual status as a star vehicle for Philippe Noiret and as a memorial tribute appropriate to the year.

As evidence of an enduring French sensitivity to past defeats, one might cite the longstanding popularity of the Asterix comics, in which the inhabitants of an unconquerable village of ancient Gauls make life difficult for the occupying army of Julius Caesar. It is perhaps significant that a major local event of 1989, in terms of media promotion at least, was the opening of a large Asterix theme park outside Paris. Even more to the point is the 1975 film *Le Vieux Fusil* ('the old gun'), directed by Robert Enrico and also starring Philippe Noiret. This film, which is loosely based on the massacre of the inhabitants of the French village of Oradour by the retreating occupying forces in June 1944, was screened during an evening of prime-time television in June devoted to commemorating the wartime tragedy. After recreating the massacre in some detail, the film becomes a healing fantasy of revenge in which the apparently ineffectual hero—a middle-aged, plump and bespectacled French Rambo—picks off the perpetrators of the massacre one by one.

Both the Asterix comics and this film show the special psychological value the very act of resistance acquires as an answer to and transformation of national defeat. Significantly, it was de Gaulle, the Free French leader during the occupation, who was far ahead of any other contender in a poll taken to determine which recent French political figure most represented the spirit of 1789.[7] The theme of a struggle against oppression was capable of transcending specific political affiliations, and hence of linking the original revolutionaries, the wartime resistance, and the uprisings in China and Eastern Europe during 1989; and it is this same theme that is hallowed in the Marseillaise—the revolutionary call to the citizens to take up arms against their oppressors which has become the French national anthem.

Later in 1989 any surviving wartime memories and fears risked being further reactivated by speculation about the reunification of East and West Germany and the types of political and economic threat a restored German superpower might pose to its European neighbours. More recent history, then, even though not necessarily mentioned in connection with the much older events being celebrated, was probably one of the motivating forces behind the particular ways in which the bicentenary was celebrated and gave added point to its affirmation of national pride and importance in 1989.

**Marking the present**

The major official celebrations, irrespective of the past events they commemorated, functioned very much as an assertion of France's claim to leadership within the modern world, with their scale, style and success serving to proclaim the present-day capabilities of the celebrating nation. The extensive coverage the main bicentenary events received from the mass media was a crucial part of this statement. Prime-time television was devoted to showing and reshowing the Eiffel Tower's birthday show, the 14 July morning military parade and Goude's evening spectacular; all three, although watched by large live audiences, were designed with their prospective television audiences in France and abroad very much in mind. The key celebrations around 14 July were international media extravaganzas; the presence of 32 heads of state and the simultaneous holding of an economic summit had ensured maximum media attention on Paris at this time. Indeed, many newspaper articles actually focused on the massive presence of the media itself as a particularly noteworthy feature of the occasion.

*Mobilising the past in a rhetoric of progress*

That the revolutionary past was being recalled largely to serve the needs of the present was very apparent in the way evocations of 1789 were used to make a rhetorical point about 1989. The past was frequently cited as a contrast by which the degree of progress achieved in the present could be measured. An obvious example of this was a widely displayed series of publicity posters for the Parisian metropolitan transport authority. All followed the basic formula evident in the one described here: opposing pictures of a sedan with its porters and a metro ticket were captioned, 'Nothing like a good revolution to get things moving: 1789 Palais Royale–Bastille 1 hr 30, 1989 Palais Royale–Bastille 8mn. Long Live Eighty-Nine.' A similar contrast in favour of the present and future was implicit in much official marking of the bicentenary, not least in the public edifices built to mark the occasion. The Arc de Triomphe, the monument to Napoleon's military victories, is now balanced by the very much bigger Grand Arche, first used for the summit that accompanied the 14 July celebrations, and dedicated to human rights; the Opera House of the Bastille puts a modern palace of culture where the medieval fortress once stood. Such contrasts present as unproblematically given a historical continuity of national identity and mobilise that continuity on the side of 'progress'.

This rhetoric of progress could also evoke the past as the origin of achievements realised in the present. This was of necessity an important theme throughout the bicentenary, given the mixed and often bloody character of the revolution and the successive swings from republic to dictatorship to a restored monarchy and, finally, back to a republic again. Typical was the Serguei cartoon in the national colours of blue, white and red which filled the back page of *Le Monde*'s revolutionary supplement for July: in it the Bastille has become an egg from which has hatched a white bird of freedom in whose forward-pointing shadow Marianne, the French republic, steps out towards a distant horizon. The achievement in the present of the freedom of speech and of publication, which had formed article eleven of the declaration of rights but had soon been countermanded by Napoleon's reintroduction of censorship (and again, more recently, by wartime censorship) was celebrated by the seventeen Parisian daily newspapers in a joint free issue on 2 May. Each paper contributed a report on revolutionary events in their usual visual and verbal style—*Paris Turf*, for example, covered Louis XVI's regulation of horseracing. Despite this historical content, the sheer number and variety of the contributing newspapers, the range of political viewpoints they represented and the fact of their friendly cooperation in this celebratory issue were calculated to speak most loudly for the present realisation of a past ideal.

However, the past can also be evoked in ways that proclaim not progress but the lack of it. 'The Bastilles still to be taken' were a standard part of the political rhetoric of both right and left during the bicentenary. The point was often made through the wearing of revolutionary bonnets and cocardes; indeed, the use of these highly charged symbolic forms was a notable feature of street demonstrations during the year by such diverse groups as schoolteachers, tax officers, prison attendants, and workers in the Peugeot and Renault car factories. The fourteenth of July in particular produced formal statements from across the political spectrum measuring the present against the ideals of the past and emphasising what revolutionary goals remained to be achieved.

The Third World, excluded from the July economic summit of the seven most developed nations, was widely proclaimed as today's equivalent of the exploited and underprivileged third estate of pre-revolutionary times; the communist leader Marchais stressed in his feature article in *L'Humanité* that although equality and fraternity had been partly achieved by leftist governments, liberty had all too often been sacrificed in the process; one article in the centralist *Le Monde* dwelt on the irony of the privileged treatment of official guests at a celebration of the bicentenary of the abolition of privilege, and another suggested that France had achieved a centralised bureaucracy rather than the people's sovereignty which had been the founding principle of the republic. Such criticisms, however, contributed indirectly to the political rhetoric of progress by implying the existence of leaders aware of the deficiencies of the present and eager to redress them.

## Preparing the future

### *Proclaiming the nation's modernity*

The bicentenary, then, was not so much a commemoration of a past revolution as the mobilisation of that past to make a statement about the present and future. The major official ceremonies and celebrations of 1989 and the monuments designed as permanent legacies of the bicentenary year were all resolutely modern in style, implicitly rejecting a nostalgic evocation of past achievements in favour of an unmistakable commitment to the future. It was significant also that the most prominent of the many exhibitions mounted in Paris for the bicentenary was not a historical one but a massive display of very recent works of art, sculpture and installations from all over the world, including a considerable number of Third World countries. This 'Magicians of the Earth' exhibition affirmed Paris's role as the modern artistic capital of the world; advertisements for it gave prominence to Otto Hahn's comment in *L'Express* that 'Paris has become once again the international cross-roads for cultural exchange'.

The emphasis on the modern was at its strongest during the official celebrations held around 14 July. Moreover, the combination of these with the international economic summit of the seven most developed nations (France, Italy, West Germany, Britain, Japan, the United States and Canada) ensured that the concerns of the present and future were to be very much to the fore throughout this period, as well as guaranteeing the presence of international heads of state, including President Bush, at the bicentennial ceremonies themselves (it was speculated that Margaret Thatcher in particular might otherwise have used the occasion to slight the French government). The opening of the official celebrations consisted of a reading of the articles of the original declaration of rights interspersed with other texts on the same theme, but this was done by several well-known French actors in present-day dress, so it was very much a modern tribute rather than a historical re-enactment. The annual 14 July military parade down the Champs Elysées was bigger than ever for the bicentenary year; but its focus was, as usual, the current state of the French armed forces, and the display of sophisticated modern technology rather than a nostalgic look at the taking of the Bastille by musket and bill-hook.

The increase in scale of this parade related to another present consideration behind the later celebration of the victory at Valmy, that of providing a boost to the morale of the French armed forces in a year in which the defeats in two World Wars were inevitably being recalled. The much publicised 'opera' designed by the avant-garde commercial artist Jean-Paul Goude for the night of 14 July was another extremely modern tribute to the bicentenary—a grand parade down the Champs Elysées involving a cast of thousands of people and many different nationalities, in aggressively modernist costumes, and intended, according to Goude, 'not to celebrate the guillotine but to show that races, tribes and countries can mix together'.[8] The anniversary of the symbolic victory of Valmy on 20 September 1792, which ushered in the declaration of the republic, was yet another major historical event commemorated in a very modern official ceremony. The selfconsciously futuristic show put on at Valmy had been commissioned from a team of controversial modern artists, and included *Apocalypse Now*-style helicopter fly-pasts, galloping wild horses symbolising liberty, and alley ways made of canvas leading across fields to selected vistas.

Similarly, the monuments destined to be the permanent legacy of the bicentenary—as the Eiffel Tower was built for the Centenary Exhibition and is now its permanent marker—represent the progressive spirit of their own time rather than any homage to the past. Some restoration and cleaning of historical buildings in Paris was carried out in anticipation of the expected influx of visitors, but the main effort went into four new monuments: the glass pyramid which forms the new entrance to the Louvre, the Grand Arche, the Bastille Opera House, and a concrete palace to house the Ministry of the Economy. All four are dramatic statements in modern architecture, in line with the official emphasis on France's role in the modern world; three of them featured in official celebrations attended by the heads of state present for the 14 July celebrations and the economic summit.

*Claiming international leadership*

Although there were mixed feelings locally about the combination of the economic summit with the official bicentenary celebrations, this combination itself was, as we have seen, extremely functional in guaranteeing the presence of major international heads of state and in securing the greatest possible international media attention; it also legitimised the security arrangements which helped ensure the celebrations rated as a triumph for France and were not violently appropriated by other political interests (as the Munich Olympics had been). As a result, the celebrations were assured of having an international impact and not just a national one. Moreover, they showed the French president acting as host to world leaders, including many from the Third World, and chairing a summit meeting of seven economically powerful nations. The dignified yet avuncular public manner which fits Mitterrand's nickname 'Tonton' (the affectionate form for 'uncle') suited his assumption of the role of elder statesman, which was made all the more securely his on this occasion by the newness of Bush's presidency, the youth of leaders such as Benazir Bhutto, and the recent defeat of Margaret Thatcher's party in the European elections. Mitterrand's taking on at the summit the role of mediator between the developed and Third World countries also contributed to the image of France as a nation of central importance in the modern world, with a correspondingly major role to play in its future.

The more obvious acts of present-day international leadership provided by the bicentenary were complemented by the less tangible inspirational leadership that could be claimed as an inheritance from the revolution along with its ideals of 'liberty, equality and fraternity'. The bicentenary celebrations, with their necessary emphasis on the original goals of the revolution, rather than the violence later committed in their name, provided a strategic reminder of this spiritual inheritance. Events elsewhere during the year, moreover, lent themselves to construction as proof of its ongoing effect. Thus, the pro-democracy demonstrations in China in May were hailed virtually as a Chinese tribute to the bicentenary of the French revolution. The subsequent dramatic political changes in Eastern Europe—the shifts in Poland and Hungary away from hardline communist governments, the flood of refugees from East into West Germany, the opening of the Berlin Wall, and finally the overthrow of the Ceausescu regime in Romania—were similarly construed as tributes to France. 'In this year of the bicentenary of the revolution, a wind of liberty is blowing . . .' as the current affairs commentator began his report for Channel One on 6 October. Such expressions became a media commonplace in the final months of 1989. Thus Mitterrand in his televised speech of New Year greetings for 1990 which closed the bicentenary year: 'We are proud of celebrating our own revolution and fight for human rights . . .

now 200 years later, the same words carrying the same hopes are upsetting other Bastilles . . . people's revolt against tyranny and the victories of democracy—no-one could have imagined so magnificent a celebration for so beautiful an anniversary'.

The patrimony evoked, and the now year-long reminders of France's claims to revolutionary initiative, made the connection seem self-evident. Conversely, a claim of responsibility for the changes in Eastern Europe made by Margaret Thatcher in mid October during her annual address to the Conservative Party Conference had provoked considerable satire at the expense of 'revolutionary Maggie' and her 'Napoleonic' delusions in both *The Guardian* and *Le Monde*.[9]

### Opening and closing themes of 1989

As anyone who has ever attended a school breakup ceremony will know, some uplifting pronouncement about the opportunities of the future is an obligatory tailpiece to the rhetoric of celebrations of past achievements. In the present case, however, preparing the future had been a major concern, already evident in the very first speech given by the president in 1989. Mitterand's New Year address to the nation had largely taken the bicentenary year ahead for granted, and had focused instead on the dangers of a narrow and parochial nationalism (here implicitly counterattacking the position taken by Jean-Marie Le Pen, leader of the neo-fascist National Front, as well as warning more generally against the chauvinist attitudes that national celebrations can foster) and on the importance of looking outwards to the wider European community and France's role in it to 1992 and beyond. This point was underlined by the strategic location from which the speech was given—not Paris, the obvious choice this year in particular, but Strasbourg, the seat of the European parliament responsible for bringing about the united Europe. The election of new representatives to that European parliament later in the year received far more extensive coverage from the local media than any single event of the major bicentenary celebrations that followed. Yet, as we have seen, these celebrations themselves were serving the needs of 1992, both in asserting France's identity to allay any fears that the forthcoming removal of national boundaries within Western Europe might provoke, and in affirming its role as 'natural' leader in the years ahead.

A similar emphasis on the future and France's role in it was central to the speech Mitterrand made on 31 December presenting his greetings to the nation for 1990. After the opening remarks mentioned above, he spoke of the existing European community of twelve nations as having already served as 'a point of reference' for the peoples of Eastern Europe and forecast the possibility that the forthcoming European federation might be even larger than originally envisaged. France's position within this, however, would naturally be a senior one ('we have the good fortune to live in a country that has had 120 years of being a republic') especially if it continued to be worthy of this inheritance.

Two final examples help put the French bicentenary into perspective. Towards the end of 1989 a fresh set of souvenirs had started to appear—keyrings and T-shirts bearing the date 1992 and a ring of twelve stars standing for the united Europe to come. Similarly, although the multiscreen tribute to the revolution inside the Pompidou Centre had closed down, outside a prominent electronic display was still busy with its countdown, by seconds, to the twenty-first century.

# PART II

# Representations and lineages

# 4

## Canons, culture and consensus: Australian literature and the Bicentenary

*Pat Buckridge*

### Resisting the treatment

Literature was something of a stranger at the Bicentennial banquet, or at least so it seems in retrospect. True, the weekly calendar of events featured occasions at which writers were present, gave readings and interviews, received prizes, attended dinners, and generally participated, as more or less prominent Australian identities, in the ongoing national event. It is true also that some of the outback events and exhibitions made evocative use of Australian bush classics like Lawson and Paterson, and that a number of plays sponsored by the Australian Bicentennial Authority—Manning Clark's *History of Australia,* Louis Nowra's dramatic adaptation of *Capricornia,* and Darryl Emmerson's play about John Shaw Neilson, *The Pathfinder*—made the national literature a part of their theme.[1] Yet despite these indirect forms of recognition, literature does not seem to have figured very much, either as a national canon to be contemplated, or as a particular activity in which Australian writers and readers engage, and which might then—in either form—have been subject to the 'nationing' rhetorics applied to Australian activities and achievements in areas such as business, sport, leisure, science and technology, and in the more spectacularly public forms of 'high culture' such as ballet and opera.[2]

This low profile for literature was surprising in one sense: Australian literature has traditionally borne rather more than its share of the burden of national self-definition, and one might therefore have expected it to be used more than it was to lend a unifying imprimatur to the varied triumphs of 'Australianity' that the Bicentenary mobilised. The fact that 'Australian Literature' did not figure in quite this way, as the site of a national–cultural consensus—but seems, on the contrary, to have emerged as one of the few sites of undisguised conflict during (or shortly after) the Bicentenary—throws an interesting light on the longer-term conditions of literary canon formation in Australia.

It is probably clearer in immediate retrospect than it was in 1988 that the Bicentennial year was not quite the harmonious chorus of national self-congratulation its official organisers may have wanted it to be, and its more trenchant critics accused it of being.[3] Even within its most highly organised structures and projects there were spaces and opportunities for presentations, statements and gestures at variance with, and in some cases strongly critical of, the consensualist optimism of the official line. This may well have been especially true of the Bicentenary in its literary dimension, for a variety of reasons.

The relationship between literature and the Bicentenary, or more precisely between literary politics and Bicentennial politics, shows that same mix of concord and discord to be found in the celebration as a whole, here in an active relation to a well-established cultural institution, that of Australian literature. To put the point more abstractly, it shows the interaction between a set of limited-term, intensively *proactive* cultural initiatives (those of the official Bicentennial program) and a set of continuous cultural processes (those of the 'literary system' in Australia), some of which were affected by the celebratory and commemorative imperatives of the Bicentenary, and some of which remained largely unaffected. This is a study, therefore, in what might be called the 'Bicentennial effect'—an impact study of sorts, which investigates the consequences of a sudden and temporary change of ideological pressure on an established feature of the Australian cultural 'environment'.

Ecological analogies aside, it is important to try to evoke a sense of the Bicentenary as something other than a series of completed projects, whether official, unofficial or 'counter-official'; to see it rather—or also—as a set of 'weak determinants', pressing upon, but not necessarily changing, existing cultural institutions and discourses in any very striking or permanent ways. There are various reasons why literature, not as a thing in itself but as a cultural system, might have been expected to provide exemplary instances of this 'weak' or limited cultural effect. Perhaps the most important of these is the coexistence of two contradictory ideologies of 'the literary' in Australian culture, and the problems this posed for any thoroughgoing recruitment of literature to the Bicentennial task.

The two ideologies—neither of which is distinctive or original to Australia, of course—might be designated as a 'rhetorical' ideology, according to which literary works can respectably be produced for public occasions or under public auspices of one kind or another; and an 'expressive' ideology, according to which true literary composition is a private act of individual expression, not to be constrained by external prescriptions as to style or subject matter. The two ideologies, though contradictory in principle, are not completely so in practice:

Australian poets like Les Murray and Bruce Dawe have shown in their writing over many years that the rhetorical ideology of the 'occasional poem' can manage to coexist quite comfortably, in the same *oeuvre* if not the same poem, with the expressive individualism of the Romantic heritage. And in the course of the Bicentennial year the surprisingly resilient Australian tradition of public reading—a tradition which flourishes in a range of modes and caters, in different ways, to both expressive and rhetorical assumptions—clearly helped to accommodate *some* public literary articulations of the Bicentennial spirit, though the *Bulletin*'s exhaustive 'Bicentennial Diary' shows relatively few such events in the calendar.[4]

In other areas, though, the rhetorical/expressive contradiction was less smoothly negotiated by the ABA team. The most visible means by which the ABA attempted to involve literature in the celebration was through its publications program. This was to consist of three elements: six 'landmarks' (new reference works of a historical or encyclopaedic kind, such as John Molony's *Bicentennial History of Australia,* Diane Bell's *Generations,* and Joan Grant's *Australopedia,* an encyclopaedia for children); nineteen 'literary commissionings'; and the prize-winning anthologies from the ABC Bicentennial Literary Awards. The literary commissionings comprised five works of fiction (by Elizabeth Jolley, Kate Grenville, Jean Bedford, Olga Masters and Robyn Davidson), a book of poetry by John Forbes, and a mixed collection of works of social and cultural history, including the *New Penguin Literary History of Australia.*[5]

The conceptual clash is intriguingly illustrated in some of the shifts that occurred between the Authority's early planning documents and final strategies. In the report of the Publications Working Group to the National Office of the ABA in December 1983, for example, it was recommended that funds be devolved to all states and territories to produce, over a two-year period, major anthologies of short pieces by writers 'whose work had not as yet been published in commercial book form and who were no longer at school'. The state/territory publications were to be sold singly and as a set, and a national anthology was also to be created from the state materials, all publication to be undertaken by a special Bicentennial press. This anthologies project, or series of projects, was seen as 'an effective way of encouraging community participation in the Bicentenary' and was explicitly preferred to the commissioning of creative literature, as the latter was felt to be 'too great a commercial risk . . . if the publication proved not to be popular'.[6]

In the event the anthologies fell by the wayside, together with the proposed press, and the Authority went for literary commissionings instead, hedging their commercial bets by approaching only authors who were already well-established as well as recently successful in the marketplace. This marked change in approach could be interpreted simply as a money-saver, or alternatively, in conventional left-political terms, as an 'elitist' move from a popular to a restricted role for literature. But it may be more useful to see in it a reflection of the unsettled public status of literature. A 'rhetorical' function for literature as public witness is fully acceptable, it seems, only when that function is also understandable in 'expressive' terms, as creative writing. Cooperative reading (and book-buying), the necessary complement to writing in producing an effective 'sharing' of nationality, is a matter of much greater uncertainty. So what begins, in 1983, as a burst of confidence in the capacity of 'ordinary Australians' to *write* the Bicentenary effectively is undermined from the beginning, and finally destroyed, by a growing anxiety about their capacity or willingness to *read* it effectively.

Similar uncertainties are evident in the reception of the commissioned works of literature too. The success or failure of the publications program would be difficult to judge in terms of its stated objective, 'to create a limited number of works that best illustrate the nature and variety of Australia's people, history and culture'. Reviewers of the novels seem to have been at a loss to know quite what to say about their 'commissioned' dimension, and most of the regular reviewers solved the problem either by ignoring it or by making a joke of it. Thus for Susan McKernan, Grenville's *Joan Makes History* is a 'not the Bicentenary novel', while Jennifer Strauss, speaking of John Forbes's *The Stunned Mullet*, asks, 'Is it a joke that has superimposed the bicentennial logo, utterly inappropriate in its pseudo-stylised patriotism to this unreclaimed product of the irreverent '60s?' Only Margaret Harris, writing of Jolley's *The Sugar Mother*, concedes that 'in its fantastic way, the novel is a triumph of good faith, playing its variations on themes much at issue in Bicentennial celebrations'.[7] In general, though, it seems fair to say that the literary commissionings were treated as something of a mild embarrassment by the Australian literary institution, as manifested in the weekly review pages.

A second ideological obstacle to using literature as an instrument of national 'epoch-making' may well have been the widely felt ambivalence about the notion of 'progress' in the cultural field. Successive sets of political and economic arrangements can be ordered into a narrative of incremental or dialectical progression towards a better state of society almost (if not quite) as readily as scientific and technological achievements. Not so with literature and the arts. The idea that Australian 'culture' in this sense has been getting better and better, that 'our writers', for example, might be said to have attained peaks of literary excellence now that should make us proud as a nation, obviously clashes rather awkwardly with assumptions about the permanent value and timeless relevance of great art, and about the triviality of those merely 'technical' elements of artworks that might be seen as exhibiting historical 'progress'—assumptions which provide crucial support for the formation of literary and artistic canons.

There is, of course, another way of constructing 'progress-narratives' for art and literature, and that is to identify the developmental aspect in semantic rather than formal/technical terms. The 'progress', in that case, is not one of increasing formal perfection or technical mastery, but one of increasing adequacy in expressing, or reflecting, some 'essential reality'. As Tim Rowse and John Docker have shown, such narratives have played a central role in Australian cultural self-description, with the true Australian landscape, or the authentic National Character as the 'essential realities' to be expressed.[8] Narratives of this kind would have been of limited use for Bicentennial purposes, however, for two reasons: firstly, they necessarily postulate a single Australian reality in relation to which the varying adequacies of other periods may be measured; secondly, such narratives tend to be two-directional. The key moment of expressive adequacy is located in the past, not in the present or the future—in Australia's case, typically, in the 'Golden Decade' of the 1890s—and the 'progress' of art and literature since the moment of achieved synthesis is often conceived rather as a decline to the present than as a move towards another epoch-making culmination in the present or future.

## Bicentenarising the Canon

What I want to argue is that Australian literature, the institution, emerged from its 'bicentenarising' treatment not, as might have been expected, with its existing canons confirmed and celebrated, but with the processes of canon formation within the literary institution more comprehensively exposed than they had been for some time. I have touched on some of the ways in which the ABA attempted to organise and motivate literary production 'for' the Bicentenary, and I would now like to consider the complementary set of moves directed at the body of writing already in existence—at reissuing, reconnecting, and reinterpreting the works of the past. But the two concerns are by no means separate and discontinuous, and indeed some of the emphasis on 'writing now' (rather than 'then') in the ABA's literary program is perhaps best understood in relation to the difficulties encountered in using the literary canon as an instrument of 'nationing'.

Those difficulties did not begin with the advent of the Bicentenary. The canon has been a problem for Australian literature for years, one that has been recognised, diagnosed and negotiated differently at different moments. In general terms, though, the source of the 'canon problem' has always been the contradiction between the popular/egalitarian/democratic meanings traditionally attributed to Australian literature and the hierarchical and exclusive nature of the 'canon form'. If

'Australianness' is epitomised in concepts such as 'the democratic spirit' and the 'fair go', and if Australian literature is held to reflect these national values, then why does Australia need—indeed, how dare Australia have—such a thing as a literary canon, understood as a select order of works from which, by definition, the ordinary, popular majority of works is excluded?

The two 'ifs' of the last question indicate the forms taken by some defences of canonicity in Australian literature: either by disputing the cultural centrality of anti-hierarchical values—as rightward-leaning critics from A.D. Hope to Peter Coleman and Leonie Kramer have done for many years—or by asserting, in 'New Critical' fashion, literature's proper independence of particular sets of social, especially political, values.[9] But if defences of the canon have tended, historically, to be mounted by cultural and political conservatives, invoking notions of timeless aesthetic value, the converse is not true—at least not until fairly recently. Progressive nationalists like the Palmers and A.A. Phillips, and even literary critics well to the left prior to the 1970s (people like Jack Beasley, Judah Waten and Mona Brand) were as comfortable with the idea of a canon as their conservative counterparts, however much they might disagree with them about its membership, and about the relationship between literature and society.

The critique of canonicity itself was a product, rather, of the New Left. In this respect, John Docker's complaint about the 'punitive drive to construct hierarchies' in Australian literary studies was the local version of a much wider tendency in contemporary Western culture which Peter Hohendahl and others have termed the 'delegitimation of the canon'.[10] This process has involved both 'unveiling' the canon as an institutional construction, and also contesting the value of particular canonical works or groups of works, and rescuing previously ignored or forgotten works; as such it has figured prominently on radical political agendas, especially those of feminist and anti-colonialist movements.

As John Guillory has argued, however, the delegitimation of the canon along these lines is premised upon 'a structural homology between, on the one hand, the distinction of the canonical from the non-canonical, and on the other, the process of inclusion or exclusion by which social groups are represented or not represented in the exercise of power'.[11] To question this premise, he adds, is not to suggest that the canon is untouched by social struggles, but to recognise that these impinge upon it only indirectly. Those works that constitute the canon at any given moment are never, he argues, unified by a single or consistent set of social, moral or aesthetic values, dominant or otherwise, but by their common function as parts of a 'discursive instrument of transmission, situated historically within a particular institution of reproduction, the school'. In this position, the literary canon operates as one of the institutional mechanisms by which access to cultural capital is differentiated (and differentially valued), and by which social relations themselves are reproduced.[12]

Application of this Bourdieu-derived conception of the canon to the Australian context would need to be approached with some caution. Guillory himself (whose own focus is mainly general, and occasionally North American) is critical of the homeostasis of Bourdieu's model; and it would, I think, be necessary to extend the notion of the school to include the university and the college to give the model any real purchase on the situation in this country. Nonetheless, the notion of the Australian literary canon as a discursive instrument for the differentiation of access to cultural capital remains an attractive one for thinking about how literary classics work in Australian culture, and also, more narrowly, about what was at stake for literature in and around the Bicentennial celebrations.

The first of these questions can only be addressed in a sketchy and tentative fashion, to provide a kind of theoretical matrix for the second. Broadly, it might be argued that what have been described as opposing 'canons' of Australian literature—'social realist' and 'psychological/metaphysical' in one formulation, 'Lawsonian' and 'Whitean' in another[13]—should perhaps rather be seen, historically, as the stratified components of a single Australian canon (itself part of a larger canon containing British and some American works as well), access to which has been differentially granted to students in Australian schools and universities at different educational levels, not as direct expressions of the literary tastes and ideological values either of distinct groups of critics, or of larger social groups or classes. Specifically, such an argument might entail the claim that whereas works of the 'social realist' tradition, from Henry Lawson and 'Steele Rudd', through Vance Palmer and Katharine Prichard, to Alan Marshall and Ruth Park, have been offered mainly to upper primary and lower secondary school students, those of the 'psychological/metaphysical' persuasion, from Christopher Brennan and Henry Handel Richardson, through Patrick White and Martin Boyd, to Peter Carey and David Malouf, have by and large been offered to upper secondary and tertiary level students. It might also argue that the successive 'levels' within the Australian canon have tended to encourage the development of distinct capacities corresponding and appropriate to the differing social destinies of those who join the workforce at age fifteen or seventeen, and those who enter the professions after several years of tertiary study.

Such a model for literary education in Australia is necessarily very speculative. The ABA itself co-sponsored a national review of Australian studies in schools in 1988 (the Bicentennial Australian Studies Schools Project), which was partly concerned with literature, and the results of this project were incorporated in a broader inquiry commissioned by the Australia Council, on 'The Use of Australian Literature in Schools'. The latter investigation, though far from exhaustive, does appear to offer some evidence for differential access along the lines proposed.[14] And what it certainly suggests, at least as a working hypothesis, is the presence of a powerful resistance, deeply embedded within the structure of contemporary Australian society, to the popular, 'democratising' impulses which emerged, predictably enough, in the various representations and discussions of Australian literature associated with the Bicentenary. There are, in other words, signs of a necessary dualism in the organisation of the Australian literary canon, a dualism which is secured by its function in the reproduction of class-differentiated skills and knowledges, and therefore not particularly susceptible to ideologically motivated efforts to abolish the 'snobbery' of canonical hierarchy in the name of national unity and cultural consensus.

I want, then, to examine and contextualise several contributions to, and instances of, the process of literary canon formation as it developed within the weakly determining framework of the Bicentenary. In doing so I hope to indicate the range of cultural strategies by which the potentially disruptive 'question of the canon' could be both asked and answered—released and recaptured, as it were—in accordance with the contradictory ideological pressures of the historical moment.

## Some new totalities: a guide and a history

The *Oxford Literary Guide to Australia*, while having no official connection with the Bicentenary, and appearing in 1987, nonetheless performs a 'bicentenarising' operation on Australian literature somewhat 'avant la lettre'. It is recognisable as that partly by virtue of its closely analogous relation to certain official ABA-sponsored initiatives which deployed 'place' as a powerful instrument of cultural consensus.

The most interesting of these is probably Angus & Robertson's 'plaque project', a program for funding the installation by local councils of some thousands of memorial plaques all over the country, wherever a literary or biographical connection could be found to link particular Australian writers to particular places. The idea originated in the ABA in 1988 (apparently as a substitute for an earlier scheme to publish a detailed literary atlas of Australia, which fell through) and it was then transported by former ABA publications coordinator Tom Thompson to the then newly merged publishing firm of Collins/Angus & Robertson, where it is presently being implemented.

The significance of 'place' or, more precisely, 'locality' in the two projects—the plaque project and the *Literary Guide*—is strikingly similar, a fact which may partly be due to the presence of connecting individuals such as Peter Pierce (the editor of the *Guide*) and Tom Thompson. In both cases, the projects define themselves partly by what they ostensibly reject, namely a hierarchical conception of literary tradition. As the introduction to the *Literary Guide* insists, 'No critical hierarchy of authors is implied'.[15]

They also define themselves by the effect they hope to produce; the *Guide's* version of this is interesting largely for its evasions and subterfuges:

> Many writers have made notable creative uses of Australian landscapes and have been as responsible as early explorers or settlers for establishing certain places within the Australian consciousness. The *Oxford Literary Guide* is intended to please and instruct in ways that are recognizably Australian, to introduce authors and their living places accurately and not necessarily with reverence. It is intended also to stimulate both further reading of their works and physical journeys to find or revisit the places where authors lived and worked.[16]

The fashionable constructivism of the first sentence evaporates when juxtaposed with the blunt didacticism of the remainder of the passage, a quality that is hardly mitigated by the patronising assurance that the sugar coating on the Horatian pill will be Australian-made, or by the remarkable assumption that literary pilgrimages are a generally popular kind of holiday. The *Guide* purports to be an instrument for revealing the literary construction of the Australian landscape, and hence, by a familiar metonymy, for revealing Australia to itself as a self-belonging social whole. The reality is that it addresses itself to two quite separate audiences: one sufficiently knowledgeable about Australian literature to accommodate the information it provides, pleasurably no doubt, into pre-existing structures of recognition; the other, a very much larger audience of those who need to be taught about Australian writers and where they lived—or rather, since the 'selective index of writers' makes that use of the book virtually impossible, about Australian places and which writers ever lived there. Hardly surprisingly, as the sales figures for the book show, only one of the audiences has been listening.

The *Guide*, in short, suffuses the land with a literary aura, linking bush and city, slum and mansion, past and present, north, south, east and west, in a vast, flat, glowing network of national cultural consensus—but only for those who already 'know' Australian literature well enough to be able to disregard literary hierarchies anyway. Of Mitcham, for example, a suburb in the foothills of the Adelaide Hills, we are told that 'detective novelist Arthur Upfield worked at a mansion here for 4 months in 1911, before obtaining a position as fourth cook in an Adelaide hotel'. Not only that. Furthermore, 'this is the suburb chosen by John Stratton, hero of Arthur Cecil Gask's *The Secret of the Sandhills* (1921), when he decides to establish himself in Adelaide and sets out to win Mary for his bride.' And finally, 'Ian Mudie was educated at Scots College here, where fellow Jindyworobak poet Flexmore Hudson was later English master for many years.'[17]

Beyond the canon with a vengeance! And yet an entry like this (which is entirely typical) ideally assumes a reader who already has a pretty clear sense of each writer's position relative to the canon; a sense that the 'Jindies' are well within it, that Upfield, though familiar, is marginal, and that Gask is unheard-of. Registering the differentials is part of the game the *Guide* offers to play with the reader; but the bulk of the literate population, those for whom the canon would normally provide, through the school system, their primary point of entry to Australian writing, are hardly in a position to play along. For them the *Guide* is almost certainly a little-read and inaccessible enigma.

It is true, nonetheless, that reading the *Literary Guide to Australia* can be a surprisingly pleasurable experience. This may be an effect of the necessary directionlessness of the process: the fact that, lacking either narrative structure or argument, and being virtually unusable as a serious reference work, it presents itself for use as an instrument of pure play, an aid to mental dawdling, *flâneur*-like, among the inconsequential bits and pieces of Australiana it assembles. To this extent, it may even be that the *Guide* is potentially a quite powerful instrument for consensualising and democratising Australian literature in the way it aims to do—more powerful, perhaps, than it will ever be able to demonstrate, simply because so few people will ever have a reason to begin reading it.

In one of the best-received academic productions of the same not-quite-Bicentennial year, Paul Carter's *The Road to Botany Bay*, a distinction is made between 'exploration' and 'discovery' as opposed modes of travelling and of knowing: '[W]hile discovery rests on the assumption of a world of facts waiting to be found, collected and classified, a world in which the neutral observer is not implicated, exploration lays stress on the explorer's active engagement with his environment: it recognises phenomena as offspring of the intention to explore.'[18]

If the *Oxford Guide*, viewed sympathetically, makes for a kind of 'exploration' of Australian writing in Carter's sense, the second contribution I want to discuss can be likened to a journey of 'discovery'. For the *Penguin New Literary History of Australia*, the country to be mapped, whatever it might be called, is very palpably already there, waiting, indeed pleading, for historiographic revision and reconstruction. The urgency derives from two sources. Firstly, there is the familiar founding conviction that the job has not yet been done *properly*. Histories of Australian literature 'have usually taken the form of "surveys" or "outlines" '; they have been 'more concerned to document, to reorder and to revalue the literature than to rewrite its history'; they have 'imitated or adapted European models'. Secondly, there is an impulse of *responsibility to the present moment*, an impulse which has characterised the 'liberal tradition' in Australian literary criticism since the 1940s: 'Each generation writes its own literature and should produce its own literary histories'.[19] In this case though, the present

moment, and therefore the nature of the project, is given added specificity by the Bicentenary, which also inflects its proposed relation to
the literary histories that have preceded it.

The most important of these looming ancestral presences is surely
the notorious *Oxford History of Australian Literature* (1981), to which
the *Penguin History* is in some respects a direct reply, ostensibly
delivered on behalf of an assumed majority of teachers and researchers
in the field who felt their historical and philological interests threatened, and perhaps—who knows?—their democratic instincts offended,
by the tone and content of the Sydney University-dominated *Oxford
History*. This largely institutional polemic may partly account for two
interesting features of the *Penguin History*: its rejection of the *idea* of
a canon (though not necessarily of canonical writers) and of the
*revaluing* function it implies, and its refusal to pronounce *summatively*,
in 'epochal' style, on the achievements of Australian literature to date.
Summation and revaluation were prominent and contentious components of the Oxford historians' conservative critical rhetoric and thus,
however suitable and conventional both might otherwise have seemed
for a Bicentennial literary history, it was inevitable, given the composition of the editorial group, that a very different rhetoric would prevail.

This different rhetoric is, above all, a rhetoric of consensus and
reconciliation. The general introduction by Laurie Hergenhan consistently positions the project not just *against* certain precedents, but
*between* them. If the *Penguin History* is less narrowly mandarin than
the *Oxford* (the argument runs), it is also less of a documentary 'survey'
than H.M. Green's two-volume history, published in 1961; and the same
centring of the project is effected in relation to Geoffrey Dutton's *The
Literature of Australia* (1964), the first 'popular history of Australian
literature', whose 'accommodating eclecticism' is to be contrasted with
the programmatic revisionism of Grahame Johnston's *Australian Literary Criticism* (1962), an 'anti-nationalist and judgemental' collection
of essays, explicitly aimed at establishing a critical canon.

In mediating between the two historiographic forms represented by
Dutton and Johnston respectively (as also by Green and Kramer)—the
'broad survey, comprehensive and annalistic', and the 'selective,
judgemental account'—the *Penguin History* also purports to transcend
the adversarial ideological stances with which the two forms are usually
roughly aligned: a 'colonial, or post-colonial nationalism' on the one
hand, a 'conservative and defensive "internationalism" ' (i.e. Euro-
centrism) on the other. In a familiar trope, these are said to be simply
two sides of the same coin, 'different symptoms of the same post-colonial uncertainty and need for recognition'. To that extent, while the
*Penguin History* professes to be 'closer in spirit to Dutton's work', it
nonetheless consistently pursues a consensual middle way between the
two sides.

The quest for consensus ranges well beyond this duality, however, to embrace several other key oppositions. Literature and history is one, as the deliberately chosen title 'literary history' (rather than 'history of literature') indicates. In a slightly awkward merging of discourses, it is claimed that 'the rewriting of history in literature has . . . involved the rewriting of *literary* history' and also that 'historians have taken more account of literature than literary critics have taken of history'. Both claims reactivate the long-held liberal distrust of 'criticism', gesturing towards a mythically large and diverse community of contributing literary historians, of which the list of actual contributors to the volume (not especially diverse, in actual fact) is the merest token. Those same claims also, of course, enact part of a Bicentennial myth of 'resolving the contraries'.

Other oppositions to be thus programmatically harmonised include high and low culture, narrative and analysis, inside and outside perspectives, and early contemporary literature. The broad rationale for this general approach is given most fully in Peter Pierce's chapter 'Forms of Literary History' in the early part of the volume, where he argues that Australian literary historiography is distinguished by its 'habit of antithesis':

> As Wilkes justly notes, dualistic and antagonistic perspectives on Australian cultural development have been endemic: colonial and national, national and international, utopian and vitalist (Buckley), vulgarity and refinement (D.R. Burns), land and language (Goodwin), and Wilkes' own ironic contrast of stockyard and croquet lawn. These embattled dichotomies reveal . . .the melodramatic temper of Australian literary histories. . .The melodramatic taking up of exaggerated positions has had the effect of postponing ways of writing literary history that might eschew dichotomy, might study the subject more purely in literary terms, or in ones less trenchantly politicised.[20]

Pierce's final sentence places the conciliatory rhetoric of the *Penguin History* squarely in the domain of cultural politics, not merely that of 'intramural disputes', as he earlier suggests. If 'eschewing dichotomy' means escaping from politics into the purely literary, and if the *Penguin History* is attempting to show the way, then we have been given a literary history worthy of the Bicentenary. In a much more active and direct way than the *Oxford Guide,* it 'consensualises' Australian literary history, collapsing its conceptual distinctions and hierarchies in a drive to achieve diversity, pluralism and flexibility.

One of the dichotomies eschewed by the *Penguin History* is the opposition between high and low culture. In making such a declaration it was setting its face directly against the uncompromising high-culturism of the *Oxford History* published seven years previously, and also perhaps against that of Geoffrey Serle's earlier 'cultural history', *From Deserts the Prophets Come,* both of which explicitly excluded 'popular literature' from their purview.[21] In the substantive chapters of the *Penguin History* the proudly proclaimed inclusion of popular literature is implemented rather sparingly—Colleen McCullough and Morris West, for example, rate one brief mention each, but there is some consideration, in two or three different chapters, of popular genres like science fiction, romance, detective fiction, and children's stories. The 'rapprochement' effected between high and popular culture in the *Penguin History* is tentative and partial, splicing the two categories together without either theorising the split it professes to heal or constructing a radically more comprehensive historical perspective.

In somewhat similar fashion, John Rickard's *Australia: A Cultural History,* another Bicentennial publication, allows its 'democratic' assumptions about Australian culture to obscure from view the reality of cultural hierarchy. Rickard's manner of incorporating literature into his urbane conspectus of Australian social and political life is clearly dictated, in part, by his earlier analysis of the 'high culture/low culture' dichotomy in which he argued, not very persuasively, that the conceptual dichotomy itself is false and misleading, and needed to be discarded for serious analysis of the diversity of Australian culture to take place.[22] The feat of intellectual legerdemain by which a whole history of institutional cultural hierarchy is thus whisked away by the power of the cultural historian's egalitarian sentiments fits neatly into the wider Bicentennial pattern of celebrating democratic consensus as a fait accompli while in the very act of displaying its practical absence. Australian literature figures in Rickard's cultural history in predominantly canonical form, as a rather short list of authors whose work provides exemplary insights into current mores, or access to the leading edge of advanced social consciousness.[23]

## High culture and popular culture: towards a synthesis

It may be worth digressing from literature briefly to sketch out a somewhat broader cultural context for the readjustments that went on around the 'high/popular' opposition within the literary system during the Bicentenary. Some of the clearest illustrations of these 'consensualising' and 'democratising' endeavours occurred in relation to the highest of the high-cultural forms: the opera. In one sense, opera in Australia was always the form best suited for staging a symbolic act of cultural levelling, since the Sydney Opera House itself, as Graeme Turner has argued, provokes and mythically resolves the tensions incident to its being, at one and the same time, a purpose-built venue for elite entertainment, and an object and site of popular cultural interests and activities.[24]

Two events in particular epitomise opera's consensualising contribution to the Bicentenary. One was the Beltana 'Opera in the Outback' in September, in which Dame Kiri Te Kanawa (a New Zealander) gave an open-air performance of operatic arias and popular songs to an audience of 9000, brought from Adelaide and elsewhere to an encampment near the little outback town of Beltana in the Flinders Ranges of South Australia. One journalist described the gala event, which included a picnic race meeting and a barbecue as well as the concert, as 'South Australia's, indeed the Bicentenary's, ultimate event', and as 'a ritual, previously unknown, where all sorts of great Aussie traditions from beer swilling to horse betting to the heights of grand operatic arias were to be enjoyed alongside each other'.[25] It was indeed a remarkably comprehensive ritual of consensus: social, political, and regional oppositions and hierarchies all subsumed in general reconciliation under the sign of the conjunction of high and popular cultures: 'It was city meets country, culture meets carnival, with a bit of rodeo thrown in for good measure.'

Even the culinary cultures were, so to speak, yoked by violence together, repeating and elaborating the 'outlandish' catachresis which formed the rhetorical essence of the whole spectacle: 'Consomme Beltana followed by rainbow trout cooked in wine or lamb shaslicks, steak and sausage served with baked potatoes and tossed salad. And they will get baked damper, pavlova, billy tea with wine, champagne, beer or soft drinks in the biggest Outback barbecue in history.'[26] Pre-publicity, descriptions after the event, even off-the-cuff responses by the participants—all conveyed a much stronger sense of the *extraordinary incongruity* of the juxtapositions than of any genuinely achieved synthesis or 'common culture'. Dame Kiri's comment, 'When I first heard about it I thought these people are completely crazy,' was allowed to stand, giving implicit sanction to the view that the celebrated reconciliations retained their power and value only to the extent that the cultural antinomies themselves remained untouched.[27]

The same Bakhtinian duality was evident in a different form a few months earlier, in the four-part television mini-series 'Melba', a Seven Network production written and directed by Rodney Fisher and starring Linda Cropper in the title role. In this 'warts and all' story of her life, Nellie Melba appears as an exemplary icon of the high/popular reconciliation in Australian culture. This is signified in various ways, and on various levels: in individual ethical terms, via the familiar 'Melbiographic' motif of her endearing 'common touch'; and through a series of homologous cultural oppositions—city/country, metropolitan/regional, British/Australian, national/international—which are also reconciled in and by her career, thereby increasing the symbolic weight of her achievement. She is finally positioned, however, not just as a representative Australian achiever, but as the mythic donor of a national high culture to the Australian people as a whole. Melba's 'gift' of such a culture—sophisticated and universal in its content, democratic and popular in its distribution and reception—is first rejected outright, on her first Australian tour, by the scurrilous philistinism of the popular press, then provisionally accepted on her third tour with the American

J.C. Williamson. And in a coda to the fourth and final instalment, an 'ageless' Melba, addressing the audience directly from a position outside history, renews her offer, in a speech that evokes both the epochalism of the Bicentenary and the mythic 'nation-ing' of high-cultural aestheticism: 'And now the time has come to say farewell. I won't say goodbye because farewell is such a very beautiful word. I'm sure you all know it is part of a prayer and means "fare thee well"—which I wish you all, and I'm sure that you wish me the same.'

### 'Speaking proper': the authentic Australian voice

An important theme in the 'Melba' mini-series was language. Regional, class-marked and nationally distinctive accents and speech idioms operate in the text as one of the codes by which Melba's culturally 'centring' role is defined. (She herself, for example, preserves her closeness to the Australian people by reverting, on suitable occasions, to a broad accent and coarse humour, while also signifying her sense of its limitations, by her confident command of other idioms and languages).

Definitions-cum-celebrations of Australian nationality in terms of the supposedly distinctive properties of Australian accent and idiom have been a constant feature of nationalist discourse for most of this century, always with reference to the variously defined and derived 'broad' or 'working-class' Australian speech. Just as persistent, over this same period, has been a counter-discourse, conveniently represented (though by no means exhausted) by the constant flow of letters-to-the-editor, editorials, columns and features in every Australian newspaper complaining about the 'lapses' and 'errors' of popular speech, usually judged with reference to standards of grammatical 'correctness' and pronunciation defined by English authorities such as Fowler and (until recently) the *Oxford English Dictionary*.

One way in which even this traditional stand-off could be 'bicentenarised' into consensus began to appear in the earliest hours of the Bicentenary, in the television special *Australia Live*. Special care seemed to be taken to ensure that within the first ten minutes of the program, the series of presenters would be seen to cover not only the full range of places but also the full range of accents that could be called Australian: from the broad 'ocker' of Paul Hogan across a spectrum of diminishing 'breadth' (tactfully disarranged somewhat on the syntagm) through Bob Hawke, Graham Kennedy (who foregrounded the procedure by displaying his 'special voice' for the occasion), David Hill, Ray Martin, Jana Wendt, Phillip Adams and Clive James, finally to reach the 'pure' Southern English vowels and breathy plosives of (Australia's own) Geoffrey Robertson.

The instance of speech returns us, by a roundabout route, to the concept with which our discussion began: the concept of the literary canon. As John Guillory observes, 'the appearance of literature as an organization of canonical texts was from the first a scholarly and pedagogical device of the classical grammarians, [who] were concerned to teach "the art of speaking correctly".'[28] It is fairly certain that the *national* literary canon has never functioned in quite this way within the Australian school system, much as its long-time champions (the Greens, the Palmers and others) may have wished it did. As in other post-colonial systems, the canon that was, and to some extent still is, used in Australian schools both to institute 'grammaticalness' and to instil a respect for 'style' has always comprised an imperial mix of Australian and non-Australian authors[29], a circumstance that has had predictable consequences not so much, perhaps, in the private book-reading habits of the adult population (which are not well documented in any case) as in the more occasional and allusive uses of literature in the public sphere: in politics, advertising, the general press, and various forms of collective interaction and display by business and professional groups.

For this reason, one of the last of the Bicentennial-originated literary projects, belatedly released in 1990, the *Macquarie Dictionary of Australian Quotations*, can be seen as a more deeply significant contribution than it might at first appear. For it is precisely as an instrument for furnishing Australians with a ready supply of literary tags and touchstones for everything from date pads to dinner speeches that such a book might well achieve some of the 'nationing' effects for the population at large that more 'academic' publications could never hope to achieve. A necessary condition of that achievement might be said to be the canonicity that confers *quotability* on texts—a further instance, perhaps, of that now familiar Bicentennial paradox by which a 'democratic' breadth of effect and access is only made possible by a restrictive hierarchy of selection and representation.[30]

'Democracy' is very much the keynote of my final example of Bicentennial 'meta-discourse'. *The Tin Wash Dish* is a recently published anthology of poems submitted for a Bicentennial poetry competition run jointly by the ABC and the ABA. In his introduction to the collection, the editor, John Tranter, who was also one of the competition judges, describes an interesting transformation of intention. From the ABC's original brief, which was to include only the 40 short-listed entries, and which would have resulted in 'a collection more or less of a kind—mainly polished, contemporary, urban lyric poetry', Tranter took up instead what he saw as 'a chance to compile a genuinely democratic collection of poems by all sorts of Australians, all living and writing in the late 1980s, about every theme imaginable, in every style and form under the Australian sun'. Thus Tranter, himself one of Australia's most cryptic and factious poets, obedient to the founding tropes of *Australia Live*, seeks to constitute a national consensus which transcends both hierarchy and conflict in Australian literature and society, aspiring to the articulation of 'an authentic Australian voice' which is at the same time 'rich with diversity'. Not surprisingly, Tranter seems less than entirely comfortable in the celebratory mode and acknowledges, without attempting to come to terms with, some of the registered non-participation and resistance to the national poetic accord supposedly embodied in *The Tin Wash Dish*.[31]

I suggested at the outset that for all the consensual rhetoric generated by the Bicentenary, and perhaps because of it, the institution of Australian literature may actually in the course of the year have become more sharply aware of its internal conflicts and hierarchies. There are symptoms of this awareness, I think, in the precarious and sometimes contradictory character of many of the syntheses constructed around Australian literature during this time: the literary guides, histories, anthologies and the like that have been looked at in this chapter. But the most direct indication of an emerging 'anti-consensual' perception of the national literature, certainly its most publicly visible manifestation, was the acrimonious controversy that flared up in February 1989, and was dubbed by the *Sydney Morning Herald,* its main 'host', the 'Great Literary Debate'.

### '*Exeunt*, pursued by a bear'

The first shot in the 'Great Debate' was fired in mid-January by Greg Sheridan, one of the *Australian*'s stable of right-wing populists, with his proud confession to being bored by canonical Australian modernists such as Patrick White and David Ireland. But what gave the debate the scope and ferocity of a major institutional crisis was the intervention of Ken Methold, deputy chairman of the Australian Society of Authors (ASA). In a satirical 'Letter from Mt Isa', read at the Sydney Writers and Readers Festival, Methold ridiculed the 'Australian literary establishment' as represented by the 'Balmain/Glebe' type of novelist—'literary' rather than 'popular', and more concerned with psychological nuance and formal experimentation than with exploring 'real' social and political issues—and by strong implication attacked the funding priorities of the Literature Board of the Australia Council which, the 'Letter' suggested, discriminated in favour of the precious, the academic, and the abstruse in Australian writing, and against realistic fictional treatments of current social issues directed at a popular market.

Methold was promptly attacked by several spokespersons for the 'literary' (read 'high cultural') reponsibilities and prerogatives of Australian writers with remarkable vehemence and a good deal of personal animus. Tom Shapcott, then director of the Literature Board of the Australia Council, was outraged by what he perceived as an assault on the principle of government funding for literature, offended by what he took to be an aspersion on his own integrity as director, personally affronted by Methold's philistine disparagement of 'the sort of writer I happen to be', and angered by 'the generalised bucketing of a whole group of Australian writers and of the work of the Literature Board'. Shapcott was vigorously supported in his 'anti-philistine' stand by Geoffrey Dutton, literary critic and editor of the *Herald*'s literary pages, and Don Anderson, Sydney academic and *Herald* columnist, all of whom found it deplorable and dangerous that such sentiments should have been voiced by an officer of the ASA—by a functionary, in other words, of the very literary system in which they themselves held prominent positions.

Methold himself, evidently taken aback by the 'establishment' response, was slow to respond, but within a fortnight a populist 'freedom-of-speech' counterattack was in full swing, galvanised especially by the other side's announced intention to move no confidence in Methold as deputy chairman at the Annual General Meeting of the ASA in mid-March.

What was most significant about the 'Great Literary Debate' was not its timing—less than a month after the conclusion of Australia's greatest (certainly its longest) affirmation of cultural consensus—and not the quality of some of the exchanges, which were almost as vitriolic as if twelve months of barely controlled spleen had been suddenly released. Though these were noteworthy in themselves, it was rather the breadth of the critique of the Australian literary system that was generated within a very short time: Methold and his supporters, mainly in the press and publishing but also in academia and at the 'grassroots' (read letters-to-the-editor), raised questions about relationships between writers, readers and markets, about public funding for the arts, about the cultural effects of censorship and defamation laws, and about the custodianship of Australian literature. Most of these issues had received only sporadic attention for a decade or more, and although all of them, hardly surprisingly, had been been put firmly on hold for 1988, it seems more than coincidental that they should have emerged—redefined, reactivated, and above all *reintegrated*—in the wake of the Bicentenary.[32]

The 'Great Debate', in other words, not only demonstrated the striking lack of 'democratic consensus' in the Australian literary institution, exposing in its display of internecine bitterness some of the rifts and hierarchies that the various Bicentennial treatments of the national literature had attempted to mask; it also provided a broader basis than might have been anticipated for a serious and continuing analysis of the Australian literary system as a whole. To this extent, the most valuable legacy of the integrating strategies of 1988 may turn out to be the possibility of a newly integrated critique.

# 5

## Manning Clark's hat: public and national intellectuals

*David Carter*

How do intellectuals behave in public during the celebration of a nation? When every history becomes a people's history, when all culture becomes popular culture, what role then for the intellectual as public figure, for the academic or professional writer as social commentator, specialist or expert? The questions can be posed in these terms with particular force in the Australian instance, for the genius of the Australian Bicentenary was, as it had to be, its spectacular democracy conducted under the sign of leisure.

As Peter Cochrane and David Goodman show in chapter 10, the forms and practices of this democratic spectacle were managed according to an inclusive, but less than consensual, 'tactical pluralism'. But even the most democratic or pluralist of national celebrations will elect its spokespersons, interpreters, and public figures of authority, functions which may or may not at any particular moment be equivalent. By examining the participation of intellectuals in the celebratory forms of national occasions we can begin to explain how, in the public sphere of the print and televisual media, certain professional intellectuals become public figures and certain public figures come to function with the authority of intellectuals. The tactical pluralism of the Australian Bicentenary created a speaking position for a singular kind of public spokesperson, the figure of the 'national intellectual'.

The two recurrent motifs of the Australian celebrations—the democracy of ordinariness and the pluralism of ordinariness everywhere simultaneously—depended for their visibility and articulation on the existence of a certain genre of national public figures who embody the nation and yet stand above it: individuals strongly marked in their individuality who can nevertheless speak to and for the nation. This embodiment (which is no casual metaphor) is more specialised than that which occurs through the narratives of popular heroes or the ubiquitous day-in-the-life portraits of the national everywhere-and-everyday (see chapter 2).

It would appear from the evidence of 1988 that the role of national spokesperson and public figure can no longer be performed by politicians or captains of industry, at any rate not in the display of their power and status, although that power might well be confirmed by a display of its bearer's ordinariness. Intellectuals, on the other hand, are now 'made' for the part and not least because of their perceived distance from quotidian or sectional power. More accurately, only a very limited number of individuals from the ranks of philosophers, authors, historians and journalists, and perhaps only one in any given national context, can play the role of national figure and public intellectual. It will be part of the exercise of the present essay to determine the limits on the 'election' of intellectuals to the role of national public figure and to describe the economy of the discourse within which they speak. Put in other terms, it will attempt to say how—rather than a statesman, industrialist or sportsman or woman—a professional academic historian, Manning Clark, became the 'hero' of the Australian Bicentenary. The journalistic cliché that Manning Clark is a 'household name' speaks directly to the nationing performed on and through his public figure.[1]

For the purposes of argument it will be useful to define intellectuals in an unfashionably narrow sense, restricting the category to its 'professionals'[2]: certain academics, non-academic professional authors and journalist-commentators, those recognised by the conventions of the media (largely) as speaking from the realm of 'ideas' or of 'culture'. Every modern national celebration will be characterised by an extraordinary proliferation of public expressions of opinion—of hopes, desires, regrets or warnings—about the national destiny. From 'prominent' and from 'ordinary' citizens of the nation these oracular utterances will crowd the daily press, the weekly magazines, television and radio specials, and special publications. But they will not all be equally author-ised or carry the same significance as to field, tenor and mode.[3] Only a small number will come to us first and foremost as the utterances of an 'intellectual', that is, as deriving their primary authority from this category rather than from that of politician, union leader, entertainer, scientist, philanthropist and so on.

National celebrations, like other forms of the public festival or ceremony of which they are a sub-genre (or super-genre?), characteristically find their own special forms within the media: the 'special feature', the 'special edition', the special offer for subscribers, or the souvenir lift-out to mention only some of those from the print world. These special forms are precisely gauged to match the significance of the occasion, according to which they are more or less set apart, typographically and editorially, from the ordinary 'news' pages. They are designed to be removed (or not) from the host paper or magazine; sold separately as well as being free inclusions; released as separate publications altogether but bearing the imprimatur of the paper or magazine; and built to last a weekend, a week, a year, a lifetime (or at least designed to *look like* something built to last so long). They are gauged, in other words, in terms of a subtly differentiated relationship to the quotidian and ephemeral qualities of their host publications. These special, occasional, celebratory or commemorative forms are those in which the intellectual will appear, and their ambivalent status between the newspaper/magazine and the book works to determine the public figure and public discourse of the intellectual.

The implied audience for intellectuals in the 'public sphere' constituted by the mass circulation newspapers and magazines will not be an audience of peers, but an anonymous public differentiated to some degree within each journal in terms of cultural capital and address—metropolitan/statewide, national, or international/tourist—but not in terms of expertise or discipline. Nor can this anonymous readership simply be identified with the 'serious' book-reading public (we need to give such operational terms their full gravity) no matter how serious or reflective a particular essay might be. For the newspaper or magazine reader is not the same as the book reader: modes of address and time-scales—the time of reading, the possibilities of re-reading—function differently to produce a quite other relationship between reading and living (and the nation). The newspaper/magazine reader can be addressed as a national subject in an *occasional* way scarcely available to the book. The reader becomes a 'celebrant'. For the book to function in this manner it must be marked in some way as a 'special' production for the occasion, and it will often become magazine-like in the process.

Focusing on the public sphere thus means a close attention to the specific forms and genres in which intellectuals appear. These are genres outside the book, as we have said, in which the intellectual will most often be recognised as being somewhere beyond home territory, making a special address, one fit for the occasion even when in excess of the prevailing discourses of that occasion: the one serious, reflective or critical note in the midst of sheer celebration. Indeed, this mix of foreignness and excess (but as a way of marking the occasion) is almost entirely predictable and functions as a generic signal for contributions by academic authors to popular celebrations in mass media forms. This is the *point* of the academic's contribution: he or she is writing from elsewhere but speaking here, for us, in a special way and just for this occasion.

Something similar applies even to the non-academic commentators: the newspaper columnists, for example, who always appear in their columns in such a way as to suggest that their 'thinking' takes place elsewhere and derives its authority from beyond the immediate occasion of the newspaper itself (this is the distinction between the columnist and the 'staffer'). The occasional essay might only be a longer form of the weekly column; but the *national* occasion is nevertheless likely to change the speaking position and therefore the relation of the utterance to its own moment. It will be both less and more: speaking more intensely to the day but also to the destiny, to past and future. In both cases, for academic and non-academic commentators alike, we might say that the public intellectuals are *self*-appointed to a position already marked out for them.

It is in the public sphere, so defined, that we see certain intellectuals produced and reproduced as public figures (or certain public figures produced *as* intellectuals), and the narrow definition of intellectuals used in the present essay is one which the public sphere itself operates. Not all commentators or spokespersons in the public sphere will figure as intellectuals in this limited sense and not all of the intellectuals who feature will do so as public figures. What governs the 'public-ity' of the intellectuals, and what governs the construction of an audience in their textual appearances, is the way they fill or are filled by concepts of the nation.

It is in this light that we can speak of a specific category of the *national intellectual*. In Australia at least, where there is no traditional public recognition of an intellectual class and no operative tradition of the philosopher–citizen (the comparison is with France), it appears that the economy of national celebration demands that there be only one or two figures at any given time who can be presented, who present themselves, as national intellectuals. On the other hand, it might be the case that the Australian situation peculiarly demands that there be *at least one* such figure. The figure of the nation is endlessly reproducable, from 'great Australians' to 'ordinary Australians'; but the figure of the national intellectual by contrast depends upon an economy of rarity.

In Australia during the 1988 celebrations, the possible candidates for the role of national intellectual were few: Manning Clark and Phillip Adams, Craig McGregor and Donald Horne perhaps, Patrick White and Geoffrey Blainey (though more in the way of negative or limit cases).[4] Of these Manning Clark wears the crown, though it is a broad-brimmed hat, 'the hat that has almost become his signature'.[5]

Such public intellectuals will appear often but seldom alone in the special features, which might be defined generically by their display of multiple voices. How, then, is the (national) intellectual related to and yet distinguished from other (national) figures? How is he—and all the potential national intellectuals are male—distinguished as both 'intellectual' *and* 'national', and thus also distinguished from other intellectuals? Partly, indeed, through sheer repetition or ubiquity, through being the one individual or one of a small number who appears on (just about) all such occasions. Manning Clark, for example, figures in the 'Australia's 200' feature of the Melbourne *Age* (1 January 1988), where he selects '88 Prominent Australians'; the 'Australia 1988: Eight Views' feature of the *Age* (31 December 1988); *Time Australia* (January 25 1988); the *Bulletin* 'Bicentenary Edition' (26 January 1988); and in *The Australian Way* (Australian Airlines) December

1987–January 1988.[6] He was also one of a small number of individuals allotted a photograph and a personal statement within the travelling Australian Bicentennial Exhibition, in the 'Today' exhibit where we were told by Clark that 'we are now all citizens in the Kingdom of Nothingness'. And although it was a commercial flop we certainly cannot pass over *Manning Clark's History of Australia—The Musical*.[7]

But repetition in itself, though necessary, is scarcely a sufficient explanation. We must also examine how Manning Clark is featured, to continue our primary example, how and why he figures. At the simplest level we can note that in the majority of cases in the special features he is given top billing, appearing first and, more often than not, noted editorially.[8] His essays and his sheer presence thereby not only achieve greatest prominence but also function by way of framing or grounding subsequent essays and commentaries. These other contributions might head off in just about any direction: indeed, the more the better, for they will typically attempt in one form or another to 'cover' the nation, whether geographically, ethnographically, or chronologically. But Clark's essays are characteristically presented so as to act as a frame in two senses: both a way in and an encompassing discourse *no matter what follows*. On more than one occasion the frame is doubled as Clark is paired with Phillip Adams, the former speaking of the past and the latter of the future, both addressing the national present through 'envisioning'.[9]

The framing function of Manning Clark's presence in the journals is both an effect and a cause of his role as national intellectual. Of course it has something to do with the particular arguments he puts forward; but even more to do with the rhetoric and the *kind* of argument, which, as will be explained further, we might call 'ethico-historical'. Indeed, in more than one way questions of specific content are relatively unimportant compared to questions of genre (in an extended sense of the term). Manning Clark's 'ideas', if not precisely his rhetoric, might be spoken by a wide range of voices without anything like the same force—or meaning—as when accompanied by Clark's 'signature'. What, then, is the source of the aura or *gravitas* that surrounds Manning Clark's words and his public figure?

For Clark and for other intellectuals in the public sphere, the aura of the 'intellectual' is not summoned via the conventions of academic or scholarly discourse except in so far as these may be present as a trace, a whiff of the study that connotes an esoteric activity happening elsewhere. But neither is the national intellectual present in the public sphere in more 'modern' guise as the specialist or expert. Although in a year that threatened to become 'the Year of the Historian'[10] it might have seemed inevitable that at least one such historian should rise to national prominence, the public presence of Manning Clark as 'Australia's most prominent historian'[11] is not that of the specialist. On such national occasions, history is not present as a discipline or a delimited field of knowledge.

For the same reason, Clark's persona is never solely that of the expert. The essays which follow Clark's framing or grounding essay, in the various special features, are usually marked as specialist precisely in contrast to his. Obviously Clark's 'expertise' as the author of the six-volume *History of Australia* is a necessary attribute of his public persona. But in the way that this persona functions publicly, expertise is less significant than experience, knowledge less significant than 'wisdom', indeed history less significant than destiny, prophecy or moral choice.

The intellectual in the discourse of the public sphere I have been describing is a category apart from that of the professional. In Manning Clark's case it absorbs the professional qualifications of his *History* into what could be more properly called an ethical realm. Indeed this is the general case, that the figure of the public intellectual and even more strongly of the national intellectual exists as an ethical category apart from the technical categories of the expert or specialist. This is one reason why calls for intellectuals to become more publicly involved seem always to function by way of offering exemplary persons rather than specific modes of institutional intervention.[12] More particularly, immanent in the aura that surrounds Manning Clark as national intellectual is a series of metonymic connections that works something like this: the history is the nation/the nation is the history; the *History* is the history; Manning Clark is the *History*; Manning Clark is the history/nation.

What do I mean? The most popular (in all senses of the word) image of Manning Clark circulated in the Bicentennial year was that which connected the life and the work: the *History* was Clark's 'lifework'.[13] This was the significant cliché that the writers and producers of *History of Australia—The Musical* turned into a dramatic principle—brilliantly by most accounts—with Clark a character in his own 'History', as historian, private individual and, anachronistically, a participant in past events. So Clark's lived history becomes his 'living' of the *History*; and in the next step, his 'epic struggle' or 'quest' for meaning becomes the nation's struggle for identity or purpose, and vice versa, the nation's struggle becomes Clark's own. The poster for *The Musical* features Manning Clark, wearing his hat and clutching his history, dancing in a chorus line alongside 'his' characters: Ned Kelly, Caroline Chisholm, Henry Lawson, Billy Hughes (and Jesus Christ), among others. It was used as a cover by *Time* for their Australia Day edition which leads off with an essay by Clark *in propria persona*. And of course Manning Clark himself appeared on stage for a curtain call on the opening night of the production.

The monumental and impossible task that *The Musical* takes on—to dramatise the history and the *History* in a few hours—adds a further

**Figure 5.1.** Courtesy *Time Australia* (Designer/Art Director: David Lancashire; Special Lettering: Godfrey Fawcett; Illustrator: Geoff Cook).

level of metonymic connections for it repeats the monumental and impossible task of the *History* itself. Both then become available for interpretation within an already familiar set of national character traits. Although they agree on little else, this aspect of *The Musical* is picked up and so put into further circulation by the reviewers of the show: 'the musical is as much about Clark himself as his history'; 'a quest of personal as well as national identity . . . reveals both the pageant of our history and one man's lifetime effort to analyse and understand

it'; 'his quest is as ambitious as that of Sturt . . . an heroic musical
. . . every Australian should see it'.[14] Or again:

> Manning Clark's *History of Australia* didn't take quite as long to write as
> the time it covers.
> But with its great length, breadth and depth, its sense of scale as vast as
> the country itself, its intensity and its romance, it might well have.[15]

These remarks are all predictable enough, and they suggest how many
intellectuals took upon themselves the major cultural project of the
whole Bicentennial celebration, the fusion of 'high' cultural and popular cultural modes. This remains the case even though the version of
the popular being performed here is arguably a specialist and coterie
one, not popular culture's popular culture. Indeed the intellectuals are
the more likely to take on this task the more they are academic or
literary, rather than journalistic, in institutional location. In the words
of Helen Thomson, the only academic among the reviewers quoted, the
musical 'represents something uniquely Australian, not just in its subject matter, but in its combination of a massive intellectual project with
popular modes of entertainment'. This is utterly characteristic of the
'deep' nationing effect achieved by critical–intellectual discourse
(rather than reporting) in the journalistic sphere.

What I described earlier as the spectacular democracy of the Australian Bicentennial celebrations can be discovered in the extraordinary
amount of signifying activity given over to revealing or representing
the co-presence of the popular and the high, the everyday and the
exceptional, the local and the international, in a wide range of cultural
forms from the postmodern collage of the travelling Exhibition, as
Cochrane and Goodman show, to Dame Kiri Te Kanawa performing
'opera in the outback', to our internationally recognised writers writing
in the special features on their city or suburb.[16] The degree to which
the ten-volume *Australians: A Historical Library* could not help being
mistaken as the official history is the degree to which it (or its
publicity) shared in this project.

A combined *Bulletin*/ABA special publication introduces the Bicentennial art program in the following, characteristic way:

> Theatre-goers, lovers of landscape and music, and those with a taste for
> terpsichore will find ample diversions during the Bicentennial year. Yet the
> entertainment is not all elitist, and will draw audiences ranging from dozens
> to hundreds of thousands. Sandra Hall reports on the combination of the
> *popular* with the *different*. (emphasis added)[17]

The primary signifier of the nation in each case is the initial term
(popular, everyday, local). But the opposed term is always necessary
and not only to give the primary term its meaning or to enable the
nation to be signified as a whole, crucial as these functions are. More
importantly, the function of the second term is to create a doubled
image of the nation, *a nation able to reflect upon itself.* This is precisely

the double space occupied by the national intellectual, and the whole array of signifying activity surrounding Manning Clark during the Bicentennial year needs to be understood in its terms. Manning Clark as a household name and, with his hat, a household *image*, is high culture in our living rooms and kitchens—and 'depth' in our everyday. Thus, in a fusion of popular and high cultural modes (which nevertheless maintains their difference), the incongruity of the scholar in the bushman's hat might be resolved. But this is only part of the story.[18]

Within this populist cultural activity, the language of quest, epic and vision which accompanies all of Manning Clark's public appearances reveals a more complicated process of nationing around the figure of the national intellectual. For each of these terms signifies the *individual* (even 'epic', for the sense is always 'one man's epic struggle'). Indeed there is a strong sense in which the discourse of Manning Clark, whatever else it does, first of all represents *Manning Clark*. The point has nothing to do with self-promotion; it depends more precisely on a sort of self-effacement (within the history). What I mean to suggest, rather, is that Clark is identified with his discourse in a way that has few parallels either among other academics or other 'prominent Australians'. Patrick White is one comparable instance, and indeed White's 'negative' presence in the Bicentenary could be seen as equivalent to Clark's 'positive' one. (My adjectives are not judgemental, nor do they imply that Clark's role was purely celebratory—obviously not.)

If this identification of self and discourse can readily be seen as a way of marking Clark's status as *intellectual*, by the same token it seems to complicate his ability to stand as a figure of the *nation*. It gives us another explanation altogether as to why Manning Clark's hat 'has almost become his signature': it is less a mark of his 'popularity', after all, than of his singularity.

Clark's presence in the special editions and features is never representative in the way that the sportsmen and women, the politicians, and even the poets are: he appears not as one historian among others but as Manning Clark. We can even risk generalising this point into a rule for the 'making' of a national intellectual. Statesmen and sportsmen might be more or less interchangeable with other statesmen and other sportsmen, telling a story of class dominance or innocent success, but the national intellectual stands in his uniqueness. Or, in more qualified terms, if there remains a sense in which Clark is present(ed) as a representative historian or intellectual, this is only because the figure of Manning Clark transcends that banal representativeness. He is, as the *Time* editor puts it, 'an unusual academic'. A 'mere' academic in the public sphere, even a mere historian, could never be so completely representative of the intellectual as Clark manages to be by so completely re-presenting Manning Clark.

This is no less evident in those places where Clark's commentary is presented as just one among a number. Thus in the *Age* 'Eight Views' feature, in which his brief commentary is given no special privilege, all the other figures are replaceable in a way that seems not to apply to Clark himself: Herb Elliot could easily be replaced by another champion athlete; James Balderstone by another business executive; even John Gorton by another ex-Prime Minister and so on.[19] But Manning Clark, here 'Professor Manning Clark' and so identified more closely than usual with the profession of academic historian, scarcely seems interchangeable with just another academic or another historian.

We might consider some of the alternatives as a way of approaching more closely the singularity of the national intellectual. Geoffrey Blainey is the only historian to rival Clark as a household name, but his singularity is less personal than political. He has 'opinions' in a way that Clark as a public figure does not, and consequently, despite his association with such projects as the Bicentenary Birthday Beacons (precisely non-official and oppositional), he has little of the aura of embodied wisdom that can become Manning Clark's. Ken Inglis, general editor of *Australians: A Historical Library*, would appear to have had strong and immediately relevant professional claims to public prominence. But these were only professional claims. Donald Horne, as the author of the very well-known work *The Lucky Country*, and someone reasonably often in the news, would also seem to be a strong candidate and his absence for the most part from Bicentennial publications and performances is initially puzzling. That he could be relied on to be critical and discordant would not in itself disqualify him from the mantle of national intellectual, as the example of Clark himself illustrates; it might then be that his chairmanship of the Australia Council tied him too closely to the domain of policy and advocacy.

A survey of the Bicentennial publications and special features suggests that the most appropriate alternative figure would not be another academic at all, but newspaper columnist, media personality, and advertising company director Phillip Adams. The possibility is a revealing one. As well as appearing alongside Manning Clark in major publications, Adams gave a number of performances all his own. These include a lead-off essay in the English *Sunday Times Magazine* Special Issue, entitled 'Australia, Who Are You?'; and a key segment at the beginning of *Australia Live* where, at Uluru, a 'spectacular symbol of reconciliation and respect', he confronts the camera and speaks to and *as* the conscience of European, urban Australia: 'it is time for our young culture to learn from the oldest living culture'. Adams is an 'unattached' intellectual, non-academic, perhaps even at times anti-academic. But just as Clark's life is tied to the national history, Adams's is tied to the (modern) national culture, popular and high, through his association with the Australian film industry. And although one suspects he falls far short of Manning Clark as a 'singular' household name, Adams too has a certain style, a signature, and even a hat (he's wearing it at Uluru and in the graphic that for a time acted as the 'signature' to his weekly column in the *Weekend Australian*). Even without the hat there's a beard and a way of dressing: a tendency to black (like the hat), something always just 'left' of the conventional. The ensemble signifies being at ease with culture, an attitude that marks Adams as later in the history than Manning Clark and what we might call the position of tragic inheritance.

The comparison makes clear that there is something more than Manning Clark's expertise or irreducible individuality at play in his election to the role of national intellectual.[20] The singularity of Manning Clark—Manning Clark as Manning Clark—is a function of that public discourse of nationing which produces intellectuals as public figures. In the first place the signs of this singularity are what mark out Clark as an intellectual in a peculiar and strong sense of the term, not simply an academic, and as an *author* not simply a historian (indeed he is thus 'authorised' pubicly to write fiction and autobiography as well as history). In the same process, he is marked out as something other than 'just' an exceptional individual, say on the level of a sporting champion, and something more than an 'individual with opinions' after the manner of a Bob Ansett or a John Bertrand. The (national) intellectual, as I have suggested, does not have 'opinions', but embodies wisdom.

The author/intellectual stands as original and as whole, qualities which depend upon the presence of a strongly marked individuality—a strongly marked *presence*, rather, which transcends individuality. These are qualities which could not be better marked in language than by Clark's characteristic and highly conventional literary language of great men with flaws, all of whom we read as a little bit of Manning Clark, made in the author's image, and *lived* by him. His authority, in other words, comes not from any institutional or sectional grounding, but from *within*. The author/intellectual is thus present as self-originating and self-contained, or better, self-embodied. It is to the question of embodiment which I now turn.

The identity of Manning Clark with his own discourse is primarily an ethical relation. It works through the category of 'the lived' in which, as we have seen, the *History* becomes Clark's life becomes the history of the nation (and so on). This is Clark's 'singular' singularity which depends for its public profile on its embodiment; I mean this 'literally': its signification on or in the body of Manning Clark. Thus the figure of Manning Clark as well as, or rather than, his words is what speaks of the intellectual: the beard and the longish, wispy white hair, conventional signs of the thinker or poet; the impassioned and wavering speech; the impression of a frail body with piercing eyes and eloquent hands; and not least the hat, describing, covering, crowning the seat of the intellect itself. The body visibly bears the burdens of knowledge and history, and yet the reader's/viewer's eye is drawn upwards towards the signs of vision and prophecy. For Manning Clark's hat is the mark of the prophet too, the custodian and bearer of secrets to whom we entrust our past and future, the guardian of our destiny, he who suffers that we may be whole. As Alan Attwood writes in *Time*, Clark's 'contemporary status is akin to an oracle, studying the entrails of a country and seeking in its past clues to the future'. As such, it is indeed a purely mythological status.

This is the network of signs from which Clark's words emanate and from which they have their authority, an authority whose substance is also *style*. Its effects recall Pierre Bourdieu's analysis of charisma, although for the intellectual we might have to distinguish a 'weak' form of this effect from Bourdieu's absolute definition:

> Charm and charisma in fact designate the power, which certain people have, to impose their own self-image as the objective and collective image of their body and being; to persuade others, as in love or faith, to abdicate their generic power of objectification and delegate it to the person who should be its object, who thereby becomes an absolute subject . . . fully justified in existing, legitimated.[21]

The kind of singular human presence, and bodily presence, which the figure of Manning Clark represents is not simply an accident of personality, although it can doubtless take a certain variety of individual forms. What matters first is that there be a style, a signature, even though the style might be otherwise. But the different styles will exist nevertheless in relation to a conventional semiotic range (hat, beard, longer hair, and so on). We might recall Augustus John and other famous, visionary hat-wearers: even when all men wore hats these men wore hats such as few men wore. The hat in this early and high-modernist phase signifies an *aesthetic* difference, anti-bourgeois and anti-commercialist; and Manning Clark's hat finds a good part of its meaning in just this system. To put in different terms a point already implied, Clark's authority as public spokesman derives from the realm of the aesthetic, not the technical–professional.

Singularity is a generic effect. Further, the representation of the singular intellectual, original and whole, is as it were a precondition for the representation of the *national* intellectual as embodiment of the lived history—the history, that is, filling and filled by the whole body, the whole individual. And as the category of the whole individual is an ethical category, a category which speaks about the relationships between experience and reflection, consciousness and conscience, so the national intellectual becomes 'national' through his identification with what we should call the *ethical* history of the nation, the construction of the nation as an ethical whole.

The framing role of Clark's presence in the special editions (a presence which is nearly always visual as well as verbal) can now be seen in another dimension. The category of the nation can bear any amount of critique, diversity or fragmentation just so long as it can be contained within the one 'body'. This is the function of Clark's language which is characteristically 'deep'. Whereas subsequent essays in a given publication will range widely over the 'surface' of the nation geographically or ethnographically, Clark's essays gather all of the nation's history into a present moment in which he speaks to our 'deepest' and 'highest' capacities as individuals, as a nation—the two are virtually interchangeable. Thus the language of the essays is typically a language of visions, dreams, faith, conscience, wisdom, spirit, tragedy and destiny—anything but the immediate, the daily, the banal:

> The loss of faith and the loss of nerve will not last forever. All serious-minded people know there is a terrible infection abroad. To sweep it away, there may be a terrible blast or a cleansing fire may sweep over the continent. It may be that, underneath the present increase of violence and barbarism, a new civilisation is beginning. Who knows? But no one is showing us the direction of the river of life. The danger is that we may all end in a billabong, from the muddy waters of which we may see the majestic river sweep by. We may not even see that river.[22]

These occasional essays are intensely nationing despite, and of course because of, their eloquent critique and despair; nationing because the language of critique is the ethical and existential language of the individual. They represent the nation as a whole, even if as a divided self, a whole which can be understood 'vertically' as present to itself rather than merely 'horizontally' as an array of so many incommensurate parts. It is an assurance that the nation has a wholeness, the assurance of self-reflection.

At the same time the tenor of Clark's occasional essays and statements defines a limited address. Appearing in the 'serious' newspapers and magazines—or as serious supplements to more popular publications—the pieces address that class of readers who are endowed, via specific forms of social and cultural capital, with the power of 'self-making' and the capacity to conceive of themselves as particular sorts of national subjects: subjects of the ethically constituted nation or the nation as culture ('all serious-minded people'). It is the activity, the *space*, of serious reflection that matters, not the particular arguments or conclusions reached; and Clark matters less because of what he says in detail than because he so completely fills that space. In this sense the broadsheets are more deeply nationing than the 'louder' uncritical enthusiasms of the tabloids where the emphasis tends to fall more on the visible dailiness of the national occasion.

What emerges most strongly from the Bicentennial year in those places where intellectuals are to be found in public, in the special features and the magazine and review sections of the newspapers, is the degree to which the intellectuals operate 'naturally' within this ethical domain rather than the specialist domain of a discipline or the political domain of the citizen, and do so in direct proportion to the national burden of the occasion. The question at this level is not that of the appropriate stance of the intellectual in public, not critique versus celebration. On either side, critical or celebratory, expertise is always ready to turn into wisdom, history into responsibility. Debate typically functions in cathartic or therapeutic terms, therapeutic in the body of the nation (see note 24, chapter 10). The history of black–white relations tends thus to appear not as an immediate political problem, but as a problem in the conscience or the memory of the nation with the Aborigines or the land as the spirit to which 'we' are as yet unreconciled. Migration or multiculturalism can play a similar role, a troubled space of conscience and spirit in the body of the nation.

It takes a troubled man to fill this troubled space. What Manning Clark does, we might say, with his whole being is performed collectively by the intellectuals in so far as they can claim to have something to say to the nation: they take upon themselves the role of conscience in the body of the nation. This role, apart and yet a part, is precisely written into the forms of the special features and supplements of a national celebration in print.

Have we come this far merely to end up with a liberalist cliché about the role of the intellectual in society? Clearly not, for the body we have uncovered is nothing apart from its traces. The presence of the intellectual as embodied conscience/conscious, as memory and reflection, as the spirit or vision which animates the body, has as its primary function to testify to the existence of the body, of the nation, itself. The discourse which thus grounds the authority of intellectuals in the specific journalistic genres we have defined is a limited one which scarcely operates outside this 'occasional' public sphere. It does not, at any rate, operate with much currency or authority in the professional intellectual domains upon which it would seem to depend for its own authoritativeness.

As such we can see it as a discourse which acts on the intellectuals as well as being acted by them. The ethical domain is that space already marked out, by the conventions of the press for example, for the performance of the intellectual; and its privilege as a site turns the academic or journalistic author (however momentarily) into a national intellectual. The position from which the intellectual speaks is always and already thoroughly inscribed in the project of nationing. So much so that the characteristic discordant notes of criticism, disillusionment and opposition that are more or less the intellectual's 'own' are less counter to than constitutive of the discourse. Viewed in this light, some of the most anti-celebratory utterances begin to look like major generic instances as they speak to an ethically constituted 'general reader' and thereby constitute the domain of the intellectual as simultaneously an ethical and national one.[23] These ethical histories of the nation need to be understood not as a deep natural language (despite their own rhetoric of embodiment) but as a specialist language after all: no less specialist than academic history or political journalism.

Have we merely arrived at another cliché, that even critique of the nation gives credence to the nation? No doubt the point is true enough but perhaps it is only a banal truth. For what we have described is not a state of predetermination so much as a process of production and exchange. In exchange for the authority and significance that the presence of the intellectual imparts, the publishers give over space to an ethico-political language knowing that it will, more often than not, run counter to the discourses of their own news pages and corporate logic (though it might be picked up in that other specialist ethical realm, the editorial). On the other hand, in exchange for the authority that comes from appearing in the 'special' places of the public sphere, the intellectual gives over any specialist or, for the columnist, any sheerly ludic or immediate political concerns, gives them over for the generalising language of the nation knowing that their 'serious' contributions will become part of the entertainment or the spectacle that *makes* the occasion.

There is characteristically a quiet form of struggle over authority and the construction of an audience in the various publications. The intellectual stands over and above the editorial site, the editor stands over and above the intellectual. This is nicely suggested in the introductory remarks to the *Bulletin*'s Australia Day edition, as Manning Clark is both privileged and contained:

> With this double, 340-page edition . . . we mark the Australia Day and year that celebrate 200 years of European settlement, two centuries stamped by achievements about which only the incurably churlish will feel no enthusiasm. At the same time we acknowledge our undoubted failures as emphasised by Manning Clark in his introductory essay. While not everyone will share all or even some of Professor Clark's disillusionment he is right to concentrate our attention on today's dilemmas as much as yesterday's triumphs . . . We also look into the future believing that if the past 200 years have not been all they should have been, the next 200 will be better, provided the good sense and spirit of the changing Australian people endure.

We should not overestimate the power of critical discourse contained as it is here by that most curious and redundant of tasks which is the intellectual's own on such occasions: to tell 'us' who we really are. All questions of history and politics will tend to become ethical questions, that is if they are to become 'national' questions and carry the authority that that suggests. As Manning Clark's rhetoric moves between optimism and despair, pride and shame, it can speak to and for all of us, all the more so because, even at the risk of melodrama, it is never bland. As ethical discourse, it speaks intimately but to our public/national selves. The 'deeper' the questions are, the more deeply the reader belongs; but, to put it rudely, the questions are thereby in danger of becoming figures of speech that belong to everyone and no-one.

At the same time we should not underestimate the power of this ethical discourse of the nation, for its whole project is aimed at the reform of the reader: to reconstruct the national subject as knowing and therefore responsible. Manning Clark's rhetoric is as much about ethical choices as about anything else. It can be no more, but also no less, effective than any other ethical discourse; no more or less capable of identifying specific injustices or inequalities and of motivating readers towards reform. It will derive its power to do so from the desires and anxieties generated by the category of the nation, and it will find the limits of its effectiveness there as well. What we can see are the workings, not simply of a 'dominant ideology', but of the genres and daily practices which govern our ongoing writing and reading of newspapers or magazines. There is no 'outside' of this discourse that still addresses the reader as national subject and still speaks to the occasion.

We noted earlier that the authority of the national intellectual is grounded in a traditional liberal conceit, the organicist notion of the intellectual as conscience and as the conscious mind in the body of the nation. We need finally to ask how this image of the intellectual survives in the era of postmodern spectacle or 'leisure in the age of technology'. On one level it is indeed residual. Manning Clark as intellectual stands as a figure of pre-industrial labour—magnificently so, for the one man has written the whole history (and the one history has written the whole man). The contrast with the ten-volume *Australians: A Historical Library*, written by a team of experts and specialists each concentrating on their little part but never the whole, couldn't be stronger. Irresistibly, Manning Clark's hat suggests itself again, this time as a sign of non-alienated labour: pre-industrial, pre-specialist, indeed utopian in that it signifies the unity of life and work. Following through this line, it appears as no accident that Clark's own vision is utopian, a 'vision of Eden' as the title of his essay in the *Australian Way* puts it: it has been the traditional privilege of the author, in the strongest sense of the term, to be granted glimpses of a possible future better world. Clark's authority still rests, ultimately, on the (monumental) word. He is a hero, still, rather than a celebrity.

But as suggested at the very beginning of this essay, the need for the figure of the national intellectual is a contemporary one, not present in 1938 for example. The signs of pre-industrial labour, then, are not so much residual as part of Clark's present meaning: his embodiment of past and future, his transcendence yet containment of the ephemeral, existential present ('the Kingdom of Nothingness'). More specifically, the figure of Manning Clark is peculiarly suited to the postmodern forms of cultural representation. More than any other public intellectual, I've suggested, Clark has a style—a *personal* style, to be sure, but still as a style something that can be read only for its surfaces. There is an element of pastiche about that hat after all. Doesn't it sit there, like so much of Clark's own language, as a quotation from elsewhere; or perhaps as a set of quotation marks surrounding the whole figure of 'Manning Clark'? The public figure, the public rhetoric, and even the *History* are available, above all in the public sphere of the media, to be enjoyed as style, to be the subjects of playful recognition rather than cognition.[24]

The hat is a complex sign, both the sign of the organic intellectual and the sign of his passing. We can see Manning Clark's role as national intellectual finally to be that of a transitional and mediating figure. In none of the earlier celebrations of 1788 did an intellectual rise to public prominence in this way and it is unlikely that a historian will play a similar role in any future celebrations. The figure of Manning Clark is transitional between changing social and cultural institutions in the forms of national celebration: between the organic intellectual and the media personality, and between 'pre-industrial' and high-tech, verbal and visual, modes for the production of knowledge. His deep embodiment of the ethical history of the nation speaks to a present lack which we are likely to mistake as peculiarly Australian. His mediating role is, firstly, to tell us that we do have a significant past ('evil' or not scarcely matters at this level); secondly, to stand as a sign for the process of 'reflection' itself, to open up that space with a 'depth' that the politicians, for example, can no longer give it.

There is no necessity for either of these roles still to be significant in the future, no inevitability that the figure of the national *intellectual* will be needed, will need to be invented, to speak to them. But the economy of representation governing national spokespersons might also prove to be conservative. The signs are mixed ones as freelance intellectual and media personality Phillip Adams takes up the wearing of the hat and strides towards the camera at Uluru.

# 6

## The unmarking of soccer: making a brand new subject

*Toby Miller*

I want to concentrate in this chapter on a special event in the history of association football (soccer) in Australia. The intention is to utilise a case study of the Bicentennial Gold Cup of Soccer to examine the interplay of discourses of policy in the areas of ethnicity, sport and nation. The chapter argues that the attempt to 'unmark' soccer from its perceived condition as a non-Anglo-Saxon sport is an exemplary instance of the will to form a single national subjectivity. But this is to be done in the context of a discourse of multiculturalism, emerging from a huge first generation migrant population. This is a site at which conflicting technologies of the subjects concerned may be seen to operate.

Soccer is chosen here because of its marked status in Australia as an ethnically differentiated practice that is 'minority'. It is also selected because the Gold Cup occurred—sometimes uncomfortably—as part of state-sanctioned festivities designed to celebrate two hundred years of white control of Australia. Soccer exhibits critical drives within a policy and media discourse of unity, drives towards the silencing of difference; or rather, its redisposal.

What is interesting to note here is the unease with which the ideal type soccer follower and player—the soccer subject—is conceived within a range of discourses. Far from soccer being a domain of bread and circuses, where difference may be permitted free play away from serious matters, a whole host of critics, policy-makers and managers clearly ascribe a significance to the sport that calls for it to be reformed. The ideal type must be unmarked from appearing 'other than Australian', a term from the discourse of immigration which in and of itself requires that the adopted subject be recast from its previous demographic underpinnings to be loving, loyal and industrious in a new locale. This is a technology for producing subjects: much more than an 'accurate' or 'inaccurate' measurement.

**A Gold Cup and Australian soccer**

The Bicentennial Gold Cup of Soccer, held in Sydney, Canberra and Melbourne in July 1988, offered a crucible for identifying the contours and parameters of these questions at a special conjuncture. The Cup provided both stresses and opportunities for marketing the code anew, a marketing which, as will be seen, involved an excoriating gaze at the self that sought to reform soccer as an 'Australian' subject.

The series saw Australia fare remarkably well in the context of its international footballing history, defeating the then world champion, Argentina, 4–1, and losing a close final 2–0 to Brazil. The print media gave the competition enormous coverage, although no commercial television network had been interested in live telecasts. Crowds were good for the final and headlines proclaimed a new sense of—or prospects for—unity that would forge additional opportunities to mould soccer as the coming local brand of football.

The Cup was a moment within the Bicentennial celebration of the English conquest of the Aboriginal land and people that exemplified many aspects of the 'Bicentennial party', as it was officially termed. But rather than being a remark on 200 years, the Gold Cup was quite overtly an attempt to produce a new context, a context in which soccer could be transformed into a state of discursive and economic parity with or superiority over its competition. The Cup was part of a promotional strategy, not always coherently or cogently conceived and executed, and itself the site of struggle, incompetence and discontinuity. It ran over with the formation of possibilities rather than memories, in keeping with the design of forming a new, Australianised sporting subject.

Before the first games of the competition, the *Australian* argued that 'Australia needs to make a strong showing to finally shrug off its country-cousin image'.[1] Which constituency was in mind—the Australian populace or the world of international soccer administration—was left unstated. After the Cup, Brisbane's *Sunday Mail* announced that the 'sleeping giant of Australian soccer had finally stirred'.[2]

The *Sydney Morning Herald* also anthropomorphised the sport via a psychologistic metaphor of maturation. It pronounced an end to 'the inferiority complex which had plagued Australian soccer throughout its history' thanks to 'the enormous potential of our national soccer team' which had been worthily transformed into 'a promotable commodity'.[3] The Sydney *Daily Telegraph* consecrated the Argentinian result as 'a new era for the round ball code'. Coach Frank Arok and team captain Charlie Yankos provided metonymic accounts of the relationship between the sport, the national team and the public. They called for a human subject to be formed that would consolidate the three levels, with the national team (the Socceroos) standing as the vehicle articulating the connection between ball, person and nation:

They've got a mission. They have to do something about the sport in this country and they are doing it. (coach, speaking of team)

The Australian people understand what we're doing and they are supporting us and lifting us when we need it. (captain, speaking of public)[4]

Again we see shifts of register that describe a complex connection between elements of the soccer subject and its adjacency to Australia, a restless set of movements grasping at an authentic location from which 'Australian soccer' can be made to interpellate a national subject in a sovereign, non-sectarian way.

## The spread of soccer

Soccer styles itself 'the world game'. And it is probably watched and played by more people than any other sport. In Australia, however, that status is problematic. In addition to soccer, Australia houses three other principal codes of football: rugby league, rugby union and Australian rules. Very clear social divisions inform this split. Soccer, league and rules are played professionally and semi-professionally as well as in recreational mode. All strive to have national competitions and minimise divisions between the interests of the six states and two territories of Australia's federal structure. Union is the only basically amateur code, primarily for fee-paying schoolboys and graduates living in New South Wales and Queensland. League is based in Roman Catholic and government schools and working-class and rural areas of New South Wales and Queensland. Rules is a cross-class indigenous code, strongest in Western Australia, Tasmania, South Australia and Victoria. Soccer is played all over, but is very much the province of ethnically differentiated clubs. Unlike league and union in particular, its organisational strength lies outside Anglo-Celts. Club titles are frequently derived from Polish, Jewish, Hungarian, Macedonian, Serbian, Greek or Italian origins.

Despite the oft-repeated incantation that more people, particularly young people, play soccer than any other winter sport in Australia, the code has not achieved the pre-eminence as a spectatorial carrier of the health of the nation which it has attained in most of Europe and Latin America. The formation of the National Soccer League (NSL) in 1977 anticipated similar developments in other codes by almost a decade, but the League's history has been ruptured. In particular, the NSL's relationship with the sport's ruling body, the Australian Soccer Federation (ASF), has often been poor. Sponsors have come and gone, commercial television has shown at best a cursory interest and the national team has stumbled since. Club bankruptcies, personal fiefdoms, aberrant patrimonial appointment procedures and arcane/archaic management practices have all been pointed to as explanations for the failure of the code to move on. But the key element, vital because of its location within a realm of wider discourses about the hetero-homogeneity of Australia, has been ethnicity.

Attempts to market the sport homogeneously—in other words, in a way that can unselfconsciously address Anglo-Celtic males—have floundered but continue remorselessly. (And this at a time when rugby league in particular has promoted itself very successfully to, for example, women across the social spectrum.) Innovations of summer soccer, of team franchising in place of ethnically differentiated club names, or management audits and new planning, are secondary to this massively powerful sense that the signified of soccer is 'new Australian'. Internal to the soccer world, debates proceed ad nauseam between polarities emphasising, respectively, the need to maintain an existing base in ethnic identity and the desirability of integration into the mainstream norms of sporting businesses. This is particularly striking given that soccer is the dominant national sport in Britain, which provides the origin for most Australian sporting public culture.

In this sense, then, soccer has a marked status as the only popular sport in Australia known by its association with a diffuse set of migrant cultures. The game is somehow transgressive because of this marking and because it stands in for a material human presence differentiated from the Anglo-Celt that problematises the power of a transplanted English language as an expression and constitution of unity. The fragility of any concept of a unitary national cultural subject is nowhere clearer than in such fractures. It is clear that being numerically powerful as a participant sport is insufficient qualification to be properly local. Rather, a structure of feeling must be invented that interpellates the game within the mythic universal Australian subject and vice versa so that it can be deployed as an agent of nation-building/*Bildung* and sport-building/*Bildung*. This can only be achieved through an appropriate symbolic cleansing of the sport's self-misrecognition as a legitimate memory of or commitment to countries and cultures that are Other.

By the time of the Gold Cup, Australia had nearly half a million registered soccer players, or one in thirty of the population.[5] A local administration had been formed as early as 1880[6] and twelve hundred clubs were in existence by 1939, following the provision of a 'large cash grant' from the English Football Association.[7] Many Australian firms paid for their employees to form soccer teams in the 1920s and 1930s in the hope that the state's labour relations apparatus would regard this as part of a social wage.[8] By the 1950s and 1960s, international games occasionally attracted crowds of more than 50 000.[9] From 1974, soccer was the fastest growing school sport.[10] As has been noted, the NSL began three years later, with sides from all capitals except Hobart, Perth and Darwin. What had begun as a game played by expatriate labourers and miners from the United Kingdom had by that time been strengthened and ordered by the influx of Italians,

Greeks and Yugoslavs after World War II, to the point where it became a sport marked by its ethnicity, by the composite migrant that came to stand for it.[11] Women's soccer, meanwhile, had seen its first interstate game in 1921, with a crowd attendance figure of 10 000. By 1988, it had 21 000 registered players and was also evidencing a divisive internecine politics.[12] It is to such difficulties that I shall now turn, because of the implications that they hold for the formation of soccer as a cultural technology for the ideal Australian subject.

### The personal politics of Australian soccer

When Australia qualified for the 1974 World Cup finals: 'It seemed there would be no stopping soccer from shedding its cinderella tag and becoming a major football force in this country. . . [but] the game slipped backwards for a while. Its European roots, its infighting and its administration threw up barriers too steep to hurdle'.[13]

Whereas crowds of more than 5000 were common in 1980, the average NSL attendance in 1988 was half that.[14] And the *Australian Soccer Weekly* (*ASW*) was arguing that the standard of professionalism at all levels—play, administration and promotion—was not commensurate with a century of history. Much of the blame for this is routinely allocated to the internal politicking of the code.[15]

Such a move psychologises political struggles by transforming them into human subjects, subjects whose failings can be slotted home to underachieved interiorities. The sport has become a person when it is held to be in a 'self-induced coma'.[16] This in turn encourages us to consider the awkward invocation of the *soma* associated with the nation (for instance, 'the body politic' or 'the health of the nation'). As Laponce notes in his study of ethnically marked soccer in Canada, there has long been a tendency to homologise, integrate and confuse the body and cosmology. Deploying bodily images can easily bring up questions of internal articulation between bits and the dominance of some parts over others, again with the united cultural subject as the whole person that justifies and totalises these components opposed to the sectionally interested subject.[17]

Such anthropomorphism subjectifies the entire topic, which in turn encourages accounts of the status of the code that follow a maturational ethos. This ethos is akin to the discursive conventions of nations and their architecture and management, if with the overdetermining urgency of this developmental psy-logic. Being a nation or a person is more usefully conceived outside this romantic rhetoric, as a question of administration: the regularised policing of discursive and material norms of unity. And so is being a sport. The comments that follow are common in their constitution of the need for and possibility of a depoliticised bureaucracy to run the game in contradistinction to present—and long-established—politicised procedures. These statements also constitute themselves as outside this political domain:

> Everyone outside Soccer who has the necessary perception to judge, knows that the same has been politics ridden for so many years past. (*ASW* editorial, pre-Gold Cup)[18]

> This is a political game, and politics is about getting the attainable. (Arthur George, President of the ASF, pre-Gold Cup)[19]

The possibility of an end to politics, the Canaan without ideology, is called for from a state of grace. The unseemly laundry titled 'politics' is located in other subjects who fail to recognise the need for oneness. Even in George's acknowledgement of the need for a grounding in politics, this is always because it comes from elsewhere. Here, the speaking subject is not political. Those articulating the presence of politics are ipso facto themselves absent from it. To speak of its dire qualities is to defer any possibility that it might be positioned in the here and now. The health of the sport, like that of the subject or the nation, is held to be beyond politics; at least it should be.

These metacommentaries function as clearing houses that will sift the worthy from the unworthy in a non-patrimonial, non-sectarian manner that knows the right words and precepts for growth: streamlined, professional, corporate, apolitical, efficient. These are signifiers of instrumental rationality that absolve subjects acting as agents within them of any trace of committed meaning outside a means–ends bifurcation. The 'good' of the nation or the code is paramount. Like distortions of the perfect knowledge available to the putative ideal consumer of *homo oeconomicus*, differences of interest and approach are inessential, discretely delineable and eradicable.

### The mark of ethnicity

While the question of administration underwrote the micropolitics of the sport, a broader social issue overdetermined the very demographic, fiscal and imaged existence of soccer: the question of ethnicity.

It has been suggested that the 1994 World Cup in the United States will see fixtures 'strategically placed in areas guaranteed to provide ethnic support; South Americans in southern California and Texas, for example, or Italians in New York'.[20] Consider that statement against plans advanced in 1989 by the company which had just been chosen to market the NSL: 'The NSL must create a new image and change its name and logo so it can be identified as Australian, modern-go-ahead and exciting . . . CLUB names should be amended where necessary to prevent ethnic recognition'.[21] Soccer in Australia is often called 'Wogball',[22] for all the mutually British origins of the game and those who label it that. Unlike almost all other sports, the soccer subject is formed as ethnic as well as gendered: this becomes both its strength and its vulnerability. For some, the principal requirement for future growth of the code is 'Australianisation'.[23] The soccer subject's self-image and status of perception by others are to be redisciplined.

This rehearses debates over the merits and demerits of ethnically organised and identified clubs, which activists within the sport see as related to a 'lack of professionalism and ability to address the Australian way of life'.[24] For the *ASW*, the problem is summed up in the expressions 'nationalistic clubs' and 'Nationalism must go'.[25] This is a nationalism not of Australia, not of the imaginary integrated local subject, but of the ethnicity of origin of club officials, players and supporters, a sign of fractured subjectivity. The soccer citizen is a split citizen, divided not only in terms of sporting affiliation or affinity, but as a trace of difference from the ideal type migrant subject with cultural, political and economic fealty fully yoked onto the local.

The Australian government's publication *Australian Sport: A Profile* contains an essay which specifically attributes soccer's problems to these most externally identifiable and unruly points of signification. It argues that:

> since those first waves of southern European migrants in the 1950s, soccer authorities have been talking of their game as Australia's sport of the future . . . Ethnic divisiveness lingered, making soccer the most politically tangled of Australian sports and keeping its potential for furthering national unity just that—potential. Soccer in the 1980s is still waiting for its future.[26]

This kind of argument is routinely deployed in sporting journalism[27] and even by Arthur George, who on retirement spoke of the 'ethnic problem'.[28] For Jeff Wells, it remains 'a disincentive to widespread community acceptance'.[29] The game fails to meet the test of 'a truly accepted part of the Australian way of life'.[30] It is even alleged that 'the ethnic base of the game' has produced crowd violence.[31] A survey of television executives, government officials and sports marketers found that terrace disturbances tied in with 'ethnic affiliations and "funny" names' to hold the code back.[32] In short, the sport is being decried as 'un-Australian'.

The problem with this critique is that it denies the utility of this lineage. *ASW* might proselytise against the system of overt Continental-ism that is club support, but the paper, like the code, is financially and culturally itself marked by that system: it is owned by an ethnic press. Shortly after his election to chair the ASF, Ian Brusasco publicly advised that he had been born 'Italo Trospero Brusasco', adding: 'I am proud of my Italian heritage and it was only after much heartache and consultation with my father that I "Australianised" it'. This was said to 'typify the identity crisis which has held back the code for years'. Much was made of the fact that Brusasco himself had played rugby union.[33] This fits into the same system of knowing the soccer subject as the one which stresses that many second-generation Mediterranean migrants have mocked arrivals who continue to follow soccer.[34]

But 1984 saw the commencement of a Sydney Ethnic Soccer World Cup, with teams from sixteen countries, including Australia.[35] And the argument remains that ethnicity is a base for the sport.[36] As former soccer official, senior public servant, national team member and Aboriginal activist Charlie Perkins once argued: 'They call us wog ball, but don't they know that the whole world is made up of so-called wogs and that they have made soccer the most popular game in the world?'.[37] Many ethnic groups have given huge amounts of money to 'their' clubs because they 'see a soccer team as an essential vehicle for establishing a community identity'.[38]

So whilst it continues to be argued or implied that the mark of un-Australianism is upon soccer, this is in many ways to deny the special meanings and strengths which that marking gives the game. Such an argument assumes an essential local quality attached to other sports which are just as fractured, but along lines that do not describe a topography of anxiety in the face of non-Anglo origins. This anxiety is to do with searching for ultimate signifieds of amity and singularity. Soccer's process is a search that is easily identified as compromised because its starting point is dispersed within geographical unity. It stands for the sorts of gaps in need of suture that were formerly associated with Catholic–Protestant dissonances in Australia but are here given the additional threatening contour of language. The national subject is under question in more obvious ways than could ever be the case with the less overt differences hinted at by divisions within other codes. Before exploring sport and ethnicity, it is as well to establish precisely how we configure such questions of identity, via a consideration of ethnicity and multiculturalism and their relationship to Australian public policy and the Bicentenary.

## Ethnicity and multiculturalism

Multiculturalism has become the response of certain liberal–capitalist states to the increasing presence of diverse ethnic populations within the national polity. As a policy initiative it is described by Mary Kalantzis as a reply to certain imperatives: 'The nation state of advanced industrial society can no longer draw its identity from a single homogeneous ethnic group. It does, as its rhetoric says, have to create cohesion out of diversity, but to do that it has to make the diverse groups appear equal.'[39]

The 1975–83 Liberal–National Party government in Australia embraced multiculturalism as a means of forestalling racial violence[40], a strategy which, according to Andrew Jakubowicz, suited an ethnic labour aristocracy and petite bourgeoisie keen to coopt migrant labour into the service of capital via an allegiance to the state prised from this promise of cultural maintenance.[41]

These left critiques of mystification—where multiculturalism drags us away from examining the economic base—have homologies on the right. Here, it is said by Geoffrey Blainey and other writers from the *IPA Review* that the policy mystifies threats to a stable political system and its singular democratic heritage that are posed by disunity and fractured loyalties.[42] This formulation identifies multiculturalism as a segment of 'The Guilt Industry', alongside support for land rights to indigenous peoples.[43] It discerns a 'multicultural industry' of unrepresentative people whose profession is the garnering of public funds in the name of the oppressed but under the real sign of rent-seeking for themselves.[44] Multiculturalism decries and denies the rich British heritage that writes history as a striving for the ultimate liberty of the market.[45]

We might do better to consider multiculturalism as a technology that classifies and redisposes. Its task is to categorise the old and the new, the retainable and the abject, the usable and the obsolete for the purposes of: government funding; tests of loyalty; and methods of distinguishing between: what needs to be assimilated; what can itself assimilate; and what should be left behind. Soccer is relatively safe terrain for the state, but the political economy of the game's relationship to other codes of football and to the commercial media draws it into a problematic relation to ethnic diversity. Multiculturalism, a technology dedicated to producing political and industrial harmony for the state, becomes a business liability for football.

Consider this against Nancy Fraser's critique of Jürgen Habermas for supporting a single public sphere. She is concerned at its potential for silencing particular categories of person by imposing a uniform mode of expression and therefore a restricted performance of subjectivity, which has major implications for women and ethnic minorities.[46] But for the managers of soccer, the public arena to be occupied is about 'Australian soccer', with each section of the syntagm to be equally forceful, but the adjective to connote an ultimate unity. A single sphere that is prepared to house soccer as adequately Australian is a desirable home. Minority status and minority definition are undesirable when contrasted with the opportunities presented by inclusion in homogenising discourses.

This technology of multiculturalism must be read in the context of the history of Australian immigration, for about 20 per cent of Australians were born elsewhere, and an additional 10 per cent are the children of migrants.[47] Many came not only as the objects of government policy, but under the particular desiring sign of state subvention.[48] This dated from the need to bolster population numbers in the light of the threat indicated by the Pacific theatre in World War II and as a source of cheap labour for industrialisation.[49] The initial aim in terms of the civic sphere was that 'migrants would become "like us" and join the Anglo-Australian monoculture'.[50] The assimilable subject eventually gave way as a desirable *telos* of immigration policy, however, to the integratable one. This imagined a melding together of different features to create the alchemically formed Australian. The Australian subject was now to be a kind of world citizen, forged from a white heat application of Mediterraneanism. But this always had its underside, as Jakubowicz points out:

> The public representation of 'the Australian public' has in part been fashioned by images of the immigrant. She has been in turn a new settler, a new citizen, a new Australian, a refugee, a migrant: the obverse image has also shadowed this formal public representation—*refo, Balt, wog, dago, slope* . . . an unresolved dichotomy, signalling at once threat, challenge, competition and a lesser form of life: deviant, underprivileged, bizarre, unnatural. Throughout there has been the fear of the enclave, so that every element of the public discourse of settlement has sought to fragment, isolate and scatter the immigrants.[51]

The contradictions within the exemplary subject of this new world are as apparent synchronically, then, as they are diachronically. Riven with different leanings and histories, it must be recuperated to certain binding logics of the political and cultural origins of Australianism. Despite the arrival of three and a half million non-English speakers since 1945, Australia remains the most monolingual advanced industrial society in the world.[52] The subcultural corollary is of disorganised, impoverished workers and an overconcentration of migrant women, in particular, in secondary labour markets.[53] As part of the contradictions enacted across the bodies of women, they have become the *locus* of culpability both for low population growth on the part of Anglo-Celtic Australians and the site of responsibility for the maintenance of ethnic homogeneity within donor cultures.[54]

## The Bicentenary and multiculturalism

I want now to examine ethnicity and multiculturalism in the context of the 1988 Bicentenary. What did the official cultural technology of celebration make of multiculturalism, this slippery sign of unity in disunity that functioned as an ordering logic for the enunciation of a disordered amalgam? In the (1979) public statement announcing the invention of the discursive unit, 'the Bicentenary', Prime Minister Malcolm Fraser advised that: 'It will be a time to reflect upon our developing and changing national identity, as a united community transformed in a remarkable way by the migration programs of the years since World War II'.[55]

From its inception, the Bicentenary was overflowing with meanings to do with pluralism and its heterogeneous virtues, a pluralism postdating the halcyon days of its reign within political science and prefacing its adoption and elaboration under the sign of textual theory's endless deferral of meaning. Amongst the five 'Aims and Objectives' of the Australian Bicentennial Authority (ABA) were two that sought 'to encourage all Australians to understand and preserve their heritage, recognise the multicultural nature of modern Australian society and look to the future with confidence. . . [and] to project Australia to the world and invite international participation with the aim of strengthening relationships with other nations'.[56]

It was presumably under these heads of power that the Gold Cup could be the carrier of Bicentenary logics. Such imperatives lead us to two comfortable sites of Bicentenary discourse:

* firstly, the ABA's choice of an *Encyclopaedia of the Australian People* to be 'its priority publication for 1988 . . . to make basic information on ethnic origins and the Aboriginal people available in alphabetic form; and to look at historic and contemporary interaction in a chronological and thematic way'.[57]
* secondly, Johnny Warren's reply to Martin Tyler's pre-Gold Cup final introduction of: 'Johnny Warren, you're such a good barometer of Australian feelings. What's going on at the moment?', with the following: 'I've just been talking in Japanese on Japanese television, and that just indicates our multicultural society'.

The first site shows the urgency for an ordering knowledge, coupled with a telling of the past, that manages the administration of peoples through a hierarchy of alphabet rather than, for example, a way of organising history that considers material equality. The second site not only encourages a rather disrespectful reading that proposes thought-disordered television commentators; it also bears witness to the immediacy of ethnicity and soccer, their always already adjacency that must be spoken even though its absence is so desired. We can encounter institutional sites that reveal counter-logics and disruptions more in keeping with the divided multicultural subject, that historicise and problematise it.

A decade after Fraser's christening speech proclaiming the ABA's *mise-en-abîme*, the High Court of Australia handed down a landmark decision over the power given to the Authority to authorise use of its logo and certain prescribed expressions (for example, 'Bicentenary', 'Bicentennial', 'Australian' and '200 years') and to seize all goods contravening this right. The case came up over anti-Bicentennial Aboriginal products organised under the theme of '200 years of Suppression and Depression'. The Court found that the relevant section exceeded the Government's constitutional authority.[58]

From a different perspective, the ABA was criticised, along with multiculturalism, for its stress on difference, for denying the nation's collective debt to the unifying force of Britain and Christ.[59] In the eyes of the then Leader of the Opposition, John Howard, this was 'guilt-inducing' at the expense of pride in achievement.[60] It was argued that the 'party' had been perverted by the influence of the left and its excoriating selfconsciousness (a selfconsciousness which was also misrecognition). Such accounts were given aetiological contour by writers like John Carroll, who argued that a significant number of Australian intellectuals opposed any glorification of their pioneering and integrative heritage because of a collective guilt attributable to their dissociation from the essences of purpose guaranteed by Christianity. Further evidence was adduced from 'their' rejection of the mother culture of Britain, itself a sign of self-hate that was then projected onto their founding heritage.[61] Fellow neo-conservative Robert Manne saw this as crucial to the nature of '1988': 'When historians look back on the Bicentenary, their most challenging task will be to explain the mood of cultural pessimism which, during this year, took hold of the intellectual class and cast its shadow across our celebrations'.[62]

The question of ethnicity—the representativeness of its demotics and the matter of their state subvention—was one of the principal *foci* for the right. For Blainey, the planning of the Bicentenary had been dominated by government fears 'of offending the vocal, richly subsidised but small multicultural lobby . . . the multicultural industry'.[63] We are seeing the same kind of sign as the one that marks 'soccer'.

### Bicentenary, sport and nationalism

One could well query the relevance of the Bicentenary to the Cup beyond its initial legitimising function: 'Bicentennial Soccer'. But the Authority was ready to position the competition after the fact as a stellar event within the broader moniker of the Sport 88 Program. James Kirk, the ABA's Chair, summed up the year by listing his selection of seven 'spectaculars', markers of the celebration's success. The only sporting event was 'Socceroos thrashing Argentina'.[64] The Cup was also highlighted in his letter of despatch to the Prime Minister attaching the Authority's final report to government.[65] In the words of one ABA self-promotion, although the Gold Cup was 'one of the biggest events on the Sport 88 calendar . . . it was successful beyond expectations'.[66] It is worth considering these sanguine summations against earlier rhetorics.

Prior to the competition, newspaper reports that few of its previous World Cup representatives would attend argued that this meant 'Brazil devalues the price of "Gold" '.[67] Rumours circulated to the effect that the Argentinian Diego Maradona was being offered A\$130 000 a game by the ASF to come.[68] As 'pessimism' about the prospects of seeing him increased, the *ASW* argued that his absence would see 'the entire series . . . fall in a heap'.[69] Confirmation that he would not play and that Brazil was not sending all its stars was held to have devalued the entire enterprise.[70] And at the same time as it had been making threatening noises about funding, the ABA itself was writing to the ASF 'to have confirmation from you of the standard of the teams you have contracted to compete. Is it the No 1 team from the 3 visitors? Is Maradona contracted to play?'.[71] As if to answer such criticisms by positioning them as outside the realm of valuable knowledge, ASF President George appeared on television to hail right-thinking viewers by advising a press conference that the absence of Maradona would only affect the 'non-soccer public'. Members of the *cognoscenti* 'would know it's a team game'.[72]

The ASF hired former national team captain Johnny Warren to go to South America for a week to find out who was actually to be sent over for the tournament. This was seen as essentially a retort to media reports that mere reserve teams would appear, raising the spectre of what the *Australian* termed 'a worthless, unproductive competition'.[73] The President of the Confederacao Brasileira de Futbol published an article in the *ASW* devoted to stilling selection/authenticity critiques.[74] These anxieties were part of a history of what Warren called the 'bad old days when overseas teams came out here to have a picnic . . . [which now were] well and truly over'.[75] This was in turn intimately related to the ambassadorial capacities for Australia of the national team.[76]

Opinions turned. Warren came to be invoked as a disinterested authority on the topic. His views that the eventual Argentinian squad was of great quality were quoted with reference to him as 'former Socceroo captain', not an employee of the tournament.[77] He wrote articles saying that the sides named were 'serious'.[78] The media discourse was transformed into that of Arthur George: to continue a critique of the competition was to be an identifiable simpleton. Viz.: 'Anybody who believes Argentina and Brazil will be in Australia for a holiday during the Bicentennial Gold Cup had better think again'.[79] The *ASW*, previously so sceptical, found the Argentinian squad to be 'of unbelievable quality',[80] '[t]he pedigree of the teams . . . cannot be questioned'.[81] It justified the status of the Cup in market terms, placing the exchange value of the visiting Latin American sides at A\$60 million.[82] This utilitarian logic extended to a form of *machismo* reportage. At a press conference on arrival, the Argentinian coach said there was '[n]o such thing as friendly games'.[83] In terms of the selection of unknowns, the 'outsider' Warren could inform ABC-TV *Sports Arena* watchers that '[p]eople have to realise teams change'.[84] Put another way, Australia was being privileged via exposure to future stars. Such contradictory pressures were also at play within the very structure of the ABA's system of support for Bicentennial sport; a tension between excellence and access on the one hand and past and future on the other.

The Authority's overall sport and recreation program was designed with a set of objectives that might be called a late reformist litany of the 'good and deserving' juxtaposed with the 'real and essential'. On one side we find 'participation by all Australians . . . community based . . . and participation of disabled people'. On the other, 'exciting . . . special, innovative events designed to . . . reinforce bonds between International, National, State, Regional and local sport and recreation groups . . . and reflect the Authority's theme of "Living Together" '. Or put another way, this combined inclusive and meritocratic priorities, reflecting those familiar dualities of equity opposed to efficiency and the development of participation versus the development of elites. This amounts to a fractured ideal subject, for ABA sport was clearly fissured. Its embodied categories bore the traces of a liberal ideology of access and quality uncomfortably adjacent to a welfarism admitting of the need for equity of outcome. The sporting citizen being hailed was the best of the best at the same time as it was the neediest of the needy. The intention is to write over contradictions about quality and elitism with a cursor carrying amelioration and a future earthly unity.

In seeking private sector funding for the program, ABA Chair Kirk called up the moneyed in terms of their fealty to national essences, that strange double move of nationalist discourse that proclaims the necessity of restabilising what is allegedly always already there. The context here was the high production values magazine, *Sport 88*:

> Sport comes naturally to Australians. It is central to our whole way of life. This taste for sport reveals some basic characteristics of our national identity, such as relaxed lifestyle.
>
> Sport is also an egalitarian pursuit in Australia. It's there for all to play and enjoy, in the spirit of giving everybody 'a fair go'. . .
>
> Every bit of assistance from sponsors is an investment in the biggest celebration in Australia's history. The ball is in the business court now . . . to step forward and support Sport 88.

Elsewhere in the publication, a link was forged between the egalitarian and the excellent. It bridged the rhetorical divide between access and output operating under the sign of meritocracy: 'It's said that sport is Australia's national religion, a relentless pursuit of competition and recreation by 16 million people. Behind the standard-bearers will be millions of active, weekend-style sportsmen and women.'[85]

Advertisements claimed that Sport 88 was 'Making the Bicentenary Great . . . Celebrating Australia's passion for sport' because it was held that 'Sport 88 is for everyone—whether your passion is watching or winning'.[86] Even competition is called into the register. Elsewhere a frequently adduced homology between the profit and loss discourse of the economy, this element of sport was routinely excluded from ABA arguments about togetherness. Rather, the ABA juxtaposed its programs as 'a balance between . . . top class, national and international, funded events and those providing opportunities for mass participation, catering to all sectors of the community, including the aged, disabled, Aboriginal, ethnic minority groups, women, youth and the able-bodied'.[87] In other words, the Authority was there to remedy market failure, the failure of spectators to support forms of sport and sporting subjects which were native and natural to the Australian, but which could be denied an adequate expression of this birthright because of the competitive subjectivity of untrammelled commercialism.

### Sport as cultural form: Australian national identity

Many accounts of sport in Australia situate it unproblematically as a central tenet of local culture, either in a welcoming or critical way. This is to reify the term 'sport', to deny the fissures—of gender, class, ethnicity, media coverage, public participation and region—which it will sometimes try to reconcile. Increasingly, though, the tensions that these fissures describe are finding expression. Debates about the value of government assistance to elite versus mass participation sport and about media coverage of male-dominated events and their presentation as carriers of national well-being have proceeded at the levels of academic sociology, parliamentary committee and the management of sporting organisations.

In 1985, Australia's Minister for Sport argued that sport had a 'dominant role in our development as a nation' because it 'cuts across race, age, sex and class and is deeply ingrained in the fabric of our society'.[88] It is instructive to put that statement against an elaboration by a senior bureaucrat appearing in the same publication:

> At present Australia has no national philosophy towards sport. Some nations use sport ideologically to show that their style of government and their style of life are superior to those of other nations; some use sport under the 'bread and circuses' syndrome to keep the people's minds off other issues; some nations have used it to overcome the effects of war; some Third World countries use sport to show that they are catching up to the rest of the world; while other national sports philosophies have racial overtones. Australia has no such philosophy and hence, as a nation, we are not at all sure why we are so involved, except that sport is a good thing—we love it—and we have to win at it.[89]

Here, the state appears to be responsible for national philosophy by enunciating or enforcing it. In the absence of such declarations, a more mystical—and inevitably unarticulated—spirit-in-dwelling propels people into sport *amour*, a proper *amour-propre* that is quintessentially Australian. Small wonder then that the *Australian* should headline the defeat of Argentina in the Gold Cup thus: 'Socceroos meet their Gallipoli'.[90]

Out of adjacent discourses there emerge significant, more essentialist shibboleths about national sporting personalities. These views were mobilised routinely during the Gold Cup in revealing ways. The Cup's viewing community was partly local and partly international. The ASF spoke of sixty million viewers, including United States and European cable networks.[91] For Arthur George, such exposure bespoke the ultimate significance of the event for the nation.[92] This overseas attention became a selling point to domestic audiences, who were told to see their own importance in terms of its recognition by others, rather after the reverse marketing done in selling continued public subvention of the film industry to government.[93] The Australian viewer was interpellated as identifying both with the national team and its fortunes and with the global interest in the contest itself. If pride in the local side was insufficient because of the nature of the sport's image, this could perhaps be countered by calling up an identification in Australia's interest in global image markets and the attention given a public event overseas, by others. But this could also be the source of self-interrogation. Consider Murray Hedgcock in the *Australian*, reporting from Britain on the lack of attention paid to the Cup by the British press: 'I'm still not quite sure whether the Australian approach to sport is totally suited to soccer: is it perhaps a bit too clever for us? . . . [S]occer really is still a graceful, complex game that is perhaps too sleek and slick and diffused for the native-born Aussie, looking for something a bit more direct, a bit more physical, a bit tougher'. He soberly quotes Australian rules identity Ron Barassi on this: 'soccer was OK but of course "isn't a bodily-contact game" '.[94]

In a different inflection of the bodily repertoire, when Frank Arok resigned as Socceroo coach nearly two years after the Cup, he talked about the unpalatable workerist fit between national identity and soccer performance:

> We have to break from this Australian way of life business which says the boys have to go out for a drink after a win. I was always against that. Look what happened after the game against Argentina in the Bicentennial Gold Cup. I was powerless to stop the hordes—the girlfriends, wives, friends and relatives—turning up at the hotel after the win. It was one big celebration encouraged by those who should know better. We had to play Brazil after that and, of course, it was impossible to recover.[95]

Of course. Men's manifest destiny to go forth and build culture is constantly restrained by the female subject and its crass temporality and materiality, the insistent female body craving strength drained from the male; all this at the expense of the perpetuation and development of the spirit-in-dwelling that is the bountiful wonder of the nation.

SBS-TV commentator Les Murray typified the Gold Cup competitors this way: Australia had 'proven resoluteness', a 'wiley' coach and 'rugged competitiveness'; Saudi Arabia had 'carefree ambition' and 'unpredictability' in keeping with being 'Asia's aristocrats'; Argentina was 'talented', 'adulated', 'modern' and possessed of 'stunning versatility'; and Brazil was 'unique' with a 'freakish penchant for improvisation' amounting to 'manifest greatness'.[96] Gold Cup publicist Warren told ABC-TV before the final that 'there is a culture gap between these two countries in the game, but the Australians shouldn't be too worried about skills'. The Sydney *Daily Telegraph* had juxtaposed the earlier contest between Australia and Brazil as one pitting 'heroic Aussie battlers' against 'the Samba dancers'.[97]

This needs to be fed further into general lines of opinion about national identity. Bruce Kapferer evaluated the Bicentenary as having the 'central theme of Australia as an egalitarian dreamland'.[98] Such an account is in keeping with John Carroll's story of Australia as bereft of heroes, grand visions and great art, a material place leavened in its hedonism by the cynicism that is held to accompany the absence of spiritual culture.[99]

Viewed in this light, self-anxious, centrally planned festivals are nothing more than markers of uncertainty. When the ABA hierarchy proclaims 'Australia is a sporting nation'[100], this is because it doesn't know what Australia is. This sense of the necessary spontaneity of an effusive rush—untrammelled—towards collective apoplectic fulfilment, disorganised but unstoppable, is equally present in the *Australian*'s lament on the quietude of local soccer crowds: 'The thinking seems to be: "My God, I can't be caught singing the national anthem. What would the person next to me think?" '.[101]

Here, a specificity can be identified and followed which turns the category into categories. In Philip Schlesinger's terms: ' "cultural identity", "audiovisual space", "national culture" function as so many useful handles; they offer respectability and brand identification for a variety of contending politico-economic projects in the cultural domain'.[102] Thus and thus alone shall we know them. Governmental campaigns on literacy, compulsory education, public arts subvention justifications, media regulation logics of self-formation are the relevant categories. That idiosyncratic Weberian Ernest Gellner reworks nationalism as 'the transfer of the focus of man's identity to a culture which is mediated by literacy and an extensive, formal educational system'. These can be seen as training modes in forming a language community which are also technologies of affiliation to the sovereign state.[103] An empty collective history (or, perhaps, a plenitude of competing histories) produces the preconditions for what Anthony D. Smith calls the 'Bureaucratic nationalisms' of countries such as Australia that must accommodate a migrant world and form a new (if always partial) subjectivity.[104] Hence the pressures on the heterogeneity (for which read non-Englishness) of soccer in Australia, pressures that were manifested so distinctively in 1988.

# PART III

# Exhibitions

# 7
## The shaping of things to come: Expo 88
*Tony Bennett*

Expositions are among the most distinctive of modernity's symbolic inventions in that, as contrived events looking for a pretext to happen, they have been obliged to seek the occasions for their staging outside themselves. While by no means solely so, the most favoured candidate for this role has been that other symbolic invention of modernity, the national celebration. The Philadelphia Centennial Exposition of 1876, marking a century of American independence, thus counts as the first in a long line of expositions held in conjunction with celebrations marking the passage of national time. A few of the examples that might be cited include the Melbourne International Exhibition held in 1888 in association with the first centenary of Australia's European settlement; the Exposition Universelle held in Paris the following year as part of the centenary of the French Revolution; and Expo '67, hosted by Montreal in the midst of Canada's first centennial celebrations. Even where the connection has not been so direct as in these instances, expositions have usually sought some way of inserting themselves into the symbolic rhythms of national histories. Chicago's 1893 World's Columbian Exhibition was thus staged to celebrate the 400th anniversary of Columbus's discovery of the Americas, while the New York World's Fair of 1939 sought its national legitimation in the sesquicentenary of Washington's presidential inauguration.[1]

Yet it is only rarely that the synchronisation of these two kinds of events has resulted in their symbolic fusion. Indeed, and especially in the twentieth century, their simultaneity has more often served to mark the differences between them, throwing into relief the contrivance of their association. For while both events are the progenies of modernity, they are ultimately conceived and organised in relation to different times. If centennial celebrations and the like tick to the clock of the nation, marking its passage through calendrical time in drawing up symbolic inventories of its achievements, expositions tick to the international time of modernity itself. They mark the passage of progress, a time without frontiers, while the inventories they organise are, at least ideally, ones which mark the achievements of the nationally undifferentiated subject of humanity.

This is not to suggest a complete dissociation of these two temporal registers. Indeed, expositions have usually aimed to overlap these two times—of nation and of modernity—onto one another by projecting the host nation as among the foremost representatives of the time, and tasks, of modernity. This was the pattern established by the Great Exhibition of 1851 and repeated in most of the major nineteenth-century expositions. Where these were hosted by metropolitan powers, the bringing together of these two times could be accomplished with some conviction. For where national time is also imperial time, its internationalisation is but a discursive hop, step and a jump.[2] The situation, however, is different where expositions are hosted by societies on the periphery of the world capitalist order. In such cases, the annexation of the time of the nation to the time of modernity requires that the former be shorn of all that is local and limiting, and thus of all that is specific to it. Where this is so, and where expositions and national celebrations coincide, the two are likely to play in different thematic registers, constantly underscoring their mutual incompatibility.[3]

An added difficulty is that there is often a third time competing with the times of both the nation and modernity: that of the host city. Again, the resulting tensions may scarcely be noticeable where the host city is the capital city of a major metropolitan power. However, they may become acute where expositions are held in provincial centres, and especially so in federal societies in view of the strong interstate and inter-city rivalries such societies characteristically generate. In such circumstances, the host city typically seeks to hitch itself directly into the time of modernity, bypassing the nation—indeed, undercutting it—in representing itself as embodying the spirit of progress more adequately than either the national capital or rival provincial cities. Where this is so—and Chicago's 1893 World's Columbian Exhibition is the most frequently cited prototype—expositions are primarily city events.[4] Caught up more in the web of local than of national politics, they are also typically sites for the enunciation of city rather than (and sometimes in opposition to) national rhetorics.

Brisbane's Expo 88 was no exception to these general rules. Indeed, as an expo held in a provincial city in a peripheral country during the midst of its Bicentennial celebrations, it was a paradigm case of the ultimate dissociation of the three times—of the city, the nation and modernity—it installed itself between. Billed as the biggest event of the Bicentenary, and granted quasi-official recognition as such, it was neither sponsored nor funded by the Australian Bicentennial Authority. Governed by a separate authority whose lines of responsibility ran, on the one hand, to the Queensland state government and, on the other, to the Bureau International des Expositions (BIE), its organisational structures were formally unrelated to those established for the Bicentenary. Moreover, its theme—leisure in the age of technology—which, in accordance with the rules of the BIE, had to be both international in conception and demonstrate the achievements of progress, allowed little connection to be made with the lexicon of nationing rhetorics so evident elsewhere in Australia throughout 1988. Visiting the Expo was, in this sense, something of a welcome relief from the discourses of 1988. The most significant concessions made to these were the Captain Cook Pavilion which, in its exhibition of Cook memorabilia, echoed to the tunes of the nation's foundation and settlement, and the Australian Pavilion—of which more later. For the most part, however, the stress fell not on the symbolic time of the nation but on the insertion of the nation into the international time of modernity.

And it fell most especially on the insertion of Brisbane into the time of modernity. The Expo motto, 'Together we'll show the world', had many resonances, accumulating in their significance as the Expo unfolded. Most obviously, it referred to the representational ambition of the exposition form—that is, to render the whole world metonymically present—as, indeed, to the aspiration that the world, in the form of tourists, would come to see this metonymic assemblage of itself. Its most crucial resonances, however, derived from its conception of the 'we' who were to do the showing. For this was, most assuredly, not the national 'we' of 'all Australians' through which we were so constantly hailed throughout the Bicentenary. On the contrary, this 'we' was intended to recruit a more local subject and organise it in opposition to the national 'we'. It was Queenslanders, and especially Brisbaners, who were hailed as the subjects of this act of showing, an act of showing in which it mattered less what we showed than that we confound all the knockers and showed that we could do it, that we could put on the Expo that the other states had proved too faint-hearted to attempt. What was to be shown, in other words, was Brisbane's capacity to put on the show.

In brief, Expo 88 was, first and foremost, an event in the life of its host city; an instrument that was both to effect and signal its transformation from a provincial backwater into a world city representing the very cutting edge of modernity—from, as two critics put it, 'backwoods into the future'.[5] And it mattered little, in this respect, if, as proved to be the case, no-one else noticed. For if Expo 88 exceeded its visitor targets, this was less because the world or even the rest of Australia came to see the show than because of the high number of repeat visits made by Queenslanders—and especially by those resident in Brisbane or its immediate environs.[6] The consequence was an Expo in which the subject of the show and its addressee were curiously intermingled; in which the primary witness to Brisbane's demonstration of its capacity to put on the show was the city itself. Characterised, in one newspaper report, as 'the drug that kept Brisbane in awe of itself for six months'[7], Expo 88 did, indeed, construct the city in a peculiarly mesmeric relationship to itself as, in watching it demonstrate to itself its own capacity to show that it could put on the show, Brisbane imaginarily leapfrogged itself over the shoulders of Sydney and Melbourne to bask in a temporary metropolitan status.

Expo 88 was, then, in all these respects, an intensely local affair. So, for the most part, were the political controversies which surrounded it. True, it did occasionally get embroiled in the national political debates which accompanied the Bicentenary. The use of an American company to provide audiovisual technology for the Australian Pavilion provoked a major political scandal, although one which had run its course before the Expo opened. Expo 88 was also a target for Aboriginal protests, although there was some difference of opinion among Aboriginal groups as to whether Expo should or should not be regarded as part of the Bicentenary and, accordingly, different views as to the appropriate political stances to be adopted in relation to it. For the most part, however, the protests which accompanied Expo's planning and execution had a local, city flavour: protests against the razing of traditional inner-city residential zones to make way for the Expo site; protests against landlords who evicted long-term tenants in order to charge inflated rents during the Expo period; allegations of police harassment of gays as part of a pre-Expo city clean-up; street marches by prostitutes in protest at the loss of business inflicted on Brisbane's night-life by the attractions of Expo; and the exertion of 'people power' in protest at the initial plans for the redevelopment of the Expo site as a tourist megapolis.

There was, as a consequence, very little criticism of Expo itself. The politics of what was shown and done there, of the kind of event it was and the nature of the experience it offered, were largely bypassed in a critical climate concerned more with either its impact on the city's economy, residential structure and public utilities or with the more general politics of the Bicentenary which, in part, Expo sidestepped. While I cannot entirely compensate for this deficit here, a consideration of the respects in which the Expo script, in organising the visitor's experience, served as an instrument for a specifically regional program of civic modernisation might go some way toward doing so.

To engage with matters of this kind, however, requires that Expo 88 be considered in relation to the longer history of the exposition form and the kind of festival of modernity it embodies. For it was this history that wrote many aspects of the Expo script, governing its conception and shaping its main contours in ways which influenced the experience of its visitors as deeply and fundamentally as any of the specifically Australian, Queensland or city resonances that were lent to that script. While an exhaustive account of the origins and development of expositions cannot be attempted here, some brief genealogical excavations of their origins and early history will pay dividends, and particularly if conducted with a view to highlighting the performative rather than the representational aspects of the exposition script. When viewed in this light, I shall suggest, expositions are best regarded as providing their visitors not, as is commonly supposed, with texts for reading, but, rather, with props for exercising.

### Evolutionary exercises

'It was only with the expositions of the nineteenth century,' Umberto Eco argues, 'that the marvels of the year 2000 began to be announced.' No matter how much earlier collections, such as the *Wunderkammern* of the sixteenth century, might have resembled modern expositions in their concern to inventorise the past, they were crucially different, in Eco's estimation, in containing 'nothing which pointed to the future'.[8] Foucault makes a similar point when he contrasts the 'utopias of ultimate development' which predominated in the nineteenth century with the earlier functioning of utopia as 'a fantasy of origins', accounting for the transition from the latter to the former in terms of the influence of a new conception of knowledge in which things are given and known in the form of 'a series, of sequential connection, and of development'.[9] If the arrangement of objects within an eighteenth-century cabinet of curiosities derived its cogency from its reference to the ideal taxonomy of the world's beginning, when everything *had been* in its proper place, the nineteenth-century exposition—and museum—points to a future in which everything *will have* arrived at its proper place.

In association with these changes—indeed, as part of them, as both their conditions and effects—the semiotic properties of the objects displayed underwent an equally far-reaching transformation. The principal semiotic value of the object in a cabinet of curiosities was thus, as Carol Breckenridge summarises it, that of its own *singularity*:

> The object in a wonder cabinet celebrated nothing but itself as rare, sensational, and unusual. Neither beauty nor history appear to have been promoted as a value by which to behold the housed object. Objects were judged according to the amazement they aroused largely because they were rare, uncommon, and even unthought of creations.[10]

By the Great Exhibition of 1851, however, the semiotic value of the object displayed is *representative*. Whether a raw material, instrument of production or finished product; whether a work of art or of manufacture; whether from Britain, India, France or America: most things at the Crystal Palace were displayed as representative of a stage within an evolutionary series leading from the simple to the complex. Subsequent nineteenth-century expositions added little to this aspect of the form except to increase its representational density via the construction of evolutionary series that were ever-more extensive and totalising in their ambit: the organisation of national pavilions into an evolutionary hierarchy of racial zones, the construction of 'colonial' or 'native' villages, and so on.[11]

All this, then, by way of saying that the underlying rhetoric of the exposition form is one of progress. A familiar point, no doubt. But what are we to make of it? Most accounts, stressing the representational functioning of this rhetoric, view it as an ideological means for the organisation of consent to bourgeois hegemony given the respects in which the evolutionary story it tells culminate in the triumphal achievements of contemporary capitalism. While not wishing to gainsay this, Foucault's comments on the relations between 'the discovery of an evolution in terms of "progress"'' and the coincident emergence of what he characterises as the 'evolutive time' constituted by disciplinary methods of training suggest another perspective from which the expositional functioning of this rhetoric might be assessed.

For evolutive time, in Foucault's conception, is not a means of representing power but is rather directly bound up with, and serves as a means for, its exercise. The differentiation of time into a series of stages (classes in a school, say); the administration of examinations to determine whether an individual may progress from one stage to the next; the retardation of the scheduled progress of those who fail to pass such tests: in these ways there is constituted a linear time whose orientation toward some terminal point allows the intervention of disciplinary exercises which prepare the individual for, and mark his or her passage through, evolutive time. 'By bending behaviour towards a terminal state,' Foucault writes, 'exercise makes possible a perpetual characterisation of the individual either in relation to this term, in relation to other individuals, or in relation to a type of itinerary.'[12] Yet—and this is the key to the relations between disciplinary power and evolutive time—behaviour is thus bent to an itinerary without end in the sense that each terminal state, once it is reached, turns out to be only a step toward a further beckoning task resulting in a 'political technology of the body and of duration' which 'tends towards a subjection that has never reached its limit'.[13]

Perhaps, then, the expositional arrangement of things, peoples and civilisations, all in sequential toil toward a beckoning future, should be viewed less as a field of representations to be assessed for its ideological effects than as an injunction, the laying-out of a task, a performative imperative in which the visitor, exercising in the intersections of the evolutionary time of progress and the evolutive time of discipline, is enlisted for the limitless project of modernity. There are, of course, many versions of this project. At expositions, however, the idea of progress has typically been thematised technologically via the projection of a line between past, present and future technologies—the latter, as in the Democracity of New York's 1939 World's Fair, doubling as progress's means and its destination.[14] In this way, in offering both an inventory and a telos, in summarising the course of mankind's advance and plotting its future path, expositions allow—invite and incite—us to practise what we must become if progress is to progress, and if we are to keep up with it. They place us on a road which requires that we see ourselves as in need of incessant self-modernisation if we're to get to where we're headed.

The theme of Expo 88—leisure in the age of technology—lent itself well to this modernising imperative. Modern expositions, Eco has argued, are most clearly distinct from their nineteenth-century predecessors in according less attention to what they show than to the means of its presentation. The international standardisation of productive technologies and, consequently, of their products deprives these of any potential competitive display value, with the result that the means of displaying are accorded an increased significance in this regard. 'Each country,' as Eco puts it, 'shows itself by the way in which it is able to present the same thing other countries could also present. The prestige game is won by the country that best tells what it does, independently of what it actually does.'[15] This was written with Montreal's Expo '67 in mind. Robert Anderson and Eleanor Wachtel, writing in the midst of Vancouver's Expo '86, confirmed this tendency in noting, of the tradition of exhibiting new inventions at expositions, that the 'invention shown is now seldom a thing; it is the method of display itself'.[16]

There are, of course, many ways in which a modernist rhetoric informed the expositionary strategies of Expo 88. Although the global nineteenth-century narrative constructions in which things, peoples and civilisations were hierarchically ranked and arranged in evolutionary toil toward the present were not much in evidence, their echoes certainly were. The construction of a Pacific Lagoon, midway between the American and Japanese Pavilions (see Figure 7.1), thus provided an imaginary retreat from the Expo sea of modernity, one in which, in however idealised and romanticised a fashion, Pacific Islanders were assigned the role of representing the backwardness from which progress had progressed.[17] Similarly, in many of the national pavilions, the time of the nation and that of modernity were articulated to one another, albeit by means of a range of presentational strategies. In the United Kingdom Pavilion, for example, their articulation took the form of a disjunction between the outside entertainment areas—stressing, in an 'authentic' English pub and an ongoing performance of cockney musicals, the traditional aspects of English life—and the interior, dominated by a hi-tech, multi-screen presentation of leisure activities in Britain. In the Australian Pavilion, by contrast, the time of the nation and that of modernity were melded together via the use of hi-tech display techniques to offer, in the Rainbowsphere (described, in the official souvenir program, as 'one of the most sophisticated audio-visual pro-

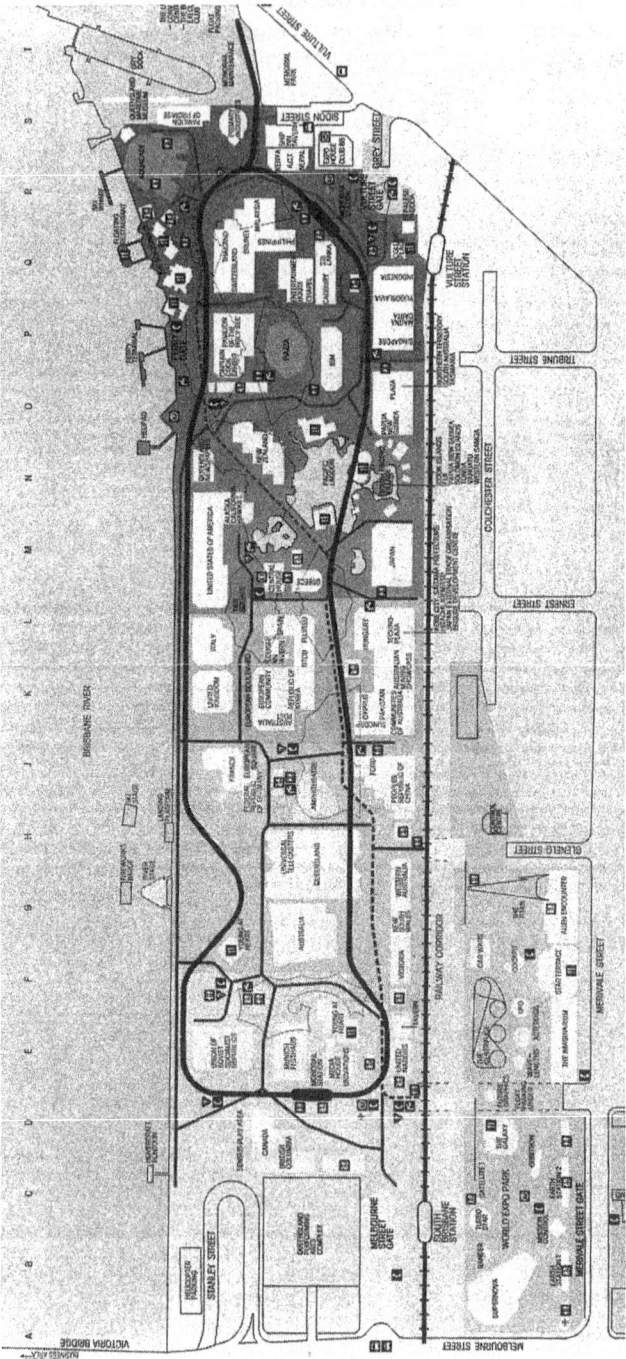

**Figure 7.1** Site map of World Expo 88, Brisbane. Reproduced with kind permission of the South Bank Corporation.

**Figure 7.2**   The 'Rainbowsphere'. Used with kind permission from Selcom.

ductions ever devised—another world first for Australia'), a kaleido-scopic portrayal of life in modern, multicultural Australia. This was complemented by an illusionistic rendition of the Rainbow Serpent legend in an animated diorama, a hi-tech version of the Dreamtime which served both to anchor national time in the deep time of Aborig-inal history while simultaneously modernising that time in technologis-ing it (see Figure 7.2).

It was, however, and in confirmation of Eco's argument, typically the technologies used in the organisation of displays that carried the theme of progress. For it was these that functioned as both the key signs and organisers of modernity. They served as the former in dividing the world up into different blocs: those whose place at the cutting edge of modernity was symbolised by their use of advanced video and computer display technologies (Europe, North America, Japan, Australia); those who, in displaying artefacts as if in a nine-teenth-century museum rather than multi-media demonstrations, were not yet modern enough to be postmodern (Russia, China); and those who, in relying solely on live performers to exhibit their culture, symbolised the past of a pre-technological age in relation to which our advance might be measured (Fiji, Tonga). And they served as organisers of modernity in embodying, in their very form, a beckoning future. 'See your past, present and future in a new dimension at the Fujitsu pavilion', the advert for one of the corporate pavilions read, where the past and present referred to a film account of human evolution and the future to the already present means of telling that account: a computer-generated 3D movie.

In this regard, then, Expo pointed to a future. Yet it also, in instantiating that future—that is, rendering it present, giving it a concrete form—afforded the visitor the means with which to practise for it and thus to engage in an anticipatory futuring of the self. The advanced interactive leisure technologies in the Technoplaza thus, in inviting the visitor to play and learn, functioned less as representations than as instruments of self-fashioning, a means for engaging in a future-oriented practice of the self, a dress rehearsal for what one is to become. The same was true of the use of advanced computer technology in the various on-site visitor information systems which rendered the future present in the form of a demand and a challenge: update yourself or get lost!

While the articulations of this futuring of the self varied from one national pavilion to another, these were all overshadowed by its embodiment in the corporate pavilions where modernity, in the form of advanced technologies of consumption, was free to be its own sign and referent. In this respect, Expo 88 confirmed a cumulative twentieth-century tendency for the corporate pavilion, once a marginal feature of the exposition form, to displace national pavilions as the organising centres of expositional rhetorics of progress.[18] If, in the national pavilions of Europe and North America, advanced leisure technologies were able to serve as signs of the nation's modernity, this was only because, in the corporate displays, such as that of the IBM Pavilion and the Technoplaza (dominated by displays of companies like Hitachi), the same technologies symbolised the internationally undifferentiated time of the multinational corporation to which national times could be annexed in a discourse of modernisation (see Figure 7.3).

Yet it was also this construction of an undifferentiated time of modernity which allowed the more local time of the city to be connected to it and thus, in a manner typical of 'second city first' rhetorics, to catapult itself ahead of the national time.[19] Tony Fry and Anne-Marie Willis correctly identified many of these aspects of Expo 88 in the prospective critique they offered some months before its commencement. The intention of the Expo, they argued, was 'to signify to the world, the nation, and the local area that the "international", in the form of the appearance of advanced modernity, has arrived'.[20] In this respect, they suggested, the event of Expo itself was (or would be) less important than its planned relation to its after-event: its 'co-option in the process of recoding the once "overgrown country town" as a modern, quasi-postmodern, progressive city'.[21] Yet, insightful though their criticisms are, Fry and Willis do not altogether escape the pull of the field of discourse they describe. Writing from Sydney, they are thus unable to resist a degree of metropolitan condescension, castigating

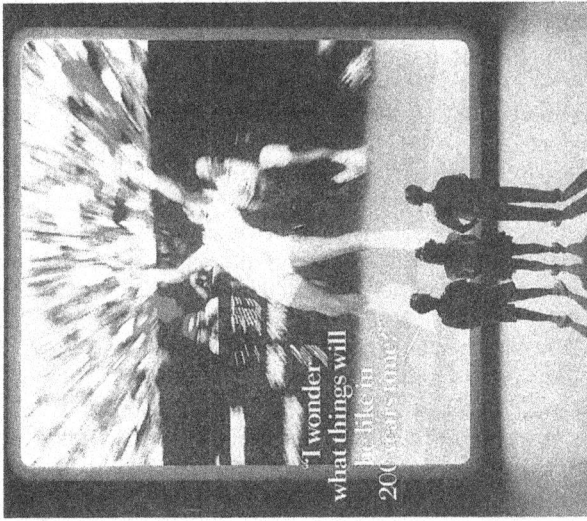

**Figure 7.3** Used with kind permission from IBM Australia Ltd.

Brisbane for revealing itself to be provincial in its very attempts to escape provinciality, as still a backwoods in its very claims to be modern, thereby necessarily showing itself to be behind the times in its failure to register the postmodernist critique of modernity's ambitions.[22]

In this, they merely anticipated the terms in which southern journalists would depict Expo—the unconvincing modern facade of a city which, in failing to disguise its backwardness, merely demonstrated its upstart qualities—thus reproducing the very discursive conditions which give Brisbane's 'second city first' rhetoric its strong local edge. Yet, as with the more general aspects of the expositionary discourse of progress, it is not merely as a set of representations that we need to assess the city aspects of Expo 88's modernising discourse. Rather, and again, we need to understand that the effectivity of such events proceeds not just via the logic of signs but via signs as parts of trainings and exercises which aim at altering less the consciousness than the conduct of individuals. Expo's significance in this regard, that is, has to be assessed less in terms of its suasive qualities than of its capacity for habituating specific norms of conduct and codes of civility oriented to the requirements of a modernised city ethos. To understand how Expo 88 functioned in this regard, however, it will be necessary, first, to expand the scope of this thumbnail genealogy of the exposition form in considering its historical role in providing a training in civics.

### Civic callisthenics

The effects of expositions, no less than those of bicentenaries, are not limited to the moments of their occurrence. Preceded by their publicity apparatuses which 'trail' their central discursive preoccupations long before their opening, expositions have proved equally important as the occasions for cultural and symbolic bequests to their host cities. Although somewhat atypical, the Eiffel Tower, a legacy of the 1889 Paris exposition, is the most obvious example. The more usual pattern, however, has been for expositions to stimulate the development of public museums, often supplying these with their buildings and initial collections. The Great Exhibition of 1851, in providing the spur for the development of London's South Kensington Museum complex,[23] thus set an example that was repeated elsewhere—Chicago's great public museums spring from the 1893 Columbian Exhibition—and often, as was the case with the establishment of Victoria's Industrial and Technological Museum in the wake of the 1866 Intercolonial Exhibition, with the South Kensington model directly in mind.[24]

In Brisbane's case, however, the museums preceded the exposition with the opening, a couple of years earlier, of the Queensland Cultural Centre with its museum and art gallery, shifted from their earlier

**The most excitement this side of World Expo 88**

All interest focuses on Brisbane's South Bank during World Expo 88. And the Queensland Cultural Centre, right beside the Expo site, is a unique and integral part of the excitement. The Centre is proud to present a six month, once-in-a-lifetime extravaganza of arts, exhibitions and entertainments throughout the entire Expo period. The four major components of the Centre, the Queensland Art Gallery, Performing Arts Complex, Queensland Museum and State Library will be on show to the world as never before.

The Queensland Cultural Centre is an initiative of the State Government of Queensland

**Figure 7.4**    Advertisement for the Queensland Cultural Centre.

premises to new buildings (see Figure 7.4). Developed on the south bank of the Brisbane River, adjacent to the Expo site, this hypermodern cultural complex symbolised the modernisation of civic life for which Expo was to pave the way. Made possible by a forcible clearance of old industrial and working-class residential areas, Expo betokened the beckoning modernisation of Brisbane that was promised in plans for the site's redevelopment, a modernisation prefigured in the shining face of the new at the Cultural Centre. Although, in this sense, preceded by its own bequest, only one part of Expo itself was envisaged as forming a part of this future: the World Expo Park, described in the official program as a 'collection of spaced-orientated rides, exhibits and amusements . . . destined to be Expo's only physical legacy' and sited directly by the Cultural Centre.

That a funfair was planned as an integral part of Expo 88 seems to have occasioned neither surprise nor objection. Nor, furthermore, was there any protest at the proposal that the fair should be left behind, nestling cheek-by-jowl with the museum and art gallery. Yet it is certain that, a century or so ago, such a proposal would have been unthinkable. Museums, art galleries and expositions then stood on one side of a cultural divide and fairs, together with other places of popular assembly, on another, and any proposal to adjoin them would have provoked outrage. Indeed, museums and the like were explicitly conceived and planned as cultural zones distinct from the world of the fair, the tavern, music hall or popular theatre.[25] David Goodman has thus tellingly argued the respects in which the mid nineteenth-century foundation and early development of the National Museum of Victoria was shaped by a dual-edged 'fear of circuses': that is, by the desire to construct a cultural space in which a rational ordering of nature would be distinct from the collections of curiosities of popular zoos, menageries, circuses and commercial pleasure gardens while also one in which civilised and decorous forms of behaviour could be distinguished from the raucousness associated with places of popular assembly.[26]

It is, in this light, important to note that at Expo 88 it was not merely the world of the fair that was brought into a harmonious relation to that of the exposition and the museum. Virtually all the other forms of popular entertainment and assembly which, in the mid nineteenth-century, would have stood on the other side of a cultural divide—the circus, remnants of freak shows (the tallest man in the world), parades and carnivals, street theatre, taverns—were enfolded into the Expo, parts of its official program.

It is not possible, here, to account in detail for the processes through which the terms of this cultural divide have been, if not undone, then certainly loosened.[27] As far as the fair is concerned, however, two developments stand to the fore, and both were incubated in the Midway zones of late nineteenth-century American expositions. The first consists in the modernisation of the culture and ethos of the fair effected by the increasing mechanisation of its entertainments and the associated tendency for those entertainments to be represented as both the realisations and projections of progress's triumphal advance. In the opening decades of the nineteenth century, popular fairs, still dedicated to the display of human and animal curiosities and still strongly associated with carnivalesque inversions of established cultural values and hierarchies, constituted a moral and cultural universe that was radically distinct from the emerging rationalist and improving culture of the middle classes. The fairs which, unofficially and uninvited, sprang up in association with the early expositions, often occupying adjacent locations, thus gave rise to a dissonant clash of opposing cultures which seriously disconcerted exposition authorities to the degree that it promised to undermine the pedagogic benefits of the expositionary rhetorics of progress.

Even when, following the initiative of Paris in 1867, fairs came to be thought of as planned adjuncts of expositions, this sense of two separate worlds remained strong. Indeed, to some degree, it became institutionalised, the integrity of the exposition's improving rhetorics being protected from contamination by the world of the fair via the construction of the latter as explicitly a frivolous diversion from the instructional and uplifting qualities of the exposition zone proper.[28]

Thus, even into the twentieth century, many of the aspects of the early nineteenth-century fair survived in the Midways of American expositions. At San Francisco's Panama–Pacific Exposition of 1915 we thus find Harry La Brecque, a famous fairground barker, hailing the passing public to visit 'the greatest show on the Midway' containing 'the long and the short, the fat and the lean, the largest, most unbelievable collection of freaks ever assembled on this earth', featuring 'Sombah, the Wild Girl, captured in deepest Africa, and Hoobooh, her savage brother'.[29] Similarly, the Midway at New York in 1939 featured an Odditorium and, in Little Miracle Town, a display of midgets while also, in the contrived underwater striptease of Oscar the Amorous Octopus, retaining the association of fairs with the illicit pleasures (burlesque, prostitution) of a phallocentric sexual order.

Nonetheless, the mechanisation of fair entertainments did enable the ideological thematics of expositions and their accompanying fairs to become more closely harmonised in allowing the latter to be enfolded within the project and discourse of modernity. If, in exposition machinery halls, progress was materially realised in displays of technologies of production, the new mechanical rides which began to be featured in the Midways from the 1890s provided a fitting complement in materially instantiating progress in the form of technologies of pleasure. The consequences of these developments were not, of course, limited to exposition fairs. In functioning as the forcing ground for new ride innovations (the Ferris Wheel at Chicago, 1893; the Aerio Cycle at Buffalo, 1901)—and often ones with futuristic references (the Trip to the Moon, also Buffalo)—which then became permanent attractions at the new fixed-site amusement parks which developed over the same period, American Midways played a significant role in transforming the culture of the fair throughout the English-speaking world. The relations between the Midways and the rush of amusement park development at Coney Island in the 1890s are of particular significance in this regard.[30] In their provision of a series of technological wonders which allowed their visitors to participate vicariously in progress and their commitment to a resolute modernisation of the ethos of the fair, they provided an example that was rapidly imitated, and often on licence, elsewhere.[31]

Once again, this did not result in a total transformation of the fair. All the Coney Island fun parks, for example, retained the symbolism of carnival, sometimes signifying their separation from the 'real world' via the rites of passage they inflicted on the visitor: visitors to the Steeplechase Park entering from the ocean side, for example, had to pass through a rotating Barrel of Fun. Nonetheless, the fact remains that, rite of passage complete, the fairgoer entered into a world whose ideological horizons had been substantially harmonised with the rhetorics of modernity. In this respect, the World Expo Park merely inherited the legacy which the nineteenth-century expositional adjustment of the popular fair bequeathed to the twentieth-century amuse-ment park. Monolithically futuristic in its resonances (its naming system was uniformly SCIFI—see Figure 7.1) and eschewing entirely any allusions to the world of carnival, the symbolic references of the Park were entirely at one with those of the Expo itself. As merely another realisation of the theme of leisure in the age of technology, the fair, here, functioned directly as part of the Expo's rhetoric. To a degree perhaps unprecedented, Expo and fair thus merged into one another, a world at one with itself, perfectly seamless in its lack of symbolic rifts or tensions.

Yet, as far as its planned adjacency to the Cultural Centre is con-cerned, it is the second aspect of the fair's nineteenth-century trans-formation that is perhaps more important. The legacy of the change I have in mind here is most evident in the conception of the World Expo Park as, precisely, a park. According to Ken Lord, its managing director, 'World Expo Park is a park in the true sense of the word. It's a place for families.'[32] The field of associations established here (fair, family, park) is, again, one made possible only by that brought into being via the development of turn of the century amusement parks and their conception as places for relaxing and strolling, for taking one's pleasures sedately. Of course, the actual forms of public behaviour exhibited at amusement parks may not always have lived up to this expectation. However, this does not gainsay the point that amusement parks were shaped into being as heirs to the work of such civilising agencies as public parks and museums—agencies which had, in part, been conceived as cultural instruments for transforming the public manners of the popular classes.

For it was not merely the ideological incompatibility of the fair and the museum which made these unlikely bedfellows in the early to mid nineteenth century. The fair, as the very emblem for the rude, rough and raucous manners of the populace, symbolised precisely those attributes of places of popular assembly to which the museum was conceived as an antidote. If fairs on the one hand, and museums and expositions on the other, were not to be mixed this was partly because they symbolised different forms of public behaviour—and different publics—which, in the view of many, were not to be mixed either. As one visitor to the Great Exhibition commented:

> Vulgar, ignorant, country people: many dirty women with their infants were sitting on the seats giving suck with their breasts uncovered, beneath the lovely female figures of the sculptor. Oh! How I wish I had the power to petrify the living, and animate the marble: perhaps a time will come when this fantasy will be realised and the human breed be succeeded by finer forms and lovelier features, than the world now dreams of.[33]

In reforming and progressive opinion, by contrast, museums and parks were regarded as precisely the instruments through which the populace would be weaned from boisterous pursuits and habits and tutored into new forms of civility. Frederick Law Olmstead, the architect of New York's Central Park, thus viewed parks as exerting 'an influence favourable to courtesy, self-control and temperance' and so as 'a gentle but effective school for citizenship'.[34] These terms were very similar to those which Sir Henry Cole had used a couple of decades earlier when commenting on the civilising virtues of museums in view of their capacity to instil respect for property and encourage the adoption of more gentle forms of public behaviour.[35] In providing for the commingling of classes, thus allowing the working classes to adopt new public manners by imitating those of middle-class exemplars, and for the mixing of both sexes and all ages, thus allowing the presence of women and children to exert a civilising influence on male behaviour, these new kinds of public space also provided a context in which visitors could practise the new forms of public bearing and civility required by new forms of urban life in which encounters with strangers were a daily experience.[36]

Expositions, of course, were regarded in a similar light: as schools for the diffusion of civilised codes of public behaviour. For Olmstead, who designed Chicago's White City, the purpose of the 1893 exposition was to offer an ideal version of an urban order, a space which could function simultaneously as a summons to civic responsibilities and as a means for practising them. Nor was this without consequence for the adjoining Midways or the fixed-site amusement parks that those Midways subsequently spawned. For over the same period in which these were ideologically renovated via the modernisation of their pleasures, their architectural organisation was transformed. Fairs had previously been temporary structures, accommodating themselves to the existing spaces of street or common, typically erected in an unplanned fashion with the entertainments jostling one another for space, thus cramming the crowd in on itself. By the 1890s, in contrast, amusement parks— whether temporary, like those which accompanied expositions, or permanent, like those at Coney Island—were laid out like cities, with vast promenades, inspection towers, and courts providing for rest and tranquillity; regulated spaces limiting the possibilities, and inclination, for rowdiness. By the turn of the century, the fair, once the very symbol of disorder, could be invoked, regularly and repeatedly, as a scene of regulation, of a crowd rendered orderly, decent and seemly in its conduct.[37] 'It is,' as one observer put it of Coney Island's Luna Park, 'the ordinary American crowd, the best natured, best dressed, best behaving and best smelling crowd in the world . . . '.[38]

By the time of Expo 88, of course, the crowd had long been tutored into such new forms of public demeanour and civility. Indeed, this became a source and sight of pleasure in itself in the form of the Expo queue whose orderly and good-natured conduct became one of the most talked-about aspects of the Expo. Yet, even though many feigned surprise at this manifestation of public civility, there was nothing new in this. From their beginnings, expositions, often planned in face of the fear of public disorder, have functioned as spaces in which a newly fashioned public (one not formally differentiated by rank) has demonstrated to itself its capacity for orderly and regulated conduct.[39] The pleasures of such a prospect have become a regular trope of exposition commentary while, in their design and layout, expositions have typically afforded their visitors vantage points from which the behaviour of other visitors might be observed and rendered a sight of pleasure, as from the monorail encircling the site at Expo 88. In these respects, expositions have offered not merely technologies whereby the visitor might engage in a modernisation of the self; they have also functioned as civilising technologies precisely to the degree that, in including their publics among their exhibits, they have provided a context in which a citizenry might display to itself, in the form of a pleasurable practice, those codes of public civility to which it has become habituated.

Indeed, in the case of Expo 88, where only a fraction of the visitor's time was spent in the display pavilions, there are grounds for arguing that this was the central pleasure of the Expo experience. Those who went again and again did so less for the sake of seeing the exhibitions than for that of roaming, rehearsing the codes of urban life in an imaginary city complete with its streets and boulevards, its sidewalk cafes and roving entertainers, cabarets and queues—all there solely for the express purpose of relaxed strolling, for seeing and looking, everyone a *flâneur*, but a *flâneur* on the move and, as simultaneously subject and object of vision, constantly open to the casual glance of other strollers.

Yet this was an aspect of Expo that had been prepared for just as it was itself a preparation. 'Brisbane,' predicted Sir Llew Edwards, chairman of the Expo Authority, 'will never be the same after Expo—shopping hours, outdoor eating, the greening of the city, our attitudes to hospitality . . . all these things will permanently transform our city.'[40] For Edwards, Expo was to serve as an instrument in the cosmopolitanisation of Brisbane, and of its populace; a cosmopolitanisation, however, in which the citizen was addressed as a consumer, and one who needed to be modernised. Alec McHoul, who didn't go to Expo, nonetheless understood this aspect of its functioning very well in contrasting its address to that of the Brisbane Show:

> It is manifestly trying so hard NOT to be like The Show that, again, the comparisons have to be made. They put each other on the agenda. Expo is where you CAN'T see sheep and cattle, produce and commodities as you move from ride to ride. It's where you CAN'T get a show bag. It's where the food is authentic and international and not cheap and nasty. It's where the beer is imported from Stow-in-the-Wold and sold in authentic pint mugs. Expo is alternative consumption: of commodities and images.[41]

However, the symbolic geography of Expo consumption is only half understood if viewed exclusively in terms of its self-distancing from the images and style of consumption associated with the traditional country fair. For if the Expo experience was an alternative to *this* style of consumption, it was also a preparation for another—and, indeed, one which was already present, just across the river, in the new Myer Centre, the face of the new in the form of a shopping development, complete with its own amusement park, where all of the video and computer display techniques and technologies evident at Expo were harnessed to a new style of consumption. Like the Cultural Centre, the Myer Centre had opened before the Expo and stood in need of only one thing: a public sufficiently modernised and tutored in the techniques of hi-tech shopping to use it. In this respect, the leisurely stroll of the would-be Expo *flâneur* was deceptive, concealing the anxious work of one bent to the task of practising new shopping mores, rehearsing new consumption codes in a custom-built environment.

I suggested earlier that Expo 88's major symbolic bequests to its host city had preceded it in the range of cultural—and, we can now add, commercial—facilities which opened their doors before the Expo commenced. Yet this is, perhaps, to distract attention from the more practical, more technological contribution it made, or sought to make, to the modernising task in the kind of re-tooling of the city's inhabitants it proposed in order to allow them to play their roles within the futures that had been arranged for them. Combining the evolutive time of discipline with the evolutionary time of progress and articulating both to the time of the city, Expo projected the future in the form of task—a new style and level of consumption—for which, in styling the consumer in the fashion of a new cosmopolitanism, its simulation of civic life provided a training.

# 8

# Expo 88: fashions of sight and politics of site

## Jennifer Craik

Histories of expositions tend to emphasise the uniqueness of individual expositions as grand events and to marginalise the politics underlying such events. Yet, the history of world expositions has been marked by controversy and contradiction. Similar conflicts, uncertainties and ambivalences have accompanied individual expositions. Common issues include haggling over funding, conflict over the site, lack of community consultation, lack of popular support for expositions, political intrigue and horse trading, and debts left after expositions.[1] Above all, while expositions are justified in terms of lofty ideals, they are rather more like popular carnivals as events. This chapter explores the politics of expositions arguing that their significance as pawns in growth machine politics far outweighs their role as signs of modernity.

The modern exposition developed during a period of industrialisation, internationalisation and modernisation, themes that are reflected in the self-congratulatory hype of expositions. The rhetoric of expositions—the official literature, public speeches, reports and media coverage—is often all that remains for the researcher. In fact, official records are largely publicity constructions of what an exposition is *supposed* to represent. These records downplay the actual circumstances in which expositions were established and held. It is all too easy to conclude that expositions were successful building blocks of nationalism and modernism. Consequently expositions have frequently been represented as a constructive force reflecting the national conscience of an epoch. There is a danger that the rhetoric of expositions supplants a close analysis of the events themselves, for such accounts cannot explain the forces behind staging expositions and fail to distinguish between formative influences and the legitimisation of such events. Expositions have been legitimated in the terms of contemporary rhetorics such as modernity, but this should not be confused with their character as events.

Expositions have been examined in relation to the emergent form of popular democratic politics. Since such events have been popular (visited by many ordinary people), expositions have been represented as a sign of populism, as the expressive capacity of a people exercised through a popular cultural festival. This chapter challenges such accounts, arguing instead that expositions are essentially anti-populist, anti-democratic, parochial exercises in partisan growth politics. The significance of expositions is far removed from the rhetorical screens superimposed on the events for rhetorical purposes.

Expositions are held for opportunistic reasons: to promote a city, to encourage trade, to acquire public facilities, and to stimulate tourism. Typically, expositions have short-term impacts (in terms of publicity, tourism, economic injections) and long-term costs (debt—usually picked up by the public purse; unusable facilities or an empty site; dislocation of local communities and residents).[2] Short-term political motives and outcomes, especially naked opportunism, are the only predictable feature of expositions. Brisbane's Expo 88 typified this pattern with an aging premier seeking to hold onto office to launch Expo, another concerned to oust him and take the credit, and a public tussle between a new premier and opportunistic lord mayor over the pecking order for the opening ceremony.

This chapter argues that expositions are the products of 'growth machine' elites wanting to stimulate further development and generate publicity for the site of the exposition. Accordingly, the exposition is organised such that the elites can further their collective and individual visibility and interests. While popular representations emphasise the 'bread and circuses' nature of the events as spectacle, opposition to the event is submerged, if not actively censored and discredited. Expositions are intrinsically political events stemming more from Tammany Hall intrigue than manifesting some abstract national ideological essence. This proposition is illustrated through the political gamesmanship that characterised the staging of Expo 88. Rather than seeing expositions as the exhibition of human progress, modernity, achievement and humanity, the argument of this chapter is that the rhetoric of expositions should be considered alongside the actual history of such events. Expositions have been marked by basic motives and grubby politics—opportunism and a potential real estate bonanza. While the rhetoric of expositions has emphasised themes of modernity, this merely flavours the politics rather than usurps it.

### Expo 88: the accidental exposition?

Most accounts of Expo 88 locate it as the apex of Australia's Bicentennial events and as the swan song of Queensland's developmentalist conservative government. This view matches the official rhetoric of the event which constitutes the official record of Expo. Yet the events that led to the staging of Expo 88 question that explanation. There was intense rivalry between the states, between the states and the common-wealth, and between various agencies embroiled in the deliberations. In no way can Expo 88 be regarded as coextensive with the plans for the Bicentenary. Rather, Expo 88 was something of an accident.

In 1974, Australia indicated a desire to stage a Category 'A' universal exposition in 1988 to the Bureau for International Expositions (BIE). Certainly, the Australian Bicentennial Authority (ABA) regarded an exposition as 'a superb centrepiece' for the Bicentennial celebrations which would provide a symbol of Australian unity, quality of life, lifestyle and achievements.[3] The question was, where would it be held, and who would pay for such an event? The commonwealth government was not prepared to fund an exposition which would cost at least $200 million. Australia was in the midst of a recession and subject to government budgetary restraint. Moreover, the commonwealth was already funding most of the planning for the Bicentennial festivities, especially through the well-endowed ABA. Although the common-wealth suggested that the ABA might wish to use its budget on an exposition, not surprisingly, the ABA was not willing to do so. Rather, the bulk of the cost of an exposition would have to be borne by the state government of the host city. In their turn, the states were unwilling to undertake such a costly exercise.

Between 1974 and 1981, there were protracted discussions as to whether or not an exposition would be feasible. Although a proposal for a special category exposition was prepared in 1979 by Queensland, the ABA and the commonwealth government showed little interest in this proposal. Most discussion centred on whether Sydney or Mel-bourne could afford to hold the event. The 1980 deadline to deliver a definite plan to the BIE led to frenzied activity and feasibility studies that indicated enormous financial costs associated with staging the event. New South Wales and Victoria were reluctant to proceed without guaranteed federal funding. A preliminary report on a Melbourne exposition anticipated that the cost would be about $310 million and leave a debt of $380–$430 million.[4] It concluded that an exposition would only be viable if the size of the debt could be offset by the 'potential residual value' of the site, that is, on its redevelopment prospects. Since it seemed unlikely to break even, Melbourne withdrew its interest in staging an exposition.

Sydney was even less keen. Then Premier Neville Wran remarked in 1983: 'I wasn't very anxious to have an expo from the beginning . . . I think the days of Crystal Palace-type exhibitions have been destroyed, certainly made anachronistic at least, by electronic media'.[5] As interest evaporated, there seemed to be no takers for a universal exposition to coincide with the Bicentenary. The ABA also discovered that France had successfully secured permission to stage a universal exposition in 1989 to mark its centenary, an event which would undoubtedly prove a much more attractive international drawcard. Since only one universal exposition could be held in a decade, according to BIE rules, Australia bit the bullet and, in December 1981, withdrew its notification to hold a 1988 exposition.

In the end, Expo 88 only happened because of political gamesmanship. The commonwealth's decision not to proceed with an exposition appalled a group of Queensland businessmen. They lobbied intensively to reactivate an exposition proposal. The possibility of a South Brisbane site was investigated in a feasibility study. The Queensland cabinet and key public servants remained sceptical although the plan was supported by some members. The lobby group then proposed a privately sponsored, Category 'B' Specialised Exposition which would be self-financing and not compete with France's exposition.

At an urgent meeting on 23 November 1982, the group convinced a reluctant Queensland cabinet to put a renewed bid to Canberra, a precondition to seeking BIE approval. The only reason this bid succeeded was because Liberal Party Prime Minister Malcolm Fraser was on sick leave with back problems. Although Fraser had given in principle approval for a Queensland exposition some months earlier, he had reiterated that 'the Queensland Government would be responsible for the raising of the total finance . . . and that there would be no financial call on the Commonwealth Government'. He also insisted that the exposition should have a national focus, that 'it would be in harmony with the overall program for the celebration of our bicentennial year' and not 'produce any imbalance in the total program'.[6] However, Fraser was lukewarm about an exposition and it seemed unlikely that he would accept this new bid. This was not the case with the Acting Prime Minister, Doug Anthony, who was persuaded by the Queensland Premier, Johannes Bjelke-Petersen, a fellow National Party member, to support the proposal. Anthony gave approval on 3 December (just four days after the revived bid). The hasty decision-making process was deliberate, to secure commonwealth support before Fraser recovered. Fraser was reportedly furious when he heard of the decision, and subsequently confirmed that he would have refused to consider the bid for a Brisbane Expo.[7]

The new proposal for Expo 88 was to stage a private sector, profit-making event. It was not a demonstration of public sector support for the celebration of national identity and international significance. The private sector lobbied hard for this event (as businessmen had done for previous expositions) motivated by short-term goals: switching effects that would inject money into parts of the local economy, increased tourism and associated revenue, the potential for individual and company benefits and the redevelopment potential of the exposition site. Of these, the latter was the golden egg. Expo 88 was an opportunity to redevelop a large, derelict site close to the CBD. Eventually, even the government was persuaded by the redevelopment potential to endorse the plan. As an editorial observed in Brisbane's establishment morning daily: 'For some in the government, Expo long ago stopped being an international exposition and became a property development operation'.[8]

This 'potential residual value' was the attraction of Expo for the business community. Consequently, when it came time to decide on the form of organisation to stage the exposition, individuals from the private sector were keen to be involved. However, it became increasingly obvious that the private sector, as a whole, was reluctant to contribute money to planning or staging Expo except where there was an obvious pay-off (e.g. securing naming rights to a pavilion, trading concessions, securing contracts and concessions, and short-term tax-free site operations). This created a problem for the Queensland government in selecting an appropriate organisational form to run the exposition. There was growing concern that expositions were not financial bonanzas. Recent expositions had left huge debts, whether publicly or privately sponsored: $1 billion in Montreal, $76 million in Knoxville, $100 million in New Orleans, and $400 million in Vancouver.[9] Most of the losses were shouldered by the public sector. While the private sector wanted to be involved and run the exposition its way, it did not want to run the risk of carrying the debt.

The Queensland government chose a single statutory authority to stage Expo. The Brisbane Exposition South Bank Redevelopment Authority (BESBRA) had responsibility for land acquisition, construction, management, and redevelopment of the site.[10] In line with the fact that Expo 88 was a Queensland initiative, the ABA was not given a place on the board, and only secured involvement after some 'nudging'.[11] Although the private sector publicly disavowed this approach, they benefited in the long run. By BESBRA's appointment of staff with entrepreneurial inclinations, and contracting out many functions to government-preferred enterprises, the private sector enjoyed the freedoms exercised by the statutory authority yet was protected by its fallback position.

Particularly significant was the appointment of Llew Edwards, former Deputy Premier and Treasurer, as Chairman of the Expo authority. Known as 'the man with the midas touch', Edwards proved to be a shrewd operator and indefatigable enthusiast. He succeeded in generating widespread support for the event despite the cynicism and complacency of many public and private sector agencies and individuals. Even so, the Queensland government ended up funding most of Expo 88 directly ($229 million) and indirectly ($493.2 million) with the macroeconomic cost estimated at $400 million–$600 million.[12] In the end, the Queensland government paid out $238 million to achieve an apparent profit of $653 000.[13] This profit was arrived at using creative and selective accounting practices (employing on-budget, off-budget techniques) which ignored costs already borne by the public sector. For example, significant costs were borne by the police force concerning security arrangements (in addition to the use of private security personnel), and the relocation and upgrading of the South Brisbane railway station was borne by the Department of Railways. Moreover, the cost of acquiring the Expo site was paid for by the government (in compulsory acquisitions) or in the form of crown land 'given' to the Expo authority and subsequently 'bought' back, in order to balance the books.

The cost of Expo 88 had been the reason why the public sector had been reluctant to support the event. It was regarded as a high-risk venture, and promoted as such by the private sector. Yet the private sector was also reluctant to underwrite Expo unless there were guaranteed returns. The fact that the public sector ended up running and financing the event suited the private sector because it minimised private sector risk and maximised its opportunities.[14]

The shadow boxing between the public and private sectors was no more clearly illustrated than by the case of World Expo Park (WEP). Conceived in 1985, the idea of a funpark adjacent to the Expo site was seen as necessary to maintain the tradition of a fair as part of exposition activities. More pragmatically, it was regarded as a way of encouraging people to the Expo site, at a time when public support was lukewarm. Despite the objections of the Brisbane City Council, the authority bought land from the railways and offered it for tender. The successful bid of $10 million was less half the asking price, and in the end, the tenderer, KFL Investments, paid only $1 million deposit.[15] The price was later renegotiated and effectively halved after the Expo authority and the tenderer both ran into cashflow problems.

KFL also obtained approval to build a 40-storey commercial building should the funpark fail. Substantial foundations—suitable for a multistory building—were laid underneath the funpark. It seemed clear that the funpark was only intended to have a short life. As a commercial venture, the funpark was a disaster. WEP only ever paid the deposit and eventually persuaded the Expo authority to buy back the site for $29.3 million. The land was leased back to WEP at $1 a year for four years, 'not bad for a $1 million deposit'.[16] In essence, the Expo authority paid handsomely to provide the grossly underutilised funfair facility. In 1989 the site was added to the Expo redevelopment site and earmarked for redevelopment as a world convention centre.[17] Because of the cost of such a centre (estimated at $150 million), the Goss government appears likely to approve the construction of a casino on the South Bank site to pay for the convention centre.[18]

In the light of this history, it is clear that the funfair was neither part of the original Expo plan nor was it intended as a permanent facility. Rather, World Expo Park was a belated, desperate and ad hoc gamble to attempt to engage popular support for Expo. In the long run, it was never likely to be a winner—and perhaps was never intended to be. The fair was publicly funded through the Expo authority, and its redevelopment will undoubtedly involve further considerable public expenditure. Instead of constituting an integral part of the Expo experience, the funpark epitomises the disingenuous planning of such events at the expense of the public.

When Expo 88 opened, however, it was not accompanied by rhetoric of parochial opportunism and greed or of the unplanned nature of the decision to stage it in Brisbane. As Expo geared up, so did the hype machine which presented it as a great opportunity to 'show the world'. Notwithstanding, the political turmoil that surrounded Expo 88 casts doubt on explanations that assume that the exposition encapsulated the national mood of the Bicentenary.

**The Expo event: we'll show the world**

The rationale of staging an exposition to coincide with the Bicentenary was that it would act as a magnet. An exposition would unite other events, generate further events, and provide a visible pinnacle of the festivities. The ABA defined an exposition as:

> a superb exposition of human achievement. An Expo brings millions of people together, either physically or through the international medium of satellite television, to delight in human endeavour and imagination. It is a breathtaking, exciting, sharing, learning experience. Sometimes an Expo is called a 'World's Fair', but an Expo is *not* a trade fair. An Expo is life today and tomorrow.[19]

The rationale of the Brisbane bid was far more specific: to enhance the tourist potential of Queensland and Australia, and to put Queensland on the map. Specifically, it was part of the Queensland Tourist and Travel Corporation's strategy to promote tourism by staging regular special events, in a way which the corporation could not afford to do by direct marketing.[20] Certain businessmen and top public servants associated with the bid saw the exposition as a catalyst for substantial investment and development, especially of the rundown South Brisbane site. Directly opposite the CBD and visible from their office windows, the South Bank represented an irresistible but untouchable real estate opportunity. All that would change with an exposition.

However, their interest was specifically in terms of promotional value, and the group favoured a tourism and leisure theme as the special category. In short, they wanted to sell Brisbane as a tourist destination and investment opportunity, and encouraged nations to participate on that basis. The proposed theme was rejected by the BIE who stressed that an exposition was *not* a trade fair and that the event was not about selling (apart from consumables associated with the event). The eventual theme, leisure in the age of technology, was a compromise to meet BIE requirements. Inevitably, it caused problems. No-one quite knew what it meant or how it could be translated into themed pavilion displays. Many participants just ignored it. Exposition functionaries lobbied energetically to persuade countries to exhibit in the face of this uninspiring theme. Numerous participants took the hint and merely presented tourist promotional displays. Thus, even the theme was cobbled together for reasons of political expediency.

Eventually, only 35 nations (including a number of very small Pacific islands) participated in addition to several themed international pavilions. Although all the Australian states and territories participated and the federal government staged an Australian pavilion, their involvement was not automatic: indeed, they 'seemed hell bent on a virtual boycott of Expo'.[21] It took Edwards two years to persuade them to participate. The states agreed grudgingly. Part of the problem was the perception that Brisbane would not succeed in staging the event. This may have contributed to the choice by BESBRA of the slogan 'we'll show the world', as a rallying point for cynical and apathetic citizens. The phrase, of course, had a certain ambiguity: who was showing what to whom?

As the visitation trends revealed, Expo 88 was primarily a local experience. About 65 per cent of the 16.5 million visits (including staff) were made by residents of Brisbane and the south-east corner of Queensland. Compared with previous expositions, Expo 88 was an intensely local phenomenon. The residents of other exposition cities made on average between two or three visits, up to six (e.g. Montreal) or seven (e.g. Spokane) visits each.[22] Brisbane residents exceeded these figures by averaging 7.8 visits each.[23] Residents with season passes made an average of twelve visits each, far exceeding expectations. This had financial implications for Expo, since extra visits contributed no revenue. The season passes proved to be a financial embarrassment for BESBRA. Not only did it underestimate the frequency of use, Expo regulars became canny in minimising expenditure on-site. In addition to this lack of revenue, BESBRA had lowered the cost of the season passes below a viable level because sales were poor. Despite the encouraging number of visits, the proportion of season pass visits imposed a financial burden on the operating costs of Expo. Although restaurants on-site did very well during Expo, most were run by overseas concessionaires who had won special taxation rights to repatriate profits. Overall, Expo was a financial drain on participants, few of whom returned any profit.

The ambivalence of Expo 88's theme, and its localised impact, typify a general crisis of expositions. Commentators and historians tend to evaluate expositions against previous expositions as if there was a common and smooth history of such events. Yet Zimmerman[24] has argued that there have been seven distinct eras of world fairs, each era adopting a special organisational theme: 1851–76 celebrating achievements; 1876–89 centennial fairs celebrating anniversaries; 1889–93 reviving a neoclassic ambience; 1893–1925 celebrating art nouveau;

1925–40 advocating modernism; 1940–67 atomic and pop art fairs; and 1967– mere expositions ('show-and-tell' extravaganzas).

Some themes and aspects of fairs have persisted. For example, the provision of popular pastimes and amusements has dominated the 'funfair' side of the event which has increasingly been separated from the 'serious side' of expositions. There has been an enduring emphasis on eye-catching displays, especially of extraordinary objects (defined in terms of quantity, gigantism, miniaturism, ritual, or prestige) and people (as technicians, craftspeople, curiosities or freaks, specimens or scientific objects, or trophies).[25] These have incorporated the quest for authenticity and typicality (recreations of events, things and cultures) to the creation of ideal conditions (from the model workers of early exhibitions to the architectural wonders of many exhibitions).

The nature of fairs changed in accordance with the political priorities of the twentieth century. Fairs became less concerned with the high-minded ideals of improvement and progress, and more concerned with consumerism, on the one hand, and mere pleasure, on the other. The latter was less of a problem: almost every fair has attracted crowds of ordinary people. The problem was to restrain the 'crass pursuits' of the masses and inject a little class into the event. As Short put it, in relation to the 1851 Exhibition, the problem was to 'allow the respectable artisan in and keep the rabble out'.[26] The aim was to elevate 'the taste of the humbler ranks of society' and keep 'the working classes away from indolence or sensual pleasure'.[27]

Gradually taste came to acquire a new meaning, referring instead to cultural appreciation, refinement, and material self-improvement. For example, the organisers of the Tasmanian Exhibition 1894–95 regarded the cultivation of art appreciation 'as a means of introducing an element of refinement into the national character'.[28] Instead of the 'backward look at many conquests already achieved' celebrated in nineteenth-century exhibitions, 'the world of the Future seeking objectification' was the orientation of the new fairs: 'titillation and sensation' became the primary emphasis.[29] According to Harris, after World War II, advertising techniques, mass media and education deprived exhibitions of their educational role. Pleasure was the primary focus. But expositions could not overtly sell goods. Elaborate charades to display the newest and the best were employed as a form of de facto advertising. The new consumer values of expositions were reflected in the giant building, shaped as a National Cash Register, which dominated New York's 1939 World Fair. The cash register displayed daily attendance figures.

A combination of motives—trade, local boosterism and political ambitions—have come to dominate the new fair: 'Business and political agendas both converge and diverge and both are refracted through fair managers and designers who have their own definition of the goals of a successful fair'.[30] Vancouver's Expo 86 symbolised the new agenda in its choice of McDonald's as official caterer; as Ley and Olds remarked, 'McDonald's stands for everything Expo stands for'. A cartoonist nicknamed the fair 'McExpo'[31], reflecting the domination of the Expo board and decision-making processes by businessmen and business objectives. Fundamentally, they saw Expo as an opportunity to crate a giant leisure ground. President Michael Bartlett commented: 'I knew how to build theme parks. There's not much difference between this and building those'.[32] The new exposition had arrived.

### Cultivating Australia through expositions: sprats to catch the whale?

Australia has had a marginal role in the staging of expositions and exhibitions. It held eight in the last two decades of the nineteenth century—Sydney 1879, Melbourne 1880–81 and 1888, Adelaide 1881 and 1887, Launceston 1891–92, Hobart 1894–95, and Brisbane 1897—but their popularity 'died out even more rapidly than elsewhere'.[33] When the idea of a Bicentennial exposition was mooted, Davison contrasts the reluctance of established 'southern' cities with the enthsiasm of the frontier state of Queensland to host the event:

> But we should not be surprised by such a contradiction for, like its predecessors, the Brisbane Expo illustrates the most persistent paradox of the exhibition movement—that its promoters were usually more interested in cultivating an image of modernity than absorbing the spirit of modernity itself.[34]

Exhibitions have been likened to a visiting card, announcing the arrival of the host city to the world, promoting trade, culture and international relations.[35] But a closer examination suggests that they are more like a driving licence, a permit to cruise the main drag and compete for a place in the international arena. Exhibitions have typically been used to promote second-rank cities. In reference to the Melbourne Exhibition of 1888, a journalist remarked that: 'In an exhibition such as ours, we not only see but are seen'.[36] The double movement of exposure to international and cosmopolitan trends vying with the display of local achievements and souvenirs was reflected in the closing speech at the Sydney Exhibition of 1879 when the Executive Commissioner declared that:

> The name of New South Wales has resounded throughout the civilised world; and by means of the display of her unparallelled resources in minerals, in manufactures, machinery, and the arts and sciences . . . ample proof is given of the great resources which form so noble a heritage . . . It remains for us to prove by our energy and patriotism that we shall prove worthy of the exalted destiny which lies before us, and that foremost in the van of great Colonies planted by the Anglo-Saxon race over all the habitable globe will be found our colony of New South Wales.[37]

The obsession with meeting international standards, the so-called cul-

tural cringe, has persisted. Displays presented the natural and manu-
factured products and artifacts of each exhibitor. For example, the
Queensland court at Sydney featured:

> an obelisk of gold, a pyramid of tin ingots, a double-storeyed pyre of sugar
> canes, a 'tree' of polished timber slabs surmounted by a broad-leafed fern,
> and another pyramid of gleaming mother-of-pearl shells. Faintly incongru-
> ous among these fruits of nature was a railway carriage constructed of
> native timbers. There was a large display of stuffed Queensland fauna, and
> in somewhat the same manner, the mummified bodies of several Torres
> Strait aborigines. Outside the court on the verandah was set a small jungle
> of potted native ferns and trees; it became a popular spot in which to
> relax.[38]

This was a typical colonial display (and echoes of it informed the
Queensland Pavilion at Expo 88). Despite its educational and enlight-
ening focus, most visitors enjoyed the more mundane, popular pleasures
on offer. While workers and children partook of the popular pleasures
offered by facilities like the Turkish Bazaar, Japanese Tea House,
Australian Dairy, Emerson's Oyster Saloon and the Austro-Hungarian
Wine and Beer Tasting Hall, Sydney's elite met under the verandah of
the Queensland court to take tea at the Floral Cafe, and listen to
concerts and the like.[39] A similar tension between popular activities
and elite cultivation marked other expositions. The Hobart exhibition
had enormous problems attracting participants and was obliged to
engage a 'Variety Fair' provided by local entertainers. Attractions
included Mr Ives' Grand Historical Naval Exhibition, performing fleas,
a shooting gallery, a gypsy tent, a doll show, dances by Miss Bromley's
and Miss Spurling's ballet schools, and concerts by the Orpheus Club.[40]

As popular events, Australia's expositions were highly successful,
attracting a large percentage of the population, though few international
visitors.[41] Financially, they were less successful—Sydney (1879) made
a loss of £103,615 2s 22d[42], Launceston (1891) made a profit of
between four and five hundred pounds, Hobart (1894–95) made no
return to investors and struggled to 'balance' the books[43], while Melbourne (1880–81) was regarded as 'an unjustifiable extravagance'.[44] A
disgruntled Hobart resident summed up the lack of financial success
when he concluded that the cost of the exhibition 'did not prove the
sprat to catch the whale'.[45]

As cultural events, the exhibitions were all promoted, and, in some
cases, proposed by, local business or agricultural leaders. The events
became a struggle between the entrepreneurial, exhibitionary zeal of
up-and-coming prosperous economic groups against the conservatism
of established elites. The rivalry between these groups accounted for
the reluctance of governments to underwrite proposals, on the grounds
that they were merely sectional promotional strategies which would not
benefit other groups. Each exhibition produced an ambivalent set of
evaluations of its success and impacts. Economically, there were few

signs that the events attracted new trade, or more visitors. Some cultural production was generated for each exhibition, and left some legacy in public collections, but largely the exhibitions were exercises in self-promotion for local consumption. Given its 'very insignificant situation in the world'[46], the Tasmanian International Exhibition 1894–95 was judged to be self-deluding, based on: 'a very subjective, ego-centric, rather short-sighted [argument], linked largely with the psychological image the Tasmanian, particularly the Hobart community, held of itself'.[47] To how many other exhibition and exposition sites have these words applied?

## Growth machines, special events and the tourist mirage

An exposition planned for tourists is a self-conscious and contrived national image. It is a pseudo-event for consumption.[48]

Expositions have been incorporated into the strategy of hallmark or special events, designed to promote a destination, generate economic and cultural activity, and potentially to enhance the profile of the destination for the future—the so-called 'ripple effect'.[49] Hallmark events include world fairs/expositions, unique carnivals and festivals, major sporting events, cultural and religious events, historical mile-stones, classic commercial and agricultural events, and major political personage events.[50] Tourism hallmark events entail acceptance by a host community, a powerful symbolic theme, marshalling of public and private resources, telescoping of time, a chameleon effect (embellishing the local community during the event), and a catalytic effect (sparking peripheral events).[51]

Central to the strategy is attracting a large number of people to an event and persuading them to part with their money. The president of Vancouver's Expo 86 had a simple formula for success: 'You get 'em on the site, you feed 'em, you make 'em dizzy, and you scare the shit out of 'em'.[52] Shortly after this declaration, he was sacked. Nonethe-less, his sentiments realistically portray the Expo experience. For example, during Expo 88, regular statistics monitored the rate of consumption:

so many hot dogs that if laid end to end, they would stretch 130 times around Expo's 2.3 kilometre track. And enough beer has slaked the dust from thirsty throats to fill 324 average-sized family swimming pools. Chips: Four Million buckets. Spaghetti: 40,500 kilograms.[53]

Of course, participants must enjoy the events themselves. Hallmark events are an extension of consumer society with its emphasis on the purchase of lifestyle and cultural capital. Getz lists several 'generic benefits' flowing from special events, including spectacle, belonging, authenticity, ritual and games.[54] This is a precondition for the targeted effects and tourism impact of events. Greatest emphasis is placed on economic activity associated with special events, although, as Hall has noted, most calculations are based on estimates of direct and related expenditure, rather than on cost–benefit analyses which take factors such as opportunity costs, leakage, administrative and social costs into account. Moreover, there has been little attention to the negative effects of, and dislocation associated with, special events. Unexpectedly, for example, these events 'provide a platform for political protest'[55] allowing aggrieved groups to gain invaluable public attention to their causes.

Hall has characterised hallmark events as 'the image makers, *par excellence*, of the twentieth century'. But although such events are justified in terms of future potential, more often than not they are constructed on images of the past, possibly working to reinforce 'conservative ideology'.[56] Hall argues that this may well have been the outcome of Australia's Bicentennial celebrations. Special events stimulate short-term activity (construction, business, government) often as part of a strategy of reinvigorating urban areas by reinvestment and gentrification. Cities that adopt such strategies have been termed 'the growth machine'.[57] Characteristically, it entails inherent tensions between the political, economic and social interests of the local elite, and financial liability and loss of quality of life for local residents. Many strategies have been developed to overcome resistance to the growth machine and encourage forms of development which the locals do not perceive to be in their best interests.

Smith and Keller[58] examined this process in the context of the New Orleans 1984 World's Fair, showing that the supporters of the fair justified it in terms of the 'trickle down effect', namely that benefits would flow down to, and through, the local economy, so that all citizens would get a prize. The excessive claims made for the fair and the lack of evidence to show subsequent benefits lead to a considerable scepticism about the strategy of special events in city growth machines. In other cases, for example, the 1988 Calgary Winter Olympics, the event was apparently welcomed by locals precisely because of the boosterism effect. The Olympics were regarded as a showcase to inject life into an isolated community.[59] Yet, expositions are expensive propositions. Even in the United States, the public sector has ended up footing a large part of the bill.

Despite the rhetorical flourishes of expositions, the experience of recent expositions suggests that they are expensive events with a few short term pay-offs but with very few guaranteed long-term benefits. Apart from the dubious publicity function, the main impact of expositions is on the fortunes of local political machines. There is little evidence of sustained economic growth nor of increased tourism as a result of expositions.

**Expo 88: the big party**

As an event, Expo 88 was a successful party so long as people did not think about it greatly. Visitation exceeded predictions and there was considerable local enthusiasm. Visitors, especially elderly people and people who had not travelled widely (or at all) outside Queensland, found that Expo put excitement into their lives. A questionnaire conducted by the *Courier-Mail* found that respondents (self-selecting and therefore not representative) were positive about Expo. An overview of the results concluded that:

> It is possible to be cynically disparaging about much of Expo's stage set-type gimmickry, the plaster and plastic, and some of the more crass manifestations of commercialism (though not about the visual effects and the efficient organisation). But the essential message is that Expo clearly enabled vast numbers of people to experience simple, basic, relatively unsophisticated pleasures which they do not normally experience in a modern urban environment . . . out-of-doors eating, drinking, walking, talking and resting. It offered the opportunity to see and be seen. It provided entertainment and educational and multi-cultural interest.[60]

Respondents nominated the festive entertainment and atmosphere as the most memorable feature of Expo, followed by the pavilions. A survey conducted by the Department of the Arts, Sport, the Environment, Tourism and Territories[61] examined responses to the Australian pavilion to determine the success of the pavilion and its displays. The results indicated that the majority of respondents rated the theme of the pavilion, the pavilion building, its staff and exhibits very highly. Almost 70 per cent of visitors were from Brisbane; of the 23 per cent who came from elsewhere in Australia, almost one-third came from New South Wales; overseas visitors accounted for 7 per cent of visits. Visits tended to be habitual; although 24 per cent were visiting Expo for the first time, 28 per cent were there for the second time, 24 per cent for the third, and 25 per cent had been four or more times. These figures underline the primarily local nature of Expo 88. Despite these positive feelings, the *Courier-Mail* survey also indicated a majority feeling (55 per cent) that locals were not being sufficiently involved in post-Expo planning.[62]

Visitors spent almost $14 each on-site, or, more specifically, $11.31 by Queensland visitors, $20.35 by interstate visitors, and $21.19 by overseas visitors.[63] Queensland daytrippers were the most frugal, spending just $10 (often taking a packed lunch), while interstate daytrippers were the most extravagant, spending $28. Brisbane was the main beneficiary of these visitors, with commercial accommodation maintaining near total occupancy during the duration of Expo. Other regions did not fare so well, particularly in the light of heightened expectations. Many had upgraded or expanded facilities in anticipation of Expo visitors and they were disappointed.

The worst affected regions were the islands of the Great Barrier Reef, adjacent coastal regions and destinations far from Brisbane. One tourist operator concluded that the Expo Authority had conned businesses to expect a bumper season.[64] Yet the Authority knew full well that experience elsewhere showed impacts to be highly localised, benefiting the immediate locality but adversely affecting other areas. For example, Expo 86 produced a 20 per cent downturn in businesses outside Vancouver.[65] An American veteran of twelve world fairs and a major concessionnaire at Expo 88, Chuck Sanders, commented that there was never any chance of a flow-on effect:

> It has never happened in any Expo city, and when I got to Brisbane and was asked to talk to the restaurant and catering people, I had to be honest and tell them to expect a 30 per cent drop in business. They were horrified. That represented a 50 per cent drop as they were expecting business to go up by 20 per cent.[66]

Overseas visitors accounted for just 9.7 per cent of visitors and 5.3 per cent of visits.[67] Many of these visitors, between 170 000 and 180 000, timed their trips to coincide with Expo. This is called destination or time switching because trips appear to be a net gain in the short term but in fact visitors are merely postponing or advancing a trip they would make anyway. In other words, they are not additional visitors in the longer term.[68] An extra 306 000 intrastate trips within Queensland and 894 000 interstate trips to Queensland were also attributable to Expo.[69] Figures for subsequent months showed a downturn in international visitation to Australia, and domestic tourism, especially to Queensland, as a consequence of switching effects.[70] Thus, there were no medium-term flow-on effects to tourism as a result of staging Expo. The Bureau of Tourism Research concluded that:

> while events such as the America's Cup defence, Expo and the Bicentennial activities can boost travel to some destinations in the short term, their effect is largely to produce changes in the timing and geographical distribution of tourism, rather than to increase the level of tourism overall.[71]

In short, the use of special events as a strategy to boost tourism and the visibility of a destination seems to be based on slim evidence, in the absence of other factors which might contribute to economic growth and city revitalisation.

### Gambling on redevelopment

This chapter has argued that, all along, Expo 88 was an excuse to redevelop the South Bank site. For the Expo Authority, BESBRA, this was a concern even before Expo had finished. In a process marked by excessive secrecy and lack of community consultation—or even with the Brisbane City Council—BESBRA selected a $200 million redevelopment proposal put together by a consortium, River City 2000, which had close links with the then government, and was headed by the then chairman of the Queensland Tourist and Travel Corporation, Frank Moore.[72] The plan, based on high-rise buildings, included an exhibition and convention centre, world trade centre, hotels, artificial island, marina, and commercial facilities, drew sustained criticism from local government, architects and planners, the media, and community.

Criticism focused on the lack of consultation, the lack of open space, the lack of activities and facilities for ordinary people, and provision for a casino on the site. This latter objection became an ongoing point of controversy. A casino was not included in the design brief, however developers and some sections of government regarded a casino as essential to ensure financial viability. Subsequently, the state government announced that a casino would be built in Brisbane when a suitable site was selected. It seems likely that the South Bank site will be chosen. This sequence of events epitomised the practices associated with the Expo site. Due to the outcry over the tendering process, however, the government was forced to cancel the tender and reopen the process. To this end, a new statutory authority, the South Bank Corporation (SBC) was established:

> to promote, facilitate, carry out and control the development of land within the Corporation Area in order to ensure that such development accords with the highest possible standards and is in the interest of the people of the City of Brisbane and of Queensland.[73]

A wider consultation and planning process was adopted to canvass the views of the local government and other interest groups. The SBC came up with a concept plan for the (now enlarged) site, a plan so vague as to make it difficult to evaluate the merits and demerits of the proposed developments. On the one hand, the SBC was charged with developing the site in the public interest. On the other hand, it was also required to secure 'the maximum prudent financial benefit for the Corporation'. To satisfy both objectives, the SBC adopted a narrow interpretation of public interest as developments that attract the public and earn significant revenue. The plan reserves half the site for open space and public uses, while orienting its design around the riverside proximity and view of the CBD across the river. Based on a theme of water, the plan creates 'a people's place parkland' for the community within a mixed-use resort for workers, residents and visitors.[74] According to the chairman of the South Bank Corporation: 'This plan will create a true landmark development for Brisbane; a successful urban rejuvenation which will become a blueprint for other cities and the most sensible and sensitive way of recapturing the essence of the Expo spirit'.[75]

The SBC plan differs from the explicit tourist orientation of the River

City proposal. On the other hand, town planning consultants' Planning Workshop, has criticised the SBC's claims, suggesting that the plan is still not conceived in relation to the character, demography or environment of the surrounding suburbs but establishes a distinct up-market clientele and users. The simple reason for this emphasis is the need to recoup development costs. The concept plan, proposed by the Gold Coast firm Media Five, includes $125 million of public facilities[76], including open space for a riverside promenade, picnic areas and waterways (including an artificial lagoon and beach); science and technology museum; historic village; aquarium; wildlife reserve; rainforest island; amphitheatre; entertainment piazza; river stage; marketplace; and sunsail structures.[77] This will largely be paid for by the public purse. The other $1000 million private sector development will include commercial and office developments, residential accommodation, a marina, and a convention and exhibition centre.

The new plan has also drawn critics, though by and large it has had a more favourable reception. The main issues have concerned the density of development, accessibility, and the need to provide more facilities for local and special interest community groups. Consequently, the plan was slightly modified to include studio apartments, tourist and student accommodation and 'more affordable' housing.[78] Brisbane's then Lord Mayor, Sallyanne Atkinson, also criticised the over-commercialisation of the site, the small proportion of residential use of the site, and the isolation of the design from the surrounding areas. The vast majority of local architects similarly 'made trenchant criticisms of the planning process, financial feasibility and design':

> 'There's never been a decent brief,' a member told the *Bulletin*. 'It's been conceived as a monolithic development and that's commercial nonsense. We do all those things in an integrated resort but they're not appropriate for this project.' As for the design, 'the plan has not evolved from the Queensland culture but proposes an Hawaiian-style resort. The main structure, 500 metres long and 13 storeys high, seems to be a deliberate contrast with that part of the city.'[79]

Undoubtedly, Brisbane will get a landmark—its 'signature'—in the development. The question is whether it will relate to the quirky and anarchistic features of 'Brisbanism' with which is is associated. If it works, then Expo 88 may leave a permanent revitalising mark on this second-order city. If not, Expo will have been just another blip which left a nasty and expensive taste in the collective mouths of Brisbanites. Either way, individuals and politicians associated with the project have furthered their ambitions and ensured that Expo 88 will be remembered as a renowned event that purportedly transformed the face of the city. As one commentator concluded:

> Brisbane's Expo might have been too much of a random assault on the senses for some, too densely packed with competitive exhibits and attrac-

tions to be comprehensible to others. But the predominant response of Australians was one of pride in the achievement. Like the Australia Day extravaganza on and around Sydney Harbour, Expo was responsible for a surge of national self-esteem and spontaneous commmunality.[80]

In a reference to the politics that commissioned Expo 88, an editorial in the *Courier-Mail* observed that the development of the Expo site will lead 'the way in the most significant redevelopment of the city's central area in recent years. There is no doubt that further public involvement is needed. At the moment, we have an eyesore. We do not want a lemon in its place.'[81]

The ambivalent course of Australia's Bicentennial Exhibition supports the proposition that the fashions of sight adopted by protagonists and analysts bear little relation to the politics and practices of the site of an exposition. As a nation-building exercise, Expo 88 was a profound flop; as parochial boosterism, it was at best a flash in the pan.

# 9

# Pioneering the past: a study of the Stockman's Hall of Fame

*Robin Trotter*

The multiplicity of history programs generated by the Australian Bicentenary resulted in a rich and telling range of discursive constructions of the national heritage. These were not only expressed in debate but materialised in concrete events, structures and projects. These, in turn, brought to the fore a diversity of perspectives focusing, inter alia, on an immigrant past, a developmental, progressive history, and a pioneering national past. The present study focuses on the Australian Stockman's Hall of Fame and Cultural Heritage Centre at Longreach, Queensland. The Hall of Fame was selected from the multitude of heritage projects for a number of reasons, the foremost being its crucial role in organising a distinctive pioneering view of the national past. In addition, a prolonged planning period and the volume of textual material generated by the project facilitates analysis of the varied forces of region, gender, race and economic interest which were critical in its shaping. At one level, the project has a mission to preserve a national heritage; at another level, its ambition is to re-create a national culture for the future.

The project was well under way prior to the Bicentenary. As early as 1974 Hugh Sawrey, a prominent outback artist, proposed the construction of a Hall of Fame to commemorate the early pioneers and to form a repository for Australian outback culture. In 1977, the Hall of Fame was incorporated as a non-profit company to enable fund-raising activities to proceed. But there were problems as Sawrey's 'vision' became the subject of conflict between competing regional economic interests. Local media reports from the 1970s and early 1980s indicate that unemployment, decreasing population and reduced services were matters of concern for inland central Queensland.[1] A tourist complex offered a remedy for the recurrent economic cycles of boom and bust characteristic of rural economies. The proposal, however, generated rivalry among the larger central Queensland towns, with various regional centres lobbying for the development to be sited in their area. Further, despite the tight control imposed by the Hall of Fame Council executive and staff, public debates concerning the proposal exhibited a marked lack of ideological consensus regarding its aims and means of achieving them.

The Longreach lobby, headed by a Dr Murphy, ultimately won approval from the Hall of Fame National Council on the grounds of the 'calibre of the people in the community, people who are prepared to get in and do a lot of work to help get the scheme off the ground and develop it into a monument to Australia's outback heritage'.[2] One response to Longreach's success was a suggestion that bribery had been involved in the Council's decision. Advocates for rival towns also questioned Longreach's suitability in respect of location, historical links with the cattle industry, and the town's ability to service the project successfully. Local media reports indicate that the Longreach Shire Council's enthusiasm waned once the project had been secured. There was a reticence in the allocation of building funds even though Dr Murphy reiterated his belief that tourism would be the 'future of the West'—a panacea which would bring to Longreach increased population, better services and improved education facilities.[3]

The Council's financial anxieties eased in 1984 when the Australian Bicentennial Authority (ABA) approved funding from the Commonwealth/State Commemorative Program for completion of the Hall of Fame as a Bicentennial project. The project's plans to retrieve, record and preserve 'the people's' culture conformed to the ABA's criteria for its heritage programs. Also, although there was a strong regional perspective to the Hall of Fame, its focus on the 'outback', promotion of the bush legend, and projection of outback pioneers as the founders of the nation, gave the project identifiable 'nationalist' credentials. In addition, the prospects of financial returns from a fresh and unique tourist attraction in the central Queensland outback made the proposition attractive to the ABA which, by this time, was expressing concern that Bicentennial funds should generate some economic return on investment.

With corporate funding of $5 million added to the ABA's $6 million contribution, the project moved into the 'fast lane', enabling the materialisation of Sawrey's 'vision splendid' within the time-frame set for Bicentennial projects. Support also came from high-profile individuals such as Dame Mary Durack and R. M. Williams; the Katter family and other large pastoral families; and political, commercial, and trade union organisations. Funds and memberships flowed from state branches of the Hall, giving grassroots support from a diverse public membership of around 10 000.[4] The Hall's governing Council in 1988 mainly comprised prominent pastoralists, with Sir James Walker as Chairman. Members of the Council included influential political figures such as Bob Katter, Sir James Killen and Roger Steele, as well as Sir Frank Moore, Chairman of the Queensland Tourist and Travel Corporation. The Council therefore represented collectively the interests of conservative political parties and regional and rural capital.

The catalyst for the Hall of Fame had been a growing conviction that the 'real' history of Australia was being lost as the old folk died and records and artefacts disappeared. Thus the Hall was not only intended as a tribute to the pioneers, it was also to form a repository for Australian culture, lore, writing, art and history. From the outset the building was planned to fulfil the function of a museum, gallery, theatre, historical library and resource centre for educational and entertainment purposes. First published in 1980, the *Stockman's Hall of Fame* newspaper was a quarterly publication designed to provide 'news' to a diverse and growing membership, as well as to inform interested members of the public of the project's objectives. The newspaper's other function has been the collection, editing and dissemination of information on the pioneers. Editorial features document the pioneering way of life and the adventures (and misadventures) of early settlers and outback characters. Histories of the great stations and their founders form a recurrent feature of the newspaper and there are even regular 'poets' pages for our twentieth-century bush balladists. The newspaper has also facilitated the development and maintenance of a social network for an ideological community—those proponents of a revitalised 'pioneering' national spirit.

To assess the nationalising function of the Hall of Fame project and its relationship to other discourses circulating during 1988 it will be useful to consider, firstly, the ideological strategies of the *Stockman's Hall of Fame* newspaper, expressed in both editorial and contributed material; and, secondly, the strategies of the Hall itself: its physical design and layout, its display techniques and exhibition content.

**The newspaper**

The goal of the project as enunciated in the *Stockman's Hall of Fame* was to focus attention on those who ventured forth with sheep and cattle and to demonstrate that these pioneers—more than Sturt, Leichhardt and others—were the 'real explorers'.[5] Initially, it was the stockmen drovers and pioneer settlers such as Kidman (the Cattle King), Williams, Tyson and Axon who were to be immortalised in the Hall, with Kidman representing the archetypal 'battler who achieved success'. As the project developed, the scope widened to incorporate lesser-known people who contributed to opening up the outback. In this way women, Aboriginal station workers, Afghan muleteers, hawkers, mail carriers, and even travelling entertainers came to be among the categories and 'types' eulogised in the pages of the newspaper. But, despite a commitment to pay tribute to the lesser-known pioneers, the newspaper displays an adulatory tone towards the great names and representatives of the pastoral families, above all toward the Cattle King himself. From correspondents who had met Kidman, or had relatives who worked for him, even those who may only have met Kidman in passing, there is an evident pride expressed in the particular relationship.

This concentrated valorisation of the 'great man' of the outback and the wealthy families founded by Kidman and his peers also generated a degree of criticism. In one issue of the newspaper, I. A. Jackson wrote, 'I read in the last HOF paper that you are writing a book about Sir Sidney Kidman and I'd like to say that each time I receive a HOF paper I feel disgusted at all the big grand names mentioned at the expense of those of the old, true pioneers'.[6] In another issue Senator Patricia Giles took the editor to task for emphasising the role of male pioneers and giving little attention to women of the outback; she also objected to the use of 'Stockman' in the Hall of Fame's title, discounting editorial comments that the paper was 'just as committed to supporting the men who were explorers, miners, timber cutters, fencers, shearers etc.'.[7]

The positioning of Aborigines also reveals problems. The newspaper's stated policy of paying tribute to Aboriginal contributions toward opening up the land is in practice almost unbelievably insensitive to the appropriation of Aboriginal land and the economic and sexual exploitation that has continued since the pioneering era, exploitation which is now well documented and publicised through the efforts of Aboriginal spokespersons, historians, journalists, writers and researchers. But the pages of the newspaper reflect none of this material.

In one article by Dame Mary Durack, however, there is an attempt to incorporate Aborigines into a pioneering role as helpers and facilitators. Firstly, commenting on Aborigines' contributions to outback settlement, Dame Mary regretted that few had emerged from history as individuals and hoped the Hall of Fame would remedy this gap in order to 'enrich our archives'. She then went on to recount her personal experiences with the Aboriginal stockmen on her family's properties. One, Pumpkin, was described as a 'remarkable stockman and skilled general handyman' who had acted as mediator between the Duracks and tribal blacks, recruiting some of these into the station work.[8] From this article, it appears that the Duracks saw their station Aborigines as 'friends and helpers'. While there is no doubt this relationship developed on some pastoral properties, it exhibits, at best, a paternalism and, at worst, a denial of Aboriginal 'rights' in respect of land, economic wealth and social status; both attitudes are indicative of a power relationship of dominance and subordination.

Dame Mary Durack's article contains one of the few positive references to Aborigines in the *Stockman's Hall of Fame* newspaper. Other references have more negative connotations. Several articles on pioneer exploits and experiences note the 'murdering' of whites by Aborigines. One article describes the Canning stock route massacre when a droving party was attacked without warning and killed.[9] Another refers to the barbaric and inexplicable actions of the local Aborigines in killing the first settler on the Humbert River.[10] There is no recognition in these accounts that a frontier 'war' emerged as blacks and whites contested access to and usage of the land, nor are explanations or motives sought for such attacks.

A denial of, or silence about, black/white conflict was a dominant historiographical tradition up until the 1960s when revisionist historians opened up new perspectives on the history of black/white relationships and black spokespersons became more vocal in expressing their people's anguish over past and present experiences. Denial of a conflictive past is a frequent response to such accounts of oppression, genocide and exploitation. Typifying this response was a letter to the newspaper from John Wilkinson:

> I am disgusted by the portrayal of our pioneers as slave drivers and oppressors of Aborigines by many academics, teachers and other public figures and I'm worried about the effect on children and overseas tourists. In most cases the pioneers respected and cared for the Aborigines who lived on the country they settled and received co-operation from them. This aspect rarely received a mention in our Bicentennial year.[11]

There are, however few articles or references to Aboriginal pioneers in *The Stockman's Hall of Fame* but where an Aboriginal presence does emerge it is depicted in negative terms (apart from the article by Dame Mary Durack referred to earlier). Accounts which depict white settlers winning the land, opening it up, and battling the hardships and dangers of the frontier make both overt and covert allusions to a hostile native element as one of those dangers. Staff of the Hall of Fame now admit there is a paucity of material on Aborigines in the resource material as well as the displays within the Hall, explaining that the deficiency is largely due to a lack of data. However, a more appropriate explanation could be the difficulty of resolving Aboriginal 'contributions' to the pastoral industry with representations depicting Aboriginal actions as antisocial and barbaric; and doing so within an overarching framework that values the 'development' of native lands and the depletion of native resources to enable wealth creation by European settlers.

On close examination, it becomes apparent that contradictions arise even as regards the principal figure to whom the newspaper pays tribute. It is not the stockman himself who is important; rather the real subjects of validation are the values and unique qualities that his life history can be made to reveal. As Bob McIntosh's letter suggests:

> I see the HOF movement with the potential to create for the young and not so young of Australia a genuine pride and confidence within themselves, drawn from the incredible feats of achievement of our bush people. The

youth of any country desperately need a sense of national history as part of their personal development. Qualities such as independence, enterprise, persistence, honesty, compassion. The HOF movement will be a powerful movement to re-emphasise these principles as a guide to our youth.[12]

This letter establishes connecting links between national history and national qualities drawn from the unique experience of the Australian bush and is reminiscent of Russell Ward's argument in *The Australian Legend* that a specifically Australian outlook originated with the early bushmen.[13] However, in Ward's apotheosis of the Australian bushman, 'mateship' was prioritised as the dominant element of the bush ethos—independence and dislike of authority being only secondary values in the construction of an egalitarian society. The Hall of Fame discourse, by contrast, has reordered the elements of the bush ethos. For example, we find in the *Stockman's Hall of Fame* reference to the notorious Captain Starlight (Harry Redford) as resourceful, restless, contemptuous of restrictions.[14] The fundamental qualities of the bush are variously described in the newspaper: 'endurance, self reliance, innovation in adversity'; 'resourcefulness, strength and unique [bush] talents'; 'tough . . . enduring . . . sharing each other's hard times . . . coping'.[15] Egalitarianism finds no place in this discourse despite Sir Ninian Stephen's words when he laid the Hall's foundation stone: 'Ask any Australian to define our national character and he will talk of the virtues of mateship, determination, hospitality, and loyalty and of not putting on side, of a fair go for all'.[16] Sir Ninian's comments are, however, more representative of a radical nationalist discourse than of the Hall of Fame's philosophy.

A further contrast between Ward's 'bush ethos' and that propounded by the Hall of Fame lies in the class perceived as the carrier of the ideal. For Ward, a quite specific class, the bush workers (comprised of itinerant shearers, shepherds, timber getters), was the bearer and disseminator of a bush ethos. But in the Hall of Fame discourse there is an ambiguity surrounding this question. On one hand, declarations of an intent to honour men and women of all classes, colours or creeds have frequently been made in the history of the Hall's development. Yet, when it comes to practice, it is Kidman and his ilk who are accorded the dominant role in the discursive strategies of the Hall of Fame. A strategy of stereotyping lesser characters has enabled their inclusion within the category of pioneers and settlers but in a subordinate position to those 'great men' who became the founders of a pastoral elite.

This privileging of heroes from a pastoral elite constructs the class as natural bearers of the national character. In many respects, this version of a national heritage is reminiscent of the 'pioneer legend' discussed by Hirst. In celebrating 'courage, enterprise, hard work, and perseverance' and the 'individual rather than collective or state enterprise', the pioneer legend, according to Hirst, focuses on the experience of the early settlers in such a way as to provide a 'conservative' and 'classless view of society', entwined with 'reverence for the past'.[17] Although Hirst documents a number of shifts in the meaning of the term 'pioneer', he argues that the legend has tended to have a levelling effect with small-time settlers and low-status selectors coming to represent the typical 'pioneer'. But the Hall of Fame discourse, in constructing its pantheon of national heroes, has chosen to highlight instead the lives of the men who founded a new pastoral class, thereby negating the levelling effect noted by Hirst.

Although the Hall of Fame's activities have focused intently on the past, there is also evidence in the newspaper texts of what Nairn has called the 'Janus face' of nationalism—the act of looking forward to the future while drawing on the past.[18] In certain articles the past is valorised on its own merits, whereas in others it is perceived as a basis for future development. Consequently, a degree of ambiguity and contradiction regarding the past can be found in both editorial material and contributions. Some parts of the movement are intent on preservation: 'We are told to forget the past and look to the future, but I sometimes consider our past the better world and can't help reminiscing, for even though times were hard, we were content to make a living and create our own entertainment'.[19] Others, such as I. Anderson in the letter quoted earlier, see the past as a model for today's youth, while some sectors of the movement perceive the past as a generator of modernisation and development.

The first issue of the *The Stockman's Hall of Fame* stressed that the Hall was not to be a 'touristy thing'. Yet, when Sir Frank Moore was appointed to the Hall of Fame's board, he proclaimed a conviction that 'outback Australia is one of our most valuable tourist assets for both the Australian domestic and overseas market'.[20] And in accepting the Hall of Fame's application for Bicentennial funding, Laurie Strange, Director of the Queensland branch of the ABA, expressed the belief that the outback offered an 'escape' from the concrete jungles, a need that the proposed Hall would meet.[21] The Hall not only had potential to benefit Longreach; it could become the 'linchpin to development of inland tourism throughout Australia'.[22] The new complex, it was believed, could even shift the tourist dollar from the seaboard to the inland and provide alternative jobs to mining and grazing. With the completion of the building, the Hall of Fame's board set a new direction: the promotion of the Hall and lobbying for the construction of a tourist corridor through western Queensland to the Northern Territory that would link 'Reef, 'Reach and Rock'.

A. D. Smith has argued that a nationalist discourse, although constructed around a commitment to the future such as that embodied in the development rhetoric of the Hall, can only achieve this by mobilising symbols, stereotypes, legends, and myths of past glory to construct a community of history and destiny to which individual aspirations can be linked. Smith has also noted how nationalist strategies identify a period of moral, social, and/or economic decline which may be rectified through reviving a sense of national pride, restoring traditional values, and removing barriers to development.[23] The Hall of Fame discourse reveals concern at a loss of bush values, particularly among 'city slickers', an anxiety that Americanisation is spreading into the outback and flooding the real Australian culture on its homeground, and fears that multiculturalism may subsume the Australian identity. This last point was put most strongly by Sir Frank Moore when the Hall of Fame launched its first publication, *The Stockman:*

> The heritage of people—that's what the HOF is all about. It remains, most passionately, the core of Australian society yet we seem to have reached a point where it has become fashionable to look after ethnic considerations and Australian governments (both Liberal and Labor over the last five years) have spent nearly $125 million on ethnic radio and television. In universities and in other academic and even political circles, we are told we 'need a new identity' . . . How about supporting the identity that we've always had and one that has stood us in good stead?[24]

## The Hall

The expectation of a tourist-led economic recovery generated by re-creating a pioneering past illustrates a particular mobilisation of relationships between past and present—or, in Patrick Wright's terms, a past–present alignment.[25] While a number of contradictory past/present alignments have been evident in the *Stockman's Hall of Fame* newspaper, the tensions between these have largely been resolved in the Hall and its displays. The Hall was conceived as Australia's 'second national memorial'[26] (the first being the Australian War Memorial). Designed to express a close relationship to the land, to capture a sense of the vastness and space of the outback, and to convey an atmosphere of homage and reverence, the Hall and its contents embody a nostalgia for the past. Yet, in practical terms, the very construction achieves the ambitions of those looking to the future. The building's construction has provided a resolution to this inherent conflict of past and present with the use of traditional outback building materials of stone and corrugated iron—icons signifying toughness, durability, strength and adaptability, and the Australian outback of the past. Inside the Hall, however, displays make use of modern technologies such as holograms, audiovisual facilities, touch screens and computer terminals.

As Ward, in *The Australian Legend*, turns to ballads for evidence of a bush ethos, the Hall of Fame turns to bush yarns, ballads and jokes, as well as reminiscences of bush life, as evidence of a distinct culture. Written records (diaries and letters) have been integrated with oral histories and stored in computer programs for visitors to access through

**Figure 9.1**   The Stockman's Hall of Fame, Longreach.
The Hall's design incorporates images of watertanks, cathedrals, shearing
sheds, windmills and rolling sand dunes with its corrugated iron roofing
standing as a metonym for the outback and its pioneers. Courtesy
Australian Stockman's Hall of Fame.

computer terminals. In addition, the skills of the past are cited as still
important. These skills and characteristics, typified in the traditional
'bush type', represent the authentic Australia to tourists. They are
valued qualities that identify 'Australianness'. It is no surprise, given
the context of this nationalising rhetoric, that these same qualities are
also cited as necessary for 'national development'.

The contradictions inherent in the pioneering ideology were evident
again in the Northern Territory's major Bicentennial event: the Last
Great Cattle Drive. This project, linking up with the construction of
the Hall, had two objectives. The first was to give 400 young men
work experience on an outback station; the second was to conduct an
authentic four-month long cattle drive across to Longreach where
proceeds from the sale of stock would be donated to the Hall of Fame.
To give work experience in a way of life claimed to be dying out and
to undertake a massive movement of cattle under antiquated conditions
had little practical purpose. In an ideological context, however, the
Cattle Drive project could be seen as having a threefold function: first,
instilling 'pioneering' values in the young men selected; second, projecting these values to a wider audience; third, linking the past to the
future.

Visitor tours of the complex are tightly structured by means of guides, self-guiding tapes, and a system of ramps that leads the visitor through the site. Starting in the theatre, an audiovisual sets a mood of patriotism and nostalgia as it celebrates the outback in images of landscape, pioneering lifestyle, and contemporary outback life. Images lifted from 'The Man from Snowy River' add a sense of excitement, even if the background of Kosciusko high country has a certain incongruity. The soundtrack is a blend of bush ballads and poetry which, when the visitor moves on out of the theatre into the main display areas, backgrounds the remainder of the visit.

The display itself provides a potted 'history' of Australia. The first tableau features Aboriginal settlement. This is described as an 'invasion' of a vacant continent with the Aborigines' movement across the landscape referred to as 'taking up the land'. This textual strategy not only establishes a symbolic precedent for the later actions of European explorers and settlers but also undermines Aboriginal claims of sovereignty. An element of fatality is suggested in relation to settlement. Cook's voyage is described as 'fateful' as is the response to his 'discovery' of the continent. Moving into the convict period, where convicts are illustrated as rogues and villains, the text refers to the 'fateful' decision of the English government to resolve its social crises by resorting to the transportation of its convicts. The heroes of this period are the pioneers of the pastoral industry, such as James Ruse (our first farmer), Marsden (our first exporter of wool) and the Macarthurs (founders of the Australian wool industry). The inclusion of a panel on Pemulwuy, an Aboriginal resistance leader, demonstrates how oppositional history can be incorporated into a conservative text and sapped of radical connotations. The display notes Pemulwuy's resistance to colonial rule but, in the last sentence, adds that his activities have been incorporated into Aboriginal legend as part of their belief system. Pemulwuy's activities are thereby heroicised in terms of a white whig 'heroes' version of history; but at the same time the textual strategy that accords him a legendary status reduces this period of black history to myth.

Of special significance is the period from the 1860s. The narrative theme developed in the displays devoted to this period focuses on the notion of explorers and settlers taking a firm grasp on the land, opening it up and establishing an Australian way of life. A display devoted to 'Unsung Heroes' surrounds the visitor with images of anonymous pioneers—men, women, children, and family groups. To find the real people here, the visitor must resort to computer terminals where searching for a name will bring up a brief biography of an 'Unsung Hero'. As the newspaper valorised the 'great men' and reduced others to categories, so the Hall displays the names of 'great men' and adorns the walls with their histories while the names and presence of others are reduced to anonymous images or are hidden within computer programs. From this period on, the pastoralists, following in the foot-

**Figure 9.2**  View of the central Hall and slab hut. Walkways along the mezzanine allow visitors to experience the Hall's sense of vastness, symbolic of the outback. Courtesy Australian Stockman's Hall of Fame.

steps of outback explorers, are introduced to the visitor as the 'cultivators of a nation', the aim here being to make new national heroes of men such as Clark, who introduced Border Leicester sheep; Mort, a pioneer of the frozen meat industry; Curr, who opened up Tasmania; and the Henty brothers, who founded the wool industry in Victoria. These men are valorised for 'improving and developing stock', 'paving the way' and 'laying the foundations' for the rural industries that made a nation.

Forming the central pivot of this section, and the ideological heart of the display, are three exhibits: a slab hut, Poet's Corner, and the Talking Drover. Entry to the hut triggers a woman's voice telling of her life and its hardships but also looking forward to the future with more settlers coming, the establishment of a church and school, and the opportunity to prosper and build 'a place for the kids'. The visitor is directed through the next display which, in simple terms, illustrates the overarching developmental theme by depicting the epic journeys of the pioneers who established the stock routes and were later followed by the bush workers and, still later, traders and finally trading groups. Next, Poet's Corner offers a place to sit and take in filmic images of cattle, horsemen and campfires while listening to Lawson's 'Drover's Wife', some bush yarns, and, of course, Paterson's 'Clancy of the Overflow'—the source for Sawrey's 'vision splendid'.

From here, the visitor moves through to a darkened alcove where a holographic image shows a drover, sitting in front of a campfire, reminiscing about life on the stock routes. Again Paterson's love of the land and the 'vision splendid of the sunlit plains extended' are central features of the monologue. The drover, typifying an outback character with his rough and ready manners and laconic speech, is an obvious bearer of the bush ethos. But the illusionary image is not as transparent as it appears. The image of the drover creates a nexus where 'pioneer' and 'bushman' legends meet. However, the qualities associated with Ward's bushman—'manly independence' and egalitarian mateship—are subject to a different ordering of values by the following display which is devoted to real-life pioneer pastoralists and drovers, from the legendary Tom Quilty and Ken Axon to more recent examples such as Mat Savage, Eric Willmot and Edna Ziginbui (one of the few women celebrated in the displays). Valued qualities ascribed to these individuals are toughness, patience, self-sufficiency and love of the land.

The remainder of the displays examine features of outback industry and services in formats that blend past and present while moving the visitor upwards towards the levels representing modern times. Here the displays move into other aspects of the outback economy: mining, communications and advancements in the pastoral industry. The tour culminates beneath the arched roof at one end of the great hall. In a small area walled off from the main hall and designated as the 'chapel', the visitor may rest, listen to the muted strains of 'Waltzing Matilda' and contemplate a massive image of stockmen silhouetted against the sunset.

Although the Hall represents the materialisation of the outback 'myth' in its architecture and displays, its architectural features also illustrate a symbolic relationship with Australia's first national memorial: the Australian War Memorial in Canberra. In front of the Hall stands a larger-than-life sculpture of The Ringer (the stockman who does the night shift) which not only signifies the pioneering ethos of independence, reliability and strength but also, in material, size, stance and positioning, recalls those memorials to soldiers which can be found in countless rural towns around the nation. The stockman's 'accoutrements' and riding gear work to reinforce the similarity, while the Hall's entrance steps and distinctive vaulted roof again have connotations of the Canberra War Memorial in their evocation of a sense of solemnity and reverence. Parallels between the memorials make the connection subtly, while the Hall's reference to itself as Australia's *second* memorial confirms the relationship.

Through setting, structure and content, the whole complex works at projecting a particular version of the bush legend—one that establishes the outback stockmen and settlers as the founding fathers who built the nation's economy by pioneering and developing rural industries. But more importantly, the legend promotes the outback pioneering spirit as the forge in which a unique national character (notably

**Figure 9.3**   The Ringer. Bronze statue by sculptor Eddie Hackman stands in front of the Hall. Courtesy Australian Stockman's Hall of Fame.

masculine) was formed and then apotheosised in two war zones: the battlefields of Europe and the ongoing battle to conquer the land. Hence the appropriateness of two national memorials to the valor of the men of the past, one in Canberra and another in the outback; one focused on an external foe, the other representing a war against internal, natural forces; both signifying national traits forged from a common experience—outback pioneering. But there are differences. In Canberra the roll of honour is open to all with no indicators of status or rank, whereas in Longreach it is only the 'officers' and 'gentlemen' whose names are on the walls while the names of 'privates' and other ranks are hidden in computer programs. In Canberra the achievements of regiments and corps are celebrated, while in Longreach it is the acts of elites.

In addition to its ideological function, the Longreach project through its relationship to local, regional and national economies reveals an economic agenda for a rural elite which is, today, under pressure from falling rural incomes and structural reorganisation. Here, it would appear, class survival is being linked to an entrepreneurial spirit which, it is claimed, is characteristic of the true pioneers. The Hall of Fame discourse proclaims a democratic view of the nation's past while celebrating the founders of an elite class and validating economic and political strategies that benefit that class in the present.

**Conclusion**

This case study has illustrated only one of the discursive strands generated by and circulated during the Australian Bicentenary, one way of 'imagining' the nation, past, present and future. However, even here there are leakages from and into a range of other debates and discourses. Late in 1989, the Hall of Fame acknowledged that there had been expressions of disappointment from various women's organisations as well as a great many individuals at the 'amount and the quality of the displays reflecting the role of women in the Hall of Fame'.[27] The initial response was a proposal to honour the Outback Women with the erection of a statue. It was hoped that a new fund-raising campaign would also stimulate 'excitement and restore the enthusiasm that people need to work for voluntary causes' while helping to keep the Hall in the public eye.

With the support of many prominent women, the concept has developed and in late 1990 the Council announced plans to construct a new wing for the Hall where 'women pioneers, drovers, station owners, nurses, teachers, publicans, pilots, cooks and others' will be honoured by reviving and maintaining their 'history, culture and lifestyle'. When launching the campaign to raise $5 million for the new wing, Alan Jones proclaimed:

> These are tough times and pioneer women prevailed in the face of unbe-lievably tough times. They couldn't afford apathy in the face of prevailing conditions . . . Our pioneering women . . . didn't seek wealth without work. They knew you couldn't get without giving. They knew that where there is no vision, people perish. Two things above all they pursued. The first was the spirit of service. Their fear, unlike ours today, was not that they may not receive their due, but rather that they may fail in their duty. The second thing was a sense of unity, unity of family, community and purpose that encouraged others around them into self sacrifice and cooperation. We need to rekindle that spirit today.[28]

It will be interesting to follow this new 'pioneering' discourse and to evaluate how today's concerns are given expression in the displays devoted to 'women's history'. Will this new direction be hijacked by an economic or tourist rationale? What will be the relationship between the new women's wing at Longreach and the development some 70 kilometres east of Longreach where Barcaldine is erecting a Workers'

Cultural Centre as a repository of Labor history? What conflicts of region, class and gender will these new projects generate? How these questions are answered will depend, in good measure, on how the contradictory bequests of 1988 are worked out in the struggles to define a usable past that will help to define how Australia's possible futures are imagined.

# 10

## The great Australian journey: cultural logic and nationalism in the postmodern era

*Peter Cochrane and David Goodman*

From its foundation, the Australian Bicentennial Authority (ABA) had to mediate a number of obvious tensions—between 200 years of nation building and 200 years of territorial occupation; between the bush legend and modern urban culture; between the British tradition and ethnic diversity; and between nationalism and internationalism—nicely embodied in the Coca Cola flag which flew on one of the unofficial First Fleet Re-enactment ships.

In a sense, all of the sackings, the squabbles and the constant palpitations within the ABA were a product of these difficult mediations. The Bicentenary would have been far less trying had it come at a high point in the Menzies era: then we would have had a solid statement of good government, cultural homogeneity and consensus. The idea of 'nation', then, was ontologically secure. Today we are part of a very different social and political landscape, one that may require a new paradigm of national representation.

At present we are living out one of the most remarkable paradoxes of the twentieth century. It involves the reduction of the nation state to a partial system, 'not a whole lived order but a willed and selected superstructure', presided over by 'architects' whose language is that of a new, populist nationalism. The powers of the nation state are cut back to make way for an 'efficient' order of production and trade by those forces, corporate and political, which most actively promote the nationalist chorus. To this end the Hawke government set about dismantling those arrangements which give most substance to the nation state: financial controls, tariff barriers, state enterprises and perhaps ownership limits for the media.

Structurally and spiritually, the nation has less substance than ever before. And yet the architects of dissolution remain committed to a 'national culture', the bottom line of which is a disciplined population, organised along national lines, for the purposes of labour and tax payments. Against this background, the national culture cannot simply be reproduced, it must be reconstituted. Its representation requires a

175

certain openness and lightness; the rhetoric around it becomes increasingly 'superficial and frenetic'.[1]

In various official Bicentennial events, there were signs that the old style, consensual representation of the nation is no longer possible. Here we pursue this idea through a study focused on the travelling Australian Bicentennial Exhibition. This was primarily about our 'journey' as a nation into the future. In it a new kind of 'imagined community' was present: one which sought to encompass a politically and culturally heterogeneous society, to accommodate people to a future of rapid and uncertain change, and to sustain the national form, while acknowledging the internationalisation of culture. The Exhibition celebrated multiple perspectives, polarities and diversities, while at the same time seeking inclusion and participation, by emphasising 'experience', 'discovery', and 'interaction'. Its cultural logic was thoroughly postmodern.

## Constructing the event

The makers of the Exhibition faced a dilemma: how to put together a program which spoke to the 200 years of white Australian history, which was in some way celebratory, and yet which took seriously the contemporary circumstances which have rendered unequivocal nationalism problematic, and unequivocal celebration of the Anglo-Saxon achievement over 200 years politically unacceptable. The Bicentenary was not a naturally occurring event. A decision had to be made that 200 years since the arrival of the First Fleet was an event worth celebrating, and then the event itself had to be invented. From the beginning, all those who entered discussions of the Bicentenary were obliged to engage in a meta-discourse about the very construction of the event to be celebrated. What, exactly, was the Bicentenary about? That had always been open to contestation.

'Deep in any human community,' Malcolm Fraser explained to the House of Representatives in April 1979, 'is consciousness of its origins and identity and its hopes and resolutions for the future.' The Bicentenary of the white settlement of Australia would be a 'time for calling to mind the achievements' of two centuries. The Prime Minister saw the celebration in the context of national cohesion, the *need* of a community for 'consciousness of its origins'. He added: 'There will no doubt be a strong emphasis on history. This must underpin any such commemoration'.[2] In this initial Liberal articulation, the Bicentenary was conceived in Burkean terms, as an affirmation of the importance of tradition and continuity in a sound community.

Bill Hayden then rose and announced the parliamentary Opposition's support for the proposed commemoration. He too stressed cohesion and community. But the sources of Hayden's thinking were different from

Fraser's, and he was not content to speak simply of community and consciousness of the past. Turning to the slightly mystical nationalism of the older Australian left, he told the House that:

> There is a distinctive Australian character. I believe it developed from the need of our pioneers to come to terms with an environment totally unlike any they had ever known. This land has moulded the national character into a style and a resilience which all of us recognise, though few are able to express it satisfactorily.

In the Labor version, the Bicentenary was to be both celebration and exploration of the distinctive Australian character, a time for 'efforts to define and identify ourselves'.[3] Achievement and consciousness of the past, distinctive character and indomitable local traditions—already there was a right and a left Bicentenary; in time both positions would fracture and complicate. Much was at stake, in that successfully established readings of the past entail strategies and attitudes in the present. But the initial conflict is always at the level of the symbolic, a fight over possession of symbols, appropriateness of metaphors, veracity of images. Was it appropriate that the First Fleet Re-enactment ships should fly the Aboriginal flag? Did a supermarket trolley adequately represent 'Living Today' in Australia? Should we display Anzacs or immigrants, and what would it mean to show both? Rarely, it must be said, has so much attention in Australia been directed towards, or so much effort been expended on, a battle for symbolic authority in representing the past.

The most profound challenge to the official construction of the event to be celebrated came from Aboriginal groups. Perhaps not since the mid-nineteenth century has the basic question of right to occupy the continent been posed with such clarity, and received such mainstream attention. Widespread consideration of the issue may turn out, to put the most optimistic case, to be one of the most important unintended consequences of the decision to celebrate in 1988.

In its published pronouncements, the ABA returned again and again to the Aboriginal question, anxiously attempting to mediate an obvious contradiction. The first strategy in this regard was to downplay the significance of the First Fleet in Australian history, and the recollection of it in 1988. This was a delicate matter—too much stress on the first settlement was clearly divisive, too little and the obvious question arose: why pick 1988? The First Fleet did arrive in 1788, the ABA's journal *Bicentenary '88* reminded us, 'However the Bicentenary in 1988 represents much more than the anniversary of this event. The Bicentenary celebrates all the people who have settled in this land over many thousands of years . . . '[4] The extent to which this denial of the First Fleet had become government policy was indicated by the vehemence of the Federal Minister for Education's attack on the privately developed plan to re-enact it. The voyage, Mr Dawkins announced, was a 'tasteless and insensitive farce', and its organisers had an 'exaggerated view of the importance of the original voyage in Australia's history'.[5] Around any contradiction in culture, anxiety develops.

## Journeys

The official reconstruction of the celebration entailed a shift in emphasis from the voyage of the First Fleet, to *all* the voyages of arrival to Australia, to all the 'people who have settled this land over many thousands of years'. The most obvious result of this strategy was to include Aborigines in the event to be celebrated and, importantly, to erase some of the distinction between Aborigines and Europeans—to recast the Aborigine (*ab origine*: from the beginning) as a journeyer too, an immigrant like us. This is a *levelling* strategy—we all go on journeys, it suggests, we are all in the end immigrants, and so everyone has an ethnic background: we all therefore have something to celebrate. It is a strategy which took shape early in Bicentennial planning. David Armstrong, the ABA's first general manager, was telling the press in 1980 that the celebration was 'as much about 40 000 years of the Aborigine and the four weeks of the Vietnamese boat people' as it was about 200 years of the British and their descendants.[6]

This theme of the journey, an abstraction of the immigration experience, played an important part in the Exhibition, which came to be envisaged as a journey through time and place.[7] The 'journeys' idea would figure in all six thematic areas, and this in turn would reflect the journey of the Exhibition itself.[8] There is a sense, then, in which the Exhibition pavilion entitled 'Journeys' can be seen as the ideological heart of the Exhibition. One entered the exhibit up some steps between two sets of objects: on the left an Aboriginal canoe at the mouth of a sacred cave, and on the right a collection of artefacts from the First Fleet ship *Sirius*, followed by crates of shipboard passenger luggage. Encapsulated in that juxtaposition was one of the central arguments of the Exhibition, and some of its most important ideological work—reconstituted as fellow journeyers, immigrants all, black and white Australians can finally celebrate together. The work performed here is the erasure of difference, of time, and of power and domination. The press kit elaborates: 'Is the Exhibition merely an expression of 200 years of European settlement? No, it includes Aboriginal beginnings, aspirations and contributions to Australia. It also includes the contributions made by the various migrant communities to their new homeland.'[9]

This amounts to an attempt to manufacture a consensual position, but it met with approval from neither left nor right critics. The left (with some exceptions) took up the Aboriginal issue strongly, and agreed not to 'celebrate in '88', but to draw as much attention as possible to the dispossession of Aboriginal land which enabled the 'Australian Achievement'.[10] The right was equally clear sighted about the fact of dispossession; some sections wished openly to confront and, on balance, endorse it.[11]

'Journeys', the strategy incorporating Aborigines into the event to be celebrated, also allowed for a celebration of the multicultural nature of contemporary Australian society. On taking office in 1983, the Hawke government gave certain new emphases to the ABA, one of them directing that attention was to be drawn to 'the sustained inter-action of cultures from all over the world' in Australia's recent history. The multicultural theme had been prominent, though, before this.[12]

The idea of multiculturalism was propagated by the Fraser government in the late 1970s, and the first issue of the ABA's *Bicentenary '88* journal in November 1980 was already offering a triumphally multiculturalist version of Australian history. An important part of the Exhibition was a fourteen-minute film called 'Celebration of a Nation'. It was shown inside a spectacular 'big top' structure on two giant three-part interacting screens. The film was a key element of the narrative of the Exhibition, for this was the only time when the audience was stationary and able to concentrate on one sequence of images. Elsewhere the logistics of 'crowd flow' necessitated constant movement.

Near the beginning of the film, after sunrise and a series of 'g'day's, we met five people who had a story of immigration to tell. There was a Greek man making cappuccino in a cafe who came to Australia as a child, and whose parents told him he was coming to paradise; a Vietnamese woman who came on a boat with her parents to escape the communists; a man whose Italian parents gave him salami sandwiches to take to school, when all he wanted was vegemite like the other children; a German woman who had known nothing of Australia before she came, though now it is her home; a man descended from eighteenth-century convicts, who talked of his ancestors as unwilling emigrants. Each was filmed firmly ensconced in an Australian environment—a comfortable home, professional surroundings, or a small business setting.

There is an equalising effect here: it seems not to matter whence one came, or what preconceptions one had, the outcome of the immigration act is assured. The sequence is socially equalising too. The cheery descendant of convicts is a besuited professional, but he is, in the extended sense of the term, an immigrant too, just like the others—2 years, 200 years, 50 000 years: what's the difference? Constituting society as a collection of ethnic minorities is, among other things, a way of stressing a horizontal perspective, one which says nothing of hierarchy or class or inequality. It also ends up privileging 'cultural' elements—the salami sandwiches and the cappuccino—rather than social relations. It is a trivialising strategy: multiculturalism is not a program for social reform but something that already exists, something pleasant, something colourful and interesting. Thus multiculturalism becomes a celebration of what is; its focus is personal, highlighting 'lifestyles', family, and religious belief.

A unity forged out of ethnic fragments? Why did the makers of the Exhibition settle on this perspective? The current museum interest in multicultural exhibitions must have had some influence.[13] But there is another more complicated answer: many of those working in the ABA and on the Exhibition were of a generation and social stratum likely to be uneasy with the received versions of Australian nationalism. What interest can tertiary-educated, young urban professionals of the late 1980s have in propagating stories of bush mateship and Anzac courage, in retelling heroic tales of national development, of mines and dams and electricity and the fortunes of the founding fathers, or even in recalling the establishment of parliamentary democracy and the triumph of the liberal state? But there is a way in which the cappuccino-loving denizens of our inner cities *are* prepared to celebrate the achievements of postwar multiculturalism, for in doing so they are in part celebrating the transformation of their parents' world into their own.

There were fragments throughout the Exhibition which lent support to the idea that a significant part of its agenda might have been a rejection of the monocultural, suburban, white-bread world of the previous generation. In the interactive video displays meant to help visitors explore the 'Futures' pavilion, there were some pointed juxta-positions—'Community' brought to the screen laughing Aboriginal children swimming together, while 'Nuclear Family' evoked a grim scene in which a two-child family was trapped by walls in a suburban home, cut off from their similarly situated neighbours by high fences which popped menacingly out of the ground. The 'Living Today' theme featured a family driving together in a car—but the car was tilted, a sign warned of a 'Slippery Road Ahead', and the faces seemed to convey alarm. A giant shopping trolley was full of oversized consumer objects, huge toothbrushes and television sets jumbled up in what could only be a comment on consumerist excess. And on the wall were plastic household objects, all upside-down or around the wrong way. These were created images of a consumer society gone wrong. Thus the second context for the Exhibition's espousal of multiculturalism was that of a generationally and socially specific critique of pre-1960s Australia—an Australia which could be castigated as monocultural, conformist, consumerist, suburban, and antisocial.

**Critics from the right**

Dame Leonie Kramer, a member of the Exhibition's 'Reference Panel', was particularly disturbed by the plans for the 'Living Today' module. In May 1987 she wrote to the Exhibition Director, Desmond Kennard, setting out her views:

> The design image of the supermarket . . . is totally inadequate to the subject. I simply do not think one can sum up all living today in Australia under the ruling concept of consumerism. If it were possible to do this, then I would feel like abandoning the whole Exhibition. Are we really suggesting that everything that has gone into the making of this country expresses itself in the notion of a consumer?[14]

These specific objections form part of a wider attack on the Bicentenary. While left criticism of the ABA mostly took the form of boycott, or argument that the whole project was ill-conceived, the right mounted a sustained program of criticism in 1984–85, in an attempt to influence the direction of planning. In December 1981, Malcolm Fraser announced that he had overturned the 'Living Together' theme, and replaced it with 'The Australian Achievement'. Fraser wanted a celebration of 'positive achievements and triumph over adversity and social problems', and went on to nominate those achievements: political democracy, free enterprise, trade unionism, educational, intellectual and technical achievements, the multicultural society, the contributions of Aborigines, and sport.[15]

The main source of conservative thinking about the ABA seems to have been the sociology department at Melbourne's La Trobe University. John Carroll and Claudio Veliz of that department have frequently criticised the left–liberal version of Australian history, a way of thinking Carroll describes as 'striving to redefine the past as a bad one, full of evil acts', writing a history conceived in 'self-hatred'.[16] This school of thought links the necessity of stressing the good and admirable in the past to the production of good citizens. Ken Baker, research fellow at the conservative Institute of Public Affairs (IPA), took up the conservative attack on the ABA program along just these lines. 'The sense of having inherited a worthy past is essential to providing the spiritual resources necessary to face the future with confidence and to feel part of a national community', he wrote. There was a danger that the minority and grievance-dominated history supported by the ABA would produce 'a generation of rootless, purposeless individuals, full of resentment against the society that has disinherited them'.[17] The simplest message of the right critique, then, was that the celebration should be celebratory. If only on pragmatic grounds, we should tell ourselves that the past was good.

Baker said the celebration should cover the 'core values, traditions and sources of national pride of Australians', those institutions and traditions which unite the nation and give society its identity: the British heritage, free enterprise, the family, Christianity.[18] In this form, the conservative critique is a kind of reiteration of late nineteenth-century liberalism—as a nation we are successful, not because of our virtues, or our prosperity, but because of our free, liberal and democratic institutions. John Howard told the National Australia Day Council on 26 January 1986 that the call by the ABA for Australians to 'undergo a process of self-assessment and resolve to correct past mistakes' was 'frankly disturbing', and nominated as achievements to be celebrated the service of Australian soldiers, the role of free enterprise, farmers, business, parliamentary institutions, the rule of law and constitutional monarchy.[19]

### Tactical pluralism

In part the conservatives were reacting to the program enunciated for the ABA by David Armstrong, who had wanted a Bicentenary which would be 'serious and broadly educational and cultural in nature'.[20] In July 1982 Armstrong promised that the Bicentennial Exhibition would include a '"warts and all" cross-section of history', and he argued for the importance of addressing 'some of the less salubrious areas of our national character, such as racism, materialism, and anti-intellectualism'.[21] But the right were also reacting against the ABA's response to the political environment around it, against the strategy of incorporation, of including all the groups clamouring for recognition within the scope of the celebrations, a strategy we have called 'tactical pluralism'.

Tactical pluralism, then, was the policy of an embattled ABA responding to all claimants and carefully balancing their presence. Internal documents reveal Exhibition planners bending over backwards to include women in every area of the Exhibition (though somehow in the final production these intentions were not quite realised). Aborigines, Aboriginal art and artefacts pervaded the Exhibition, as did images of multiculturalism. But there was also a mining drill bit, a display on BHP, and a copy of the Australian constitution. Everything seemed to be included, nothing was given priority. This seeming lack of hierarchies of significance led critics like the IPA's Baker to complain that the ABA's image of Australia was one of a 'land of incoherent diversity'.[22]

In the Exhibition film, multicultural images are reconciled with the British tradition: we see French schoolchildren at Villers Bretonneux singing 'Waltzing Matilda'. This is a village where the heroism of the Diggers is still remembered. Then follows film of diggers fighting and dying in World War I, World War II and Vietnam, to the unifying strains of a French girls' choir, also singing 'Waltzing Matilda'. The three wars are one war. The choir is stirring. It is powerful stuff. After this interlude the film moves on, picking up the multicultural thread, among other things, once again. But the Digger tradition persists. It recurs several times, momentarily in the form of a Light Horseman in an Anzac parade, and finally in the form of an old Digger in an open car responding to the applause of the crowd on Anzac Day. These are Anglo-Saxon punctuations amid 'paragraphs' of smiling ethnic faces. Alternatively, one could read the sequence as a more complicated statement suggesting that the British tradition is a thread winding through our history, winding through the film, a thread which binds up our differences and holds us together; the spinal column of the ethnic body. The latter interpretation is perhaps unlikely, though there is no dialogue to resolve it.

The Exhibition was conceived as a show of very few words.[23] Most of the objects on display were not labelled, and there was little connecting or scene-setting text to be found. In part, this was a reflection of contemporary thinking among museum professionals— their great fear of 'museum fatigue', 'information overload'; their sense that objects communicate better than words, and that displays should as far as possible be interactive, 'hands on', engaging senses other than mere sight. Thus the aim became an evocative and expressive, rather than a documentary, style of presentation.

The idea of assembling objects without texts, or with minimal text, had a noble intention behind it: interpretation was not to be imposed, so no-one would be alienated; there was to be no information overload, so no-one would be intimidated. And yet, ironically, this most open of Exhibitions became closed, for unless one approached it already know-ing certain things, one would leave mystified rather than enlightened. Explained and contextualised, the stump-jump plough, Lloyd Rees's pallett and easel, or the Aboriginal artworks would be of great interest to many. Unlabelled, or obscurely labelled, they become merely winks to the knowledgeable.

The idea was that objects are more democratic than words. The assemblage of objects allows the unimpeded operation of tactical pluralism, for no text can discriminate or qualify inclusion. The visitor was encouraged to 'experience' the display. But objects do not really speak for themselves, and the wordless museum promotes mystification and speculation rather than enlightenment. This was particularly unfortunate in the case of the Aboriginal artefacts. A letter to the Melbourne *Age* from a country schoolteacher in December 1987 com-plained of the incoherence of the experience: 'the exhibits attempt to communicate a series of impressions, somewhat along the line of abstract art, without the benefit of any explanatory texts or orderly presentation'.[24]

Director Kennard wrote back in some annoyance, but did agree in passing that 'it was my intention to provide . . . a cameo approach which will leave the viewer with a series of impressions about the Australian achievement and innovation'.[25] The theory was that objects in their propinquity would provide a series of impressions out of which, democratically, the spectator could make what s/he would. 'Where else in the world', the Exhibition's 'Information Sheet' asked plaintively, 'could one find Captain Cook's telescope, armour from the Kelly gang, Dame Nellie Melba's tiara, an Aboriginal breastplate, a stump-jump plough and a dingo trap all within walking distance of each other?'[26] The more difficult question of what meaning or meanings might be associated with such an assemblage was not to be asked.

## Reflections

Despite the exclusive style, it was intended that much of the Exhibition's appeal would lie in a kind of inarticulate thrill of recognition. As one Melbourne *Herald* reporter perceptively put it, 'the Exhibition's power lies in its ability to stir feelings which have been dormant since the last time you saw a box of MacRobertson's Old Gold Chocolates and a stump-jump plough'.[27] But if you were too young or recently arrived in the country to have previously seen either of these things, there would be no feelings to be stirred. The Exhibition film also had no narration, and there were, apart from the five immigrants discussed above, very few words spoken. It presented the viewer with a series of brief encounters with different images structured around some broad themes—immigration, colonial history, war, entertainment, disaster, the natural environment—and flanked by morning and evening.

It almost seems as if the highest ambition of the Exhibition was that people should be able to come in and recognise the familiar. Recognition rather than cognition became the goal, for the ABA and Exhibition eventually seemed to reject an educational role. *That* acquired divisive and political overtones in the Armstrong era. The Authority aimed, instead, to reflect, to mirror back to people images of themselves and the objects around them. In 1985, replying to Ken Baker, John Reid firmly rejected any suggestion that the ABA should 'go beyond its role as expounder' and take on one as 'director of the collective view'. The people, he said, had a right 'to determine the form and content of their own celebration'.[28] This way of thinking became more dominant under the Kirk ABA, and found its expression in the Exhibition. 'It's about you and for you', says the publicity sheet. *'You may even see something of yourself'*.[29] That would be the key moment, the moment of self-recognition. It became important for the Exhibition to stress that it was not imposing anything on the communities it visited. Part of the exhibition area was given over to the community at each town, and local displays were organised, local groups performed in the outdoor theatre. In the space reserved for local exhibits was the guarantee that this was not some controversial view imposed from Sydney; one could come to view familiar, local, artefacts and images.

How to explain this outcome? The Exhibition became preoccupied with avoiding controversy. Almost anything *said* would have been controversial, almost any theme would have been more congenial to either left or right agendas for the event. The solution was to avoid *saying* anything by simply aggregating objects and images without words, and to avoid favouring one side or the other by the strategy of 'tactical pluralism': responding to all claimants, including a little of everything. Another way that the Exhibition deflected criticism was by adopting a jokesy, parodic tone in dealing with its subject matter. The 'Australian Identity' exhibit was got up as a gaudy old-time picture palace—you entered as you would a theatre, past a sign which said 'Enter the Palace of Dreams'. Inside were arranged, without comment, objects ranging from Ned Kelly's armour, and characters from the *Magic Pudding*, to a collection of hats from notable Australians, among them Edna Everage. A row of grotesque figures sat watching excerpts from Australian movies and Cinesound newsreels in the 'theatre'. In a way, the attempt to say something about the 'Australian Identity' had already been abandoned. The question was raised, but the answer was only to gesture towards statements that have already been made, behind a protective wall of irony. We the spectators were distanced from direct comment on the Australian identity like viewers of a film—the metaphor of the exhibit was an appropriate one. This is not to say that an exhibit *could* usefully have made statements about Australian identity, but by using the title, and then referring ironically to pre-existing stereotypes, the exhibit appears to have tried to have things both ways.

In the main film, and in other parts of the Exhibition, there was something of a preoccupation with past fashion, modes of consumption and recreation. Nothing denotes the past more clearly than quaint costume, outmoded dance styles, antiquated household objects. It is the pastness of the past which is valued, it seems, its distance and difference from us; and in a way this facilitates a very contemporary-minded mode of self-congratulation. 'Having trivialised the past by equating it with outmoded styles of consumption, discarded fashions and attitudes', Christopher Lasch writes, 'people today resent anyone who draws on the past in serious discussions of contemporary conditions.'[30]

Other critics, too, have explored this paradox of modes of contemporary fascination with the past which yet rest upon a denial or refusal of history. Susan Sontag's discussion of the aesthetic mode she 25 years ago called 'camp' seems directly relevant to the style of the Exhibition. 'Camp', she wrote, 'sees everything in quotation marks.'[31] There was something of this in the ironic mode of parts of the Exhibition: a safe revelling in the already ironic (Dame Edna), in the *look* of the Old Gold Chocolate box. But irony is a way of seeing; one has already to be inside to appreciate it. 'Camp is esoteric', Sontag observed, 'something of a private code', a badge of identity even, among small urban cliques. This, too, fits our sense of the closedness of this Exhibition;

the distance between the intentions of its creators and the readings of it available to its audiences.

Reflection and parody lead us into postmodernism. There are several respects in which the Exhibition shared the aesthetics of postmodernism. Firstly, the kaleidoscope approach, the ambition only to provide a 'series of impressions', the abandonment of a master narrative, and the frequent collage-like use of pre-existing statements (films/objects/images) are all the standard devices of high postmodernism. Perhaps it is not surprising that a group of design professionals called together on a project like this should gravitate toward this kaleidoscopic, ironic, collage-like mode of presentation, a mode which quotes all styles but endorses none. The culture is permeated by images presented in this form—advertising and rock video-clips are prime examples—and Fredric Jameson has argued that it is 'essential to grasp "postmodernism" not as a style, but rather as a cultural dominant'.[32] So one is not surprised when images from the Exhibition film turn up on television in a Qantas commercial and an advertisement for Swan Lager. Postmodern culture is an internally mobile collage, characterised by the easy transference of imagery from one site (and form) into another. That is one of the means by which it has become the 'dominant cultural logic' of our time.

The Exhibition's senior curator, Peter Emmett, has described it as 'an Exhibition about choices, polarities and diversities'.[33] The polarities expressed themselves sometimes as simple, uncomplicated opposites. At other times they seemed to express a troubled ambivalence: endorsement was followed by qualification, enthusiasm by caution, celebration by a warning. Polarities were everywhere: in the film, Aboriginal music is contrasted with orchestral sound; there is sadness contrasted with happiness, there are disasters counterposed with good times; there is war and sacrifice alongside peace and leisure. The 'Journeys' module contrasted two 'worlds', the European and the Aboriginal. The 'Living Together' module situated war posters and memorabilia alongside anti-conscription pamphlets and a photograph of Women Against Rape in War outside the Melbourne Shrine of Remembrance. Centre-stage in the 'Environment' module was a stump-jump plough—a voice at an exit warned against the destruction of forests. The 'Futures' module was a foreboding exhibit: 'it doesn't look good. We're polluting the earth and destroying nature—trees, the fish, the sea.'[34] But 'Futures' was situated alongside the CSIRO/Australia Post display which was a celebration of technology and science. The 'Celebration of a Nation' film bathed us in the visual splendour of Australia, while the 'Living Today' module conveyed something of the jostle, the noisiness and nastiness of city life. Nothing was concluded; there was always the possibility of another opposition.

The idea of the mirror was the second postmodern presence in the Exhibition. Postmodernism is premised upon the claim that there is nothing new to say, no new forms to be created, only the old ones to be quoted. Everything is mediated—the entire 'Living Together' module was 'the social and political history of Australia as reflected in the media'.[35] And the picture-palace setting for the 'Australian Identity' module ran clips from well-known films to 'show aspects of our identity'. Is it too far-fetched to see the Exhibition as another manifestation of the postmodern architecture of mirrors?

Thirdly, there is the relationship of postmodernism to the past. Postmodern cultural production is all about the past, it endlessly quotes the past, but again seems premised upon a denial of history. The past becomes a ragbag of images to be ransacked in any order; 'nostalgia art', writes Jameson, 'gives us the image of various generations of the past as fashion-plate images, which entertain no determinable ideological relationship to other moments of time: they are not the outcome of anything, nor the antecedents of our present; they are simply images'.[36]

What kind of a national celebration does the postmodern form of the Exhibition frame? One of the tensions of the contemporary period is between the increasing power and influence of transnational communications and economic forms, and the parallel and apparently contradictory reassertion of virulently nationalist ideologies—the idea gaining in importance just as the reality ebbs away. At the level of intellectual argument and aesthetic development, however, nationalism is out of favour. If modernism coincided historically with the heyday of nationalism, and a belief in the importance of increasing production in an industrialising world, as in the 1920s, postmodernism coincides with a period of critique of nationalism, and a belief in the importance of improving communications in the era of the microchip.

The Exhibition adopted in its presentation some of the strategies of the postmodernist critique of nationalist myths and images. Its fragmented form, its parodic voices, its bombardment of visitors with sights and sounds in obstinately non-linear sequences amounted, in accumulated effect, to a refusal to subscribe to any univocal, unironic or unqualified account of the nation and its characteristics. All that can be said, in the end, is that there is diversity—perhaps, beyond that, we can infer that diversity is not a bad or a dangerous thing. These are not trivial messages; but there are stern critics of the side-effects of the open discourses of postmodernity.

### The great divide

The achievements and problems of the Exhibition cannot be separated from its reception in the various centres visited. Comments here are based on time spent at the Exhibition during its stay in Albury and Geelong, and subsequent press discussion of its 'failure' to draw and charm crowds. The Exhibition presumes a country audience. It was conceived as the key event in 1988 for those outside the major cities, for people who would not have easy access to events like the Tall Ships, Expo 88, the Bicentennial Air Show, sporting events, concerts and major exhibitions centred in the cities.

There is a need to consider the Exhibition operating in this country environment. For in this setting one of its charms was hard to miss: it aroused a professional and knowledgeable interest among visitors in its mechanics, machinery and equipment—the Kenworth trucks, the compressors, the cables, the tenting and so on—which no doubt links up with a country concern with machinery in general, and haulage and storage in particular. This contrasts sharply with not uncommon hostility to the exhibits themselves: for example, an Albury taxi driver told us he thought there was a lot of abstract art in it which the boffins from Sydney University might understand but which he did not. Another man told a friend (angrily) that he expected the 'Living Today' pavilion to be 'all cars' because of the motoring mural on one of its exterior walls: 'I got in there and it was all bloody rubbish.' The 'rubbish' theme was reiterated again and again: 'Most of this stuff I could pick up, lyin' around between here and my place. What do they want to cart it around the country for?' One observed a special kind of contrast between 'junk' and 'equipment', between waste (of time and money) and expertise (in design and performance). A lot of people thought the equipment was the best part of the Exhibition.

A second striking feature of the Exhibition's impact was its confrontational character. In the Theatre, on one occasion, a family man growled as the film began to the clicking sound of the Aboriginal percussion: 'Any more of this Aboriginal stuff and—'. At that point his wife silenced him. He had obviously been to other pavilions to confront a number of Aboriginal artefacts, paintings and posters. From others there came the suspicion that the Exhibition had 'a lot of immigration stuff in it', as one woman in the food tent told us. Aborigines, conservation, the future, and multiculturalism were repetitive if not constant themes. The sheer persistence was confronting. And the message was tolerance, caring.

Whether people got the message is another question. The Exhibition was definitely experienced as a cacophony of sounds and a kaleidoscope of momentary images. Its effect as a composition was abstract. This was reinforced by free movement around the Exhibition: people did not see everything, they saw things in various orders, they could pick and choose, get tired or angry or excited, go away or go elsewhere. Crowd problems, for example, meant that some people chose to miss entire pavilions and their themes.

An important part of this was the way the Exhibition's artefacts prevailed over its words. People read little of what little there was to read; very few made use of the $2 or $5 catalogues. They might listen to what little there was to listen to, but the aural cacophony in several of the modules reinforced the abstract visual nature of the Exhibition because it was difficult, almost impossible in some cases, to hear anything in particular.

In another instance a woman said she thought it sacrilegious to have a leadlight of Mary with ram's horns on her head. She was certain it was Mary because it was a 'church window'. It was, in fact, a copy of a stained glass window from Sydney Town Hall, representing a view of European progress in Australia. In this window, 'New South Wales 1788–1888', one finds an Australian version of Britannia (tall, flaxen and wholesome), draped in a Union Jack, wearing ram's horns to symbolise the export economy. But it was like a church window, so it had to be Mary.[37] For the Exhibition, a fundamental problem follows form this. It is a cognitive one: ordinary people, of a common sense, practical orientation and without a 'lateral intellectuality' and a vocabulary of historical symbolism, simply cannot come to grips with this style. Indeed, very few people could—everybody got lost somewhere along the way in this jungle of images. We might argue, then, that a major flaw in the Exhibition was the disjunction between 'style' and audience; it was the 'great divide' separating the urbane Exhibition creators from a mass audience.

## Conclusion

If the Bicentenary began in parliament with a bipartisan affirmation that there was a united Australian community, that there was more to bring us together than to draw us apart, it ended in the final form of the celebration in a postmodern affirmation of diversity. We were all included in the celebration, we could all recognise ourselves in the Exhibition, but there was less talk about one national community. The incorporative strategy of the ABA did not seek consensus, merely inclusion, did not seek statement, merely representation. There was almost a desperate note to the imperative of inclusion in ABA rhetoric. 'The handicapped, the aged, the shut-in, others who for a variety of reasons find it difficult or impossible to join in', John Reid explained in 1985, 'have all been contacted and are working at their contributions'.[38] All *must* be drawn within the circle.

It might be that the Exhibition marked a new 'sophistication' and 'maturity' in thinking about and representing the Australian scene—a distancing from the old stereotypes and a recognition, in its silences, of the genuine difficulties of speaking in a consensual voice in a complex politically, ethnically, and socially divided society; an authentic pluralism in many ways new to Australian discourse. This was not an uncritical 'celebration of the nation'. People may have got from it a *qualified* sense of nation and achievement, but the Exhibition was not a statement of uncomplicated patriotism. Probably its like could never have appeared, under government sponsorship, in the American Bicentenary. The fact that Dame Leonie Kramer and others on the Exhibition Reference Panel were unhappy that their advice was ignored in the planning stages may reflect the creative freedom allowed the planners. The makers of the Exhibition may have responded pluralistically to outside influence, but they were clearly not the marionettes of the Reference Panel, nor of outside lobby groups.

On the other hand, there is an inclination to say that enormous effort and vast amounts of money were spent on something rather insubstantial, something that will not linger in the mind. Certainly the Exhibition's version of history did not provide the conceptual tools for dealing with its own warnings about the problems of consumerism, pollution, technological danger, and the tensions around multiculturalism. Any evaluation of the Exhibition will involve prior assumptions about the nature or possibility of 'community' in the postmodern age—about whether it exists, and about how it can be represented and spoken for.

# 11
## Postscript 1991—explicating openness
*David Goodman*

The New South Wales 'First State 88' exhibition, a multi-million dollar 'supershow', was on display at Darling Harbour from March to July 1988. The walk through the exhibition began in an early nineteenth-century courtroom, where the visitor was sentenced by a mechanical judge to transportation for seven years. One then walked into the lower decks of a convict ship. The stench, noise and gloom of the ship were soon left behind, however, and one emerged onto the dock at Sydney, into a bright new day, birds singing. Rapidly leaving servitude behind, the visitor moved into an even more brightly lit room: there was a brass band playing as one observed first the celebration of the centenary of 1888 and then the celebration of Federation in 1901. The joy subsided only slightly as one walked into a room full of handicrafts from around the world and pictures of smiling faces of people from all nations, as the walk-through history concluded with the multi-cultural achievement.

Then there was a series of thematic displays on aspects of life in New South Wales, past and present: the outdoors, manufactures, work, sport, entertainment, the arts, finance, and of course, finally and at some length, the beach. Leisure and recreational activities were central; the financial world was depicted as baffling and nonsensical, and one was left with the vague impression that work really belonged to the nineteenth century rather than the present. The walk-through ended with two multiscreen displays on the Australian Telescope and Aussat. The future, it appeared, was principally to be imagined in terms of improved communications. The teleology of our history began with the convict ship and ended with the satellite, the one as imprisoning as the other was liberating.

Finally, one entered a theatre for the 'Showscan' film, a new technology which allows for especially realistic presentation—children were warned to block their ears when the thunder cracked. The film went right back to the beginnings: 55 million years ago, when the continent emerged; 40 000 years, when Aboriginal settlement began;

and 200 years, when Europeans began the 'hard work of building a new state'. Again we saw a lot of leisure time activities, from opera to water skiing. 'At the heart of this culture', the narrator intoned, 'is a utopian idea of play.'

There in Darling Harbour, as part of the new tourist precinct, 'First State' was faced firmly in two directions. On the one hand, in the tourist context, the 'supershow' had to be about the distinctively Australian: 'we need to hang on to our heritage, and whatever makes us different', the narrator of the film warned. On the other hand, domestic requirements were that the exhibition be a celebration of diversity: the film talked approvingly of 'a lot of different people learning to live together, like we are today'. Distinctiveness for the international market, diversity as a safe answer to the pressing national question of what it was that ought to be celebrated in 1988—there in the postmodern environs of Darling Harbour, in this enormously popular exhibition, were dramatised some of the complexities and contradictions involved in representing the Australian nation today.[1]

In celebration, one strand of cultural anthropology has long maintained, a society is committed in some way to the telling of a story about itself to itself. The images circulated and displayed in the course of the various Bicentennial events enacted solutions to ideological dilemmas about national representation. The journey, the spectacle, the panorama became the characteristic forms of a powerful impulse to a form of symbolic inclusiveness which characterised the official celebrations. On the eve of the Bicentennial year David Burchell pondered how it was that, with so many 'progressive people' involved in work on aspects of the Bicentennial program, it appeared in the end as only 'a hotch potch of therapeutic devices interspersed with gestures towards cultural diversity and racial reconciliation'.[2] How was it that critical ideas proved so ineffective?

Part of the answer might lie in the incorporative powers of large bureaucracies, and there were some well-publicised instances of censorship or suppression of critical ideas and themes. But the deeper answer surely lies with the kinds of critiques available: specifically, the legacy of those critiques of earlier unitary definitions of the Australian nation which consisted mainly of pointing to diversity and to those who were 'left out' or marginalised by dominant versions of Australian history and self-definition. The legacy of those critiques was an interest in the demolition of boundaries, the opening up of the planes of representation. Chapter 10 argued that there was an intersection here with the discursive strategies of postmodernism. 'The idea that all groups have a right to speak for themselves, in their own voice', argues David Harvey, 'and have that voice accepted as authentic and legitimate is essential to the pluralistic stance of postmodernism'.[3] There was and is a radical edge to this new mode. The symbolic inclusions it made possible are not trivial, and not without 'real world' implications. But there are limits to the grip that critiques which are just about inclusion can have. For new official pluralist ideologies in Australia easily incorporate such critical discourses as part of a depiction of the nation as a happy diversity, a mobile postmodern collage of difference.

The rapidity of change in Australia has blinded some to its extent. We are still, three years after the Bicentenary, coming to terms with the new kinds of representation of the nation which were tried out in those celebrations. In 25 years we have progressed as a nation from White Australia and the refusal of citizenship to Aboriginal people, to official multiculturalism and its 'management of the consequences' of cultural diversity. We have also progressed from relative communications isolation to a capacity to watch the TV news from the great metropolitan centres in our homes, 'live'. What has been involved in these shifts has been an altering of the boundaries of the nation—its new permeability and openness mirroring a new permeability to the movements of capital—and a new way of thinking about its content. There has been here some paradoxical convergence of the liberationist discourses of the 1960s and 1970s, with their stress upon openness and the removal of boundaries, and the new economic rationalism, in the view of which the artificial political and cultural boundaries of an older and more sentimental world have to be cut down. The hopes for the tourist industry are also a part of this turning to openness: where once our national salvation was thought to lie in fortress-like exclusion and protection, it is now seen in openness to the gaze and the trading of the world. Meaghan Morris has shown some of the symbolic consequences of this in her study of the panorama form of the 'Australia Live' broadcast and its depiction of Australia as a 'space wide open' for tourists, photography, and money.[4]

Financial deregulation through the 1980s has been one aspect of the material background to these new senses of openness. The floating of the Australian dollar in the mid 1980s was a key symbolic moment in this opening of the boundaries of the nation. Members of the Hawke government always spoke of the move as one of courage and disciplined realism. 'This Government did a very brave thing . . . floating the dollar', Mr Lamb told the House of Representatives.[5] Yet this accommodation to the reality of the international market was not to be allowed to affect domestic social democratic goals. 'It is a simplistic notion', Paul Keating explained, 'that deregulated labour markets and deregulated financial markets go hand in hand'.[6] Here was a dilemma which was to recur: how to combine distinctive national traditions and conditions with a new and disciplining openness to the world?

One characteristic response has been a stress on internal diversity. The planners of the Bicentenary were always eager to stress its decentralised character, 'to achieve a grassroots Bicentenary'.[7] There is perhaps a paradox here in the centrally organised and authorised grassroots celebration. It may be that centrally organised celebrations are not the appropriate form for a multiculture—certainly central acknowledgements of diversity are poor substitutes for genuine emanations of it. This paradox was embodied in the empty tents taken around the country by the ABA's Travelling Exhibition, for local displays in each visited town—the centre providing the space to legitimate the local. But there are also parallels with other aspects of what David Harvey refers to as post Fordist–Keynesian economic and cultural life.[8] After modernism, the postmodernist argument goes, there is an acceptance that change is a permanent condition, and that small and specific solutions rather than grand ones will be the most effective. We now address public housing needs not with massive towers in the sky, but with small infill additions to the existing fabric of the city. We now imagine our nation not as a monolithic entity with a describable set of characteristics, but as a diversity of small things, each 'contributing' its small part to the whole.

There is an emerging orthodoxy in Australian public life, then, which advocates openness and plurality as not only existing Australian characteristics, but as normative goals the achievement of which it is properly the business of the state to facilitate. This emerging mode of representation stands in some tension with a residual older orthodoxy, which now in general belongs only to conservatives and to some sections of the left ('there is a national interest' argue David and Wheelwright[9]), which continues to argue for a unitary definition of the nation, for the importance of a single national tradition. This can be in terms of an Australian way of life, ethos or prosperity, or in the more austere terms of some *Quadrant* and *IPA Review* authors, who often stress the merits of the legal and political systems and the freedoms of democratic life. Variants of these views would, as Castles et al. point out, have passed unremarked as orthodoxy only 30 years ago, but are now increasingly embattled.[10]

We can distinguish relatively closed representations of the nation from relatively open ones. By 'relatively closed' representations I mean statements of the form 'Australia is an X nation/society', or 'the Australians are an X people'. In the 1950s, radical nationalism tended towards such closed statements, seeking to define the national ethic in class-conscious and anti-imperial terms. The '"typical Australian"', wrote Russel Ward, 'is a practical man'[11]. By the 1980s, progressive200 descriptions of Australia, acutely conscious especially of the gender- and race-based exclusions from the older representations, were turning instead to openness as the key descriptive term.

Richard White's 1981 *Inventing Australia* put forward an influential argument that there are and have been no true representations of or attributions of characteristics to nation or national identity, and that attempts to construct or impose them are to be understood merely as operations of power, jostlings among intellectual and artistic elites, and local reiterations of international ideas. All versions of the essential

Australia, White argued, are 'necessarily false'.[12] While the final chapter of *Inventing Australia* expressed suspicion about the motives behind the emergence of official policies of multiculturalism, the implication of White's scepticism about monistic definitions had to be a position which saw the only true descriptions of the nation as plural, open, provisional and inclusive. Such a conclusion is also drawn in John Rickard's more recent *Australia—A Cultural History*, where we find the argument that in Australia 'in the attempt to proclaim one authentic cultural tradition there was an element of ideological compulsion'. The 'recognition of diversity', Rickard writes, 'has already enriched the totality of the culture'.[13] Historians such as these occupy positions of scepticism with regard to previous formulations of unitary national character, and openness with regard to future development.

The problem for the critics of closure is to imagine the completely open nation, a 'nation without nationalism', to take the formulation of Castles et al. in *Mistaken Identity*. In practice this has proved difficult. The Wollongong authors argue that multiculturalism means a 'celebration of cultural diversity as a continuing feature of Australian society', and that it is 'currently the dominant discourse in the attempt to define the nation'.[14] They see multiculturalism as progressive in its attempt to 'define the nation in non-nationalistic, non-ethnocentric terms', but regressive in that it trivialises serious issues of structural inequality, and because it 'does not question the need to define the nation and to draw boundaries of inclusion and exclusion'. The authors are critical of the celebration of an already achieved pluralism inherent in multicultural ideology, which they see as masking real social inequality and assymetrical relationships to central institutions. Multiculturalism is thus seen as, at best, a way-station on the road to the transcendence of national identity and loyalty: 'The step beyond multiculturalism is the transcending of national identity, the denial of its necessity'.[15] Significantly, the authors believe that the new multiculturalism will 'not sustain a nationalism able to perform its traditional ideological function'.[16] They argue that our goal has to be 'community without nation'. But as the one optimistic possibility for the future, they look forward to a combination of the best features of the 'national Australian tradition' (a 'fair go' interpreted as social justice for all) and of multiculturalism (cultural self-determination and cosmopolitan identity).[17]

The return of the analytic category of the 'national Australian tradition' at the end of *Mistaken Identity* is indicative of the difficulties inherent in attempting to think through the possibilities of openness, while at the same time maintaining a critique of the here-and-now ideological effects of the celebration of openness as something already achieved. A similar tension can be observed in the 1987 *Windows onto Worlds* report on Australian Studies in the tertiary curriculum, which sought to elaborate a nationalism not wedded to any particular content, an Australian culture which was processual, 'a sequence of practices' not an essence of bunyips and eucalypts. 'By staying open to the new and different, Australian culture is never in danger of being complete.'[18] The authors of the report defend suitably defined versions of patriotism (love of country, exemplified in environmental concern), nationalism (a desire for national independence) and nativism (a concern for access to 'our physical and human heritages').[19] These good varieties of nationalism will allow us to combine in some way an endless respect for difference within the nation, with a pride in collective difference from other nations. Critical response has been either to doubt the efficacy of the nationalism in the face of the commitment to openness, or to doubt the commitment to openness in the face of the nationalism. The marriage is widely seen to be unstable.

The architects of the Bicentenary celebrations were torn in the same way as these authors between the reiteration of the old unitary stories about the Australian identity and a newer paradigm which spoke only of diversity. The television spectacular 'Australia Live', the ABA *Annual Report* recorded, 'told us something about our past; it took us on a magic carpet ride to parts of our continent we had not seen; it brought overseas leaders and heads of state into our homes in a relaxed way; and most of all it gave us a sense of optimism about being Australian'.[20] The fluidity was symptomatic. The new politics, we are told, consists of social movements which 'have a loose and fluid structure', and which 'form spontaneously and can disappear quickly'.[21]

More like Ninja Turtle fans than Collingwood supporters. And in Australia it has not only been ockerdemic populists who have lamented the change. Melbourne's *Arena* magazine has been keeping an eye on the increases in the levels of abstraction evident at different levels of Australian life. Paul James argued there some years ago that the postmodernist critique of nationalism was complicit with the openness brought about by the internationalisation of capital and the 'dissolution of the old, closed national form'.[22] He noted further the changed quality of contemporary nationalism, its 'more open, abstract' character.[23] Gerry Gill has written similarly of the 'current enchantment with openness' which 'does not distinguish between the genuinely liberating and the emergence of a new order of domination which requires the dissolution of the older structures and boundaries'.[24] This kind of argument has still not received the attention it deserves in Australian cultural studies, preoccupied as they often are with either the defence or the critique of older unitary definitions of the Australian nation.[25] The complex consequences of the changes towards openness in thinking about the nation have yet to be fully debated or comprehended.

The Bicentenary thus came at a particularly interesting time in Australian public life, as newer forms of representation partially replaced older ones. The task of analysis was to assess these competing languages, and to provide some understanding of the less familiar contours of the newer of them. Those who saw in the celebrations merely another attempt to reassert a unitary nationalism were often puzzled by the form of the celebrations and talked despairingly of the vacuousness. John Murphy argued that, in comparison with the resurgence of conservative British nationalism, 'the Australian Bicentenary fades somewhat, the pallid official amnesia being a much more hesitant form of nationalist history than Thatcherism'. The comparison may be unhelpful, if the Australian celebrations are seen to be different in kind. Murphy laments an 'alarming vacuity' in the content of 'Australia Live', but Meaghan Morris found in contrast that 'a certain dullness was . . . a generic feature, and not an aesthetic flaw, of *Australia Live*'. In this case the understanding of the genre of the cultural text determines the readings which are made of it.[26]

If the *Windows onto Worlds* authors and the architects of the Bicentenary attempted to combine the new respect for difference with older nationalist categories, others are interested in developing critiques of the implications of the new ideologies of openness which do not fall back into the terms of the older unitary nationalism. The mere acknowledgement of diversity, in an open and uncritical way, will not continue to be a progressive form of representation.

The ongoing arguments about postmodernism provide a useful frame within which to assess these changes in Australian national representation. David Harvey's anxiety about the double-edged qualities of postmodernism is oddly familiar to a student of the Australian Bicentenary: 'A mode of thought that is anti-authoritarian and iconoclastic, that insists on the authenticity of other voices, that celebrates difference, decentralization, and democratization of taste . . . has to have a radical cutting edge.'[27] But Harvey also worries that postmodernism disempowers those voices even as it allows them to speak, by shutting them off from 'more universal sources of power'.[28]

The most successful analyses of the Bicentenary were those which recognised that a new discourse was being tried out, somewhat tentatively in places, in the celebrations, and which attempted to probe the limits of that discourse. The inclusive and incorporative strategies of openness surfaced in other areas. Jill Matthews, reviewing the representation of women in the Bicentennial histories, concluded that 'good intentions are part of the problem', while Kay Daniels criticised the *Australians 1888* volume for presenting a 'mosaic of different regions, industries, occupations and social groups' without providing understanding of how they became that way.[29] The openness of some of the official Bicentennial projects did not appear to have satisfied their critics.

The Bicentenary in Australia in 1988 enacted new as well as old forms of national representation: the new were open, inclusive, panoramic, and Australian critics are only just beginning to explore their implications. The new forms were a clear advance on the older nationalisms, and their recognitions of difference were not trivial. But they did not even begin to address the fundamental underlying issue of the Bicentenary, the celebration of the invasion of someone else's land. And many began to feel that in their empty, undiscriminating openness, there were few possibilities of liberation.

# Notes

## Introduction

1 Benedict Anderson, *Imagined Communities: Reflections on the Origins and Spread of Nationalism*, Verso, London, 1983.

2 For a full discussion of the 1888 celebrations, see chapter 1 of Graeme Davison, J.W. McCarty and A. McLeary (eds), *Australians 1888*, Fairfax, Syme and Weldon Associates, Sydney, 1987.

3 The *Argus* thus indulged in a prolonged editorial lament at the fact that Cook was little known, and his deeds only scarcely commemorated, in England.

4 See Nicos Poulantzas, *State, Power, Socialism*, Verso, London, 1980.

5 See Gavin Scouter, 'Skeleton at the Feast', in Bill Gammage and Peter Spearritt (eds), *Australians 1938*, Sydney, Fairfax, Syme and Weldon Associates, 1987.

6 For details of the respects in which Phillip's correspondence was transmogrified into a fictitious landing-day speech, see Julian Thomas, '1938: Past and Present in an Elaborate Anniversary', in Susan Janson and Stuart MacIntyre (eds), 'Making the Bicentenary', *Australian Historical Studies* 23 (91).

7 *The Bicentenary: The Official Magazine*, Australian Bicentennial Authority, Sydney, 1987, p. 5.

8 *The Bicentenary*, p. 8.

9 See, for example, Peter Cochrane and David Goodman, 'The Great Australian Journey: Cultural Logic and Nationalism in the Postmodern Era', in Janson and MacIntyre.

10 Mona Ozouf, *Festivals and the French Revolution*, Harvard University Press, Cambridge, Mass., 1988, p. 54.

11 Ozouf, p. 11.

12 Ernest Renan 'What is a nation?' (1882), in Homi K. Bhabha (ed.), *Nation and Narration*, Routledge, London and New York, 1990, p. 11.

**Chapter 1**

1    Cited in H. Kohn, *Prelude to Nation-States: the French and German Experience, 1789–1815,* New York, Van Nostrand, New York, 1967, p. 83.

2    A.D. Smith, 'State-making and nation-building', in John Hall (ed.), *States in History,* Blackwell, Oxford, 1986, pp. 228–63.

3    Federal expenses specifically for the Centenary in Canada were Can \$85.5 million, given in Canadian Centennial Commission, *6th and Final Report,* 1967–68; for the Australian Bicentenary Aus \$198 million, see Denis O'Brien, *The Bicentennial Affair,* ABC, Sydney, 1991, p. 119. But there were also special initiatives, such as in Canada Expo '67 (Can \$200 million), and in Australia the construction of the new Parliament House (Aus \$1.1 billion) and a road building program (\$2.5 billion).

4    R. Bothwell, 'Centennial year', *The Canadian Encyclopaedia,* Hortig, Edmonton, 1985 pp. 308–9; American Revolution Bicentennial Authority (ARBA), *The Bicentennial of the USA: A Final Report to the People,* vol. 1, 1977, p. 58.

5    ARBA, p. 33.

6    On these internal conflicts, see H. Tennant, 'Are we going to be late for our own birthday party?', *Maclean's Magazine* 16 November 1964, p. 24; Judy LaMarsh, *Memoirs of a Bird in a Golden Cage,* McLelland and Steward, Toronto, 1968, ch. 8.

7    In the US, for example, there were nearly 12 000 approved projects, and a limited survey suggests that 70 per cent of costs was financed by local government and private funds, see ARBA, pp. 77–88.

8    LaMarsh, p. 184.

9    W. Zelimsky, *Nation into State,* University of North Carolina, Chapel Hill, 1989, ch. 2.

10    ARBA, p. 102.

11    National Archives of Canada, Records of the Centennial Commission, RG 69, vol. 39, International Development Programme, 26.1.1967.

12    Australian Bicentennial Authority (ABA), 'Australian Bicentennial celebrations', *Australian Foreign Affairs Record* 56 (1), January 1985, p. 9.

13    See Zelimsky, p. 102.

14    Quoted in *Maclean's Magazine* 18 May 1963, p. 1.

15    Canadian Centennial Commission (CCC), *3rd Annual Report,* 1964–65, p. 7.

16    J. Dusche, 'The American tragicomedy', *Saturday Review* 1 July 1972, pp. 28–33.

17    See J. Warhurst, 'The politics and management of Australia's Bicentennial year', *Politics* 22 (1), May 1987, pp. 8–18.

18    *IPA Review* 30 (1), Winter 1985, p. 49.

19    J. Warner, 'The rediscovery of America', *Saturday Evening Post* April 1977.

20    *Centennial Facts: General Information on the Centennial of Canadian Confederation, 1867–1967,* Canadian Centennial Commission, Ottawa, September 1965, p. 38.

21    CCC, *6th and Final Report,* p. 8.

22    O'Brien, pp. 30, 38–9.

23    *IPA Review* 30 (1), pp. 49–51.

24 Warhurst, p. 13.
25 J. Michener, 'A slice of cake in every hamlet', *New York Times* 5 April 1975, p. 29.
26 CCC, *6th and Final Report*, p. 7.
27 LaMarsh, pp. 179, 190.
28 P. Spearritt, 'Celebration of a nation', *Australian Historical Studies* 23 (91), 1989, p. 7.
29 ARBA, vol. 2, p. 23.
30 Dusche.
31 Dusche.
32 William Buckley Jr., 'Living up the 200th', *National Review* 9 July 1976, p. 751.
33 ABA, p. 29.
34 Ken Baker, 'Reply to John Reid,' *IPA* 39 (1), 1985, pp. 51–3.
35 On local re-enactments, see D. Lowenthal, 'The Bicentennial landscape: a mirror held up to the past', *Geographical Review* 67 (3), July 1977, pp. 253–67.
36 For the financial support, see CCC, *4th Annual Report*, 1965; also LaMarsh, pp. 181–3.
37 S.M. Crean and M. Rioux, *Two Nations*, Lorrimer, Toronto, 1983, chs 2, 3.
38 S. Alomes, *A Nation At Last?*, Angus & Robertson, North Ryde, NSW, 1988.
39 See H. Kissinger, 'America and the world: principles and pragmatism', *Time* 27 December 1976, pp. 41–3, and the reprints of articles by Archibald Macleish and H. Commager in *Current*, 185, September 1975, pp. 3–25.
40 See C. Van Woodward, 'The ageing of America' *American Historical Review* 83, 1977, pp. 583–94.

## Chapter 2

1 Meaghan Morris, 'Panorama: the live, the dead and the living', in P. Foss, (ed.), *Island in the Stream: Myths of Place in Australian Culture*, Pluto Press, Sydney, 1988, p. 165.
2 Lance Campbell, 'The sun and the sea, and a life worth living', *Courier Mail* 27 January 1988, p. 9.
3 Pierre Bourdieu, *Choses Dites*, Editions de Minuit, Paris, 1987, p. 24.
4 Roger Chartier, 'Social figuration and habitus: reading Elias', in his *Cultural History*, Polity Press, Oxford, 1988, p. 88.
5 Norbert Elias, *The Civilizing Process, Volume 2: State Formation and Civilization*, Blackwell, Oxford, 1982, pp. 309–10.
6 I have borrowed this threefold formulation with some amendments from Chartier, p. 11.
7 Kim Haighton, 'Magna Carta seeks baron with a spare million dollars', *Weekend Australian* 23–24 January 1988, p. 3.
8 D.D. McNicholl, 'The First Fleet's finest hour', *Australian* 19 January 1988, p. 4.
9 Michael Beach, 'My oath, this is true blue ceremony', *Australian* 27 January 1988, p. 11.

10  Edward Said, *The World, The Text and The Critic*, Faber, London, 1984, p. 8; emphasis in original.

11  Bourdieu argues that '...the notion of habitus as an incorporated and thereby individuated social, aims to displace the scientifically absurd opposition between individual and society'. See Bourdieu, p. 43; my translation.

12  Said, p. 8.

13  Morris, p. 165.

14  Stanley Morison cited in Jeremy D. Popkin, 'Journals: the new face of news', in R. Darnton and Daniel Roche, (eds) *Revolution in Print: The Press in France 1775–1800*, University of California Press with New York Public Library, Berkeley, 1989, p. 151.

15  Heather Brown, 'A bet and a beer—a great day for ordinary people', *Australian* 27 January 1988, p. 8.

16  Clifford Geertz, *The Interpretation of Cultures*, Basic Books, New York, 1973, p. 30.

17  'Day in the life of Australia II', *Australian* 21 January 1988, p. 3.

18  'Twenty-four hours in the life of Australia' *Australian,* 25 January 1988, p. 3.

19  Peter Smart, 'This ancient, untamed land', *Courier Mail* 27 January 1988, p. 9.

20  'This ancient, untamed land still waits and watches', *Australian* 21 January 1988, p. 1.

21  Benedict Anderson, *Imagined Communities: Reflections on the Origins and Spread of Nationalism*, Verso, London, 1983, pp. 19, 31.

22  The concept of 'mental tools *(outils mentaux)*' is taken here from the French *Annales* historian, Lucien Febvre, who coined the expression in the 1930s in order to formulate a historical method concerned with the technologies, categories and 'equipment' which would demarcate the 'limits of the unthinkable'. This method became part of the more general project now known as the 'history of mentalities'. For commentary on this and its relationship to specific practices of reading which are germane to the argument being developed here, see Roger Chartier, 'Intellectual History and the History of *Mentalités*: A Dual Re-evaluation', in *Cultural History* (1988).

23  Samuel Taylor Coleridge, *Biographia Literaria or, Biographical Sketches of my Literary Life and Opinions*, Dent, London, 1971, p. 169.

24  A.D. Smith, *The Ethnic Origins of Nations*, Blackwell, Oxford, 1986, p. 178.

25  This argument is developed in much more detail in my *Entertainment, or the Policing of Virtue*, Routledge, London (forthcoming).

26  Jeffrey Minson, 'Ethical Culture in the Government of Sexual Harassment', unpublished draft, Division of Humanities, Griffith University.

27  Robin Kent, *Aunt Agony Advises: Problem Pages Through the Ages*, Allen, London, 1979.

28  Max Harris, 'The nation that got it wrong', *Weekend Australian* 6–7 February 1988, p. 8.

29  Geoffrey Blainey, 'Triumph of the great majority', *Weekend Australian* 30–31 January 1988, p. 20.

30 Frank Moorhouse, 'The bush, the bloody bush', *Bulletin* 26 January 1988, p. 218.
31 Elizabeth Eisenstein, *The Printing Revolution in Early Modern Europe*, Cambridge University Press, Sydney, 1983, p. 95.
32 Daniel Roche, *The People of Paris: An Essay in Popular Culture in the Eighteenth Century*, Berg, Leamington Spa, 1987, p. 217.
33 Eisenstein, p. 93.
34 Anderson, pp. 39–40.
35 Anthony Smith, *The Newspaper: An International History*, Thames and Hudson, London, 1979, pp. 27–28.
36 Michel Foucault, '*Omnes et singulatim*: towards a critique of political reason', in *The Tanner Lectures on Human Values*, Stanford University Press, Stanford, 1979, p. 248.
37 Foucault, p. 250.
38 *Courier Mail* 27 January 1988, p. 8.
39 *Courier Mail* 27 January 1988, p. 25.
40 *Australian* 26 January 1988, p. 9.
41 *Australian* 26 January 1988, p. 9.
42 For those who have not been trained in this national practice of reading, this is the brand name for the main manufacturer of one of the great Australian inventions: the rotating clothes line.
43 Another brand name which has become both 'naturalised' and 'internationalised' via Greg Norman and Paul Hogan.
44 *Australian* 26 January 1988, p. 7.
45 Morris, p. 161.
46 Foucault, p. 250.
47 Foucault, p. 250.
48 In Heinz-Dietrich Fischer, 'Entertainment—an underestimated central function of communication', in H.D. Fischer and S.R. Melnik (eds), *Entertainment: A Cross-Cultural Examination*, Hastings House, New York, 1979, pp. 4–5.
49 Michel Foucault, *Power/Knowledge: Selected Interviews and Other Writings, 1972–1977*, Bantam Books, New York, 1980, pp. 73–7.
50 Paul Carter, 'Invisible journeys: exploration and photography in Australia, 1839–1889', in Paul Foss, (ed.), *Island in the Stream: Myths of Place in Australian Culture*, Pluto Press, Sydney, 1988, p. 52.
51 Carter, p. 53.
52 Paul Carter, *The Road to Botany Bay*, Faber, London, 1987, p. xx.
53 A.D. Smith, (1986) p. 206.
54 Benedict Anderson has pointed out to me that this was not the case with the first generation nationalist movements, those in the Americas in the 1770s and 1820s, in which people prided themselves on their novelty in the spirit of Year One. The US Declaration of Independence doesn't mention the American people, let alone an antique past. This way of thinking is more common to second-generation intra-European nationalism and subsequent developments (private correspondence).
55 Stephen Castles et al., *Mistaken Identity: Multiculturalism and the Demise of Nationalism in Australia*, Pluto Press, Sydney, 1988, p. 128.

## Chapter 3

All transcripts off air and translations are by the author.

1    Michel Vovelle, 'Rien n'est joué', *Le Monde de la Revolution Francaise* 12, December 1989, p. 6; Francois Furet, 'Tout est dit', *Le Monde de la Revolution Francaise* 12, December 1989, p. 7.
2    Jacques Siclier, 'Radio Television Supplement', *Le Monde* 1–2 January 1989, p. 29.
3    James Markham, 'In Versailles, a Noncelebration' *International Herald Tribune* 30 June 1989, p. 1.
4    Claude Quétel, 'La Bastille Telle Quelle', *Le Monde de la Revolution Francaise* 7, July 1989, p. 12; Guy Chaussinand-Nogaret, 'La Bastille Rêvée', *Le Monde de la Revolution Francaise* 7, July 1989, p. 13.
5    See, for example, Philippe Bouche 'Journal d'un Amateur', Alain Houlou, 'Où est passé l'Etat-nation?', *Le Monde* 15 July 1989, pp. 8, 11; Bruno Peuchamiel, Georges Marchais, 'Editorial', *L'Humanité* 14 July 1989, pp. 2, 3; André Ribaud, 'Les Rois de l'Homme et du citoyen', *Le Canard Enchainé* 12 July 1989, p. 1.
6    Cf. Colin Mercer, 'Liberté, Publicité', *Australian Left Review* 111, July/August 1989, pp. 33–6.
7    Mercer, pp. 33.
8    Interviewed by Mary Blume, 'Bicentenary Supplement', *International Herald Tribune* 13 July 1989, p. iv.
9    Dominique Dhombres, 'Maggie la "révolutionnaire" ', *Le Monde* 15–16 October 1989, pp. 1, 3; Michael White, 'Thatcher rallies party to basics', *The Guardian International* 14 October 1989, p. 1; Ian Aiken, 'Commentary', *The Guardian International* 14 October 1989, p. 3; Andrew Rawnsley, 'Blackpool Sketch', *The Guardian International* 14 October 1989, p. 24.

## Chapter 4

1    *Review: Australia's Bicentennial Arts Program, 1988*, ABA, Sydney, pp. 161–332.
2    'Overview' pieces by Maria Prerauer (*Australian*), Paul McGillick (*Australian Financial Review*), Michael Smith (*Age*), and others highlighted the generally 'spectacular' direction of ABA arts funding. See *Review 1988*, pp. 738–56.
3    For an interesting 'proleptic' critique of the Bicentenary as an attempt to engender 'an appeal to nation-ness ... through the simple stacking of icons', see Martin Thomas, 'Centennial dreamings: the tyranny of a discourse', *Age Monthly Review* December/January 1987–88, pp. 3–6.
4    The 'Bicentennial Diary' was published in *The Bicentenary: The Official Magazine*, a joint *Bulletin*/ABA publication, in 1987, pp. 85–175.
5    ABA 'Fact Sheet', issued 26 May 1986.
6    Information contained in a Report of the Publications Working Group to the National Office of the Australian Bicentennial Authority, 2 December 1983, in Kit ABA-PUB-3, Institute for Cultural Policy Studies, Griffith University.

7   McKernan, 'Fantasy of the female', *Bulletin* 3 May 1988, p. 127; Strauss, 'A mixed kettle of poets', *Age* 24 April 1988; Margaret Harris, 'It's a wise child', *Australian Book Review* 98, March 1988, pp. 32–33.

8   Tim Rowse, *Australian Liberalism and National Character*, Kibble Books, Sydney, 1978; John Docker, *In a Critical Condition: Reading Australian Literature*, Penguin Books, Melbourne, 1984.

9   See, for example, Leonie Kramer (ed.), *Oxford History of Australian Literature*, Oxford University Press, Melbourne, 1981, 'Preface'.

10  Docker, p. 173.

11  John Guillory, 'Canonical and non-canonical: a critique of the current debate', *ELH* 54, Fall 1987, pp. 483–527.

12  Pierre Bourdieu, 'Cultural reproduction and social reproduction', in J. Karabel and A.H. Halsey (eds), *Power and Ideology in Education*, Oxford University Press, New York, 1977, pp. 487–511.

13  John Docker, chs 4, 5; Ian Reid, 'Discharging the canon? Australian literature in schools', *Journal of Australian Studies* 12, October 1989, p. 21.

14  Ian Reid et al., *The Use of Australian Literature in Schools: A Report of a Preliminary Investigation Conducted on Behalf of the Literature Board of the Australia Council*, Centre for Studies in Literary Education (Deakin University), February 1989.

15  Peter Pierce (ed.), *The Oxford Literary Guide to Australia*, Oxford University Press, Melbourne 1987, p. xv.

16  Pierce, pp. xv–xvi.

17  Pierce, p. 147.

18  Paul Carter, *The Road to Botany Bay: An Essay in Spatial History*, Faber & Faber, London, 1987, p. 25.

19  Laurie Hergenhan (ed.), *The Penguin New Literary History of Australia*, Penguin Books, Melbourne, 1988, pp. xii, xiii.

20  Peter Pierce, 'Forms of Australian literary history', in Hergenhan, p. 86.

21  Geoffrey Serle, *From Deserts the Prophets Come: The Creative Spirit in Australia, 1788–1972*, Heinemann, Melbourne, 1973, p. xi.

22  John Rickard, 'Cultural history: the "high" and the "popular" ', in S.L. Goldberg and F.B. Smith (eds), *Australian Cultural History*, Cambridge University Press, Cambridge, 1988, pp. 178–189.

23  See, for example, Rickard's comments on Patrick White, and on Xavier Herbert, Thomas Keneally, Christopher Koch and Blanche D'Alpuget, in John Rickard, *Australia: A Cultural History*, Longman Cheshire, Melbourne, 1988, pp. 257–8, 261.

24  J. Fiske, B. Hodge and G. Turner, *Myths of Oz*, Allen & Unwin, Sydney, 1987, pp. 155–62.

25  Tim Lloyd, 'Opera in the Outback', *Adelaide Advertiser* 5 September 1988.

26  Diane Beer, 'Beltana bash a hit', *Adelaide News* 20 July 1988.

27  '7.30 Report' ABC television, 5 September 1988.

28  Guillory, p. 501.

29  See, for example, the *Queensland School Readers, Grades I–VIII* (1948), facsimile ed., Department of Education, Brisbane, 1989. Also S.G. Firth, 'Social values in the New South Wales primary school, 1880–1904', in R.J.W. Selleck (ed.), *Melbourne Studies in Education*, Melbourne University Press, Melbourne, 1970.

30  Stephen Torre and Peter Kirkpatrick (eds.) *The Macquarie Dictionary of Australian Quotations* Macquarie Press, Sydney, 1990.
31  John Tranter (ed.), *The Tin Wash Dish*, ABC Publications, Sydney, 1990, pp. 1–2.
32  Material from the *Sydney Morning Herald* Monday, 20 February and Saturday, 25 February 1989. The Saturday issue publishes articles on both sides of the question by Don Anderson, Oliver Freeman, Ross Fitzgerald, Robert Pullan, Ken Wilder and Geoffrey Dutton.

**Chapter 5**

1   Charles Manning Hope Clark (1915–1991) was Emeritus Professor, Australian National University. His death was announced while this essay was in preparation.

    Clark's publications include *A Short History of Australia* (1963), *In Search of Henry Lawson* (1978) and, most famously, the six-volume *A History of Australia* (1962–87). He also published two autobiographical books and his *Collected Short Stories* (1986). He won numerous literary awards.

2   Cf Brian Head, 'Introduction: intellectuals in Australian society', in Brian Head and James Walter (eds), *Intellectual Movements and Australian Society*, Oxford University Press, Melbourne, 1988, pp. 3–8.

3   These terms are derived from M.A.K. Halliday's analysis of speech situation types in *Language as Social Semiotic*, Edward Arnold, London, 1978; and their discussion in John Frow, *Marxism and Literary History*, Basil Blackwell, Oxford, 1986. The public utterances by intellectuals in the celebratory forms of the Bicentenary are marked by their insertion into the peculiar field of 'national celebratory rhetoric' which is neither the professional sphere nor that of the dailiness of the newspaper; by the tenor of an exchange between *national* subjects (and within this, between certain kinds of national subjects: 'serious readers' in colloquial terms); and by a rhetorical mode governed by metaphors of embodiment, whatever the political direction of the utterance.

4   Phillip Adams: 'Film Maker, Author, Broadcaster' (*Who's Who in Australia, 1988*); director of advertising company, Mojo MDA; Commission for the Future, 1985; Australian Film Commission 1983–90; Film Board, Australia Council, 1972–5; consultant to Australian Bicentennial Committee; author of *The Unspeakable Adams* (1977), *More Unspeakable Adams* (1979), *Un-Censored Adams* (1981), *The Inflammable Adams* (1983), *Adams Versus God* (1985).

    Geoffrey Blainey: Professor of History, University of Melbourne; Literature Board, Australia Council, 1973–74; publications include *The Rush that Never Ended* (1963), *The Tyranny of Distance* (1966), *The Causes of War* (1973), *Triumph of the Nomads* (1975), *A Land Half Won* (1980), *The Blainey View* (1982), *All for Australia* (1984). The last expounds Blainey's controversial views on immigration.

    Donald Horne: Emeritus Professor, University of NSW; Chairman, Australia Council, since 1985; editor variously of *Quadrant* and the *Observer*, publications include *The Lucky Country* (1964), *God is an Englishman* (1969), *Time of Hope* (1980), *The Story of the Australian People* (1985),

*The Public Culture* (1986), *The Lucky Country Revisited* (1987). Horne has also published fiction and autobiography.

Craig McGregor: journalist, author; publications include *People, Politics and Pop* (1968), *Profile of Australia* (1966), *The Australian People* (1980). He has also published fiction.

Patrick White: the Nobel Prize-winning novelist.

5  Alan Atwood, 'Irreverent Anthems', *Time* 25 January 1988, p. 11. As Patrick O'Farrell remarked, in an obituary piece, the hat was 'not, strangely, R.M. Williams Akubra in style', *Australian Book Review* July 1991, p. 5.

6  'Manning Clark's 88 Prominent Australians', *Age* Colour Souvenir, 1 January 1988, pp. 2–7; 'Australia 1988: Eight Views', *Age* Bicentenary Souvenir, 31 December 1988, p. 15; Manning Clark, 'The beginning of wisdom', *Time* (Australia) 25 January 1988, pp. 12–15; Manning Clark, 'What do we want to be and what should we believe?', *Bulletin* Bicentenary edition, 26 January 1988, pp. 10–11; Manning Clark, 'A vision of Eden', *Australian Way* December 1987–January 1988, pp. 31–7. Clark also gets to speak in the ABA special publication, *The Bicentenary*, in his role as consultant to the Parliament House Construction Authority, in a feature article on Parliament House which he describes as 'a place of inspiration and instruction for all Australians' (p. 14).

For later manifestations of Manning Clark's public persona see 'The bookworm's guide to the essential library: Donald Horne and Manning Clark each choose 50 books every civilised Australian should read...', *Australian Magazine* 25–26 February 1989, pp. 44–53; Pru Goward, 'Clark', *Australian Way* June 1990, pp. 8–11; Catherine Lumby, 'Manning's graceful life', *Sydney Morning Herald* 29 September 1990; Sandy Yarwood, 'Who will take up the mantle of Manning Clark?', *Bulletin*, 22 October 1991, pp. 83–5.

7  *Manning Clark's History of Australia–The Musical* by Tim Robertson, Don Watson and John Romeril, opened 16 January 1988, Princess Theatre, Melbourne. For discussion see P.P. McGuiness, 'After the musical, we can forgive Manning's myths', *Times on Sunday* 24, January 1988, p. 2; Hilary Glow and James Waites, 'His story of Australia', *New Theatre: Australia* March–April 1988, pp. 180–1; Donald Horne, *Ideas for a Nation* Pan, Sydney, 1989, pp. 229–30.

8  In the *Age* Bicentenary souvenir, for example, he is listed on the cover behind only the Prime Minister; in the 1 January 1988 Colour Souvenir his contribution is highlighted on the front cover, and his list of 88 prominent Australians is presented in a band across the top of six of the Souvenir's eight pages. More significantly, Clark's essays lead off the segments in *Time*, the *Bulletin*, and the *Australian Way*. In *Time* he is featured on the cover and in the editorial; in the *Bulletin* and the *Australian Way*, he is signposted editorially.

9  See, in relation to Clark's essays listed in previous footnote, Phillip Adams, 'The next 200 years', *Australian Way* December 1987–January 1988, pp. 44–50; 'It's time for a declaration of independence', *Bulletin* 26 January 1988, pp. 298–300.

10  Chris Healy, 'History, history everywhere but...', in Susan Janson and

Stuart Macintyre (eds), *Making the Bicentenary*, Special Issue of *Australian Historical Studies* 23, October 1988, p. 180.

11  *Time* 25 January 1988, p. 1.

12  See, for example, Miriam Dixson, 'Thoughts on thinkers', *Weekend Australian* 28–29 July 1990, p. 24.

13  *Time* (editorial), p. 2.

14  These quotations in order are from: Alan Attwood, *Time* 25 January 1988, p. 11; Helen Thomson, *Australian* 18 January 1988; Barry Oakley, *Times on Sunday* 24 January 1988, in *Review: Australia's Bicentennial Arts Program 1988*, ABA, Sydney, 1989, pp. 174 & 176.

15  John Larkin, *Sunday Press* 24 January 1988, in *Review: Australia's Bicentennial Arts Program 1988*, p. 177.

16  Cochrane and Goodman in the present volume; the *Bulletin* Bicentenary edition features essays on the national, state and territory capitals and one on the bush by writers including Elizabeth Jolley, Morris Lurie and Frank Moorhouse. The *Sunday Times Magazine* Special Issue Australia 200, 17 January 1988, features Peter Carey on Sydney. See the chapter by Patrick Buckridge in the present volume.

17  Sandra Hall, 'A question of balance', *The Bicentenary* Australian Consolidated Press, Sydney, 1988, p. 19.

18  As will become evident, I can agree only partially with Noel McLachlan who sees Manning Clark's hat as a residual sign of 'precocious ockerism'. From a review of Clark's second autobiographical volume, *The Quest for Grace*, in the *Weekend Australian* 20–21 October 1990, Review p. 6. Cf Geoffrey Blainey's account of Clark's emergence into writing: 'The Manning Clark school of history', *Scripsi* 6 (1), p. 64.

19  The eight views are those of Lily Brett, poet; Herb Elliot, athlete; Robyn Williams, presenter of the ABC's 'Science Show'; Professor [sic] Manning Clark; James Balderstone, chairman of BHP; Sir John Gorton, former PM; Bob Ansett, managing director; John Cain, Victorian Premier.

20  Robyn Williams seems to be the hardest of the other seven in the *Age* feature to imagine replacing and interestingly he also has some minor claim to the status of national intellectual although his 'base' in science journalism seems to be too narrow—less and less so perhaps as science and the environment come to be linked to questions of national destiny. He also appears in the *Australian Way* special edition; and see his 'Looking beyond the rubbish-tip era', *Sydney Morning Herald* 27 January 1988, p. 15.

Craig McGregor is another name mentioned earlier. He seems to function in much the same way as Manning Clark but his constituency, as it were, scarcely extends beyond Sydney. See his 'The dreaming's over', *Sydney Morning Herald* 1 February 1988, pp. 36–7; 'Not a day for pride or shame', *Sydney Morning Herald* 26 January 1988, p. 3.

21  Pierre Bourdieu, *Distinction: A Social Critique of the Judgement of Taste* (1979), trans. R. Nice, Harvard University Press, Cambridge, Mass., 1984, p. 208.

22  *Bulletin* 26 January 1988, p. 11.

23  See, for example, Dorothy Green, 'Jubilee—jubilate?', *Age Monthly Review* December 1987–January 1988, pp. 14–16.

24  See Cochrane and Goodman this volume.

## Chapter 6

1 Daizy Gedeon, 'If Krncevic gets a chance, so will Socceroos', *Australian* 7 June 1988, p. 26.
2 Geoff Stead, 'Sleeping giant has finally stirred', *Sunday Mail* 24 July 1988, p. 54.
3 Mike Cockerill, 'Why 28,000 fans can't be wrong about soccer's future', *Sydney Morning Herald* 19 July 1988, p. 45.
4 Quoted in Mike Hurst, 'World champs stunned by gallant Socceroos', *Daily Telegraph* 15 July 1988, p. 67.
5 David Mazitelli, 'Major Events', in Department of Sport, Recreation and Tourism and Australian Sports Commission (DSPRAT and ASC), *Australian Sport: A Profile*, AGPS, Canberra, 1985, p. 70; and Australian Bicentennial Authority (ABA), *Sport 88: A Guide to Bicentennial Sport & Recreation*, n.place, n.d., pp. 33–4.
6 DSPRAT–ASC, p. 185.
7 Tony Mason, 'Some Englishmen and Scotsmen abroad: the spread of world football', in Alan Tomlinson and Garry Whannel (eds), *Off the Ball: The Football World Cup*, Pluto Press, London, Sydney, Dover, New Hampshire, 1986, p. 78; and Angus Cameron (ed.), *The Second Australian Almanac*, Angus and Robertson, Sydney, 1986, p. 207.
8 John Goldlust, *Playing for Keeps: Sport, The Media and Society*, Longman Cheshire, Melbourne, 1987, p. 57 n. 50.
9 Cameron, p. 208.
10 John Warren, *John Warren's World of Australian Soccer*, Liahona Books, n.place, 1980, p. 7.
11 Mike Jenkinson, 'Social Impact', in DSPRAT–ASC, p. 26.
12 *Australian Soccer Weekly, Australian Soccer Annual*, n.place, 1988, pp. 45, 68.
13 Brian Mossop, 'Best foot forward', *Australia's Sport 88*, ABA, Sydney, 1988, p. 34.
14 Mike Cockerill, 'End of the decade prompts a backward glance for soccer', *Sydney Morning Herald* 29 December 1989, p. 33; and Greg Blake, 'NSL over 500,000', *Australian Soccer Weekly* 9 (347), 1988, p. 4.
15 'Editor', *Australian Soccer Weekly* 9 (347), 1988, p. 10.
16 Mike Cockerill, 'We can beat the world's best, says Arok', *Sydney Morning Herald* 5 July 1988, p. 40.
17 Jean Laponce, 'Nation-building as body-building: a comparative study of the personalization of city, province and state by Anglophone and Francophone Canadians', *Social Science Information* 23 (6), 1984, pp. 977–8, and 988.
18 'Editor', *Australian Soccer Weekly* 9 (341), 1988, p. 10.
19 Quoted in Mike Cockerill, 'Review is revolutionary, says Sir Arthur', *Sydney Morning Herald* 18 June 1988, p. 67.
20 Stan Hey, 'World Cup 90', *Marxism Today* June 1990, p. 43.
21 Stefan Kamasz quoted in Ray Gatt, 'Kid keeps an eye on the door of the lolly shop', *Australian* 6 December 1989, p. 39.
22 K.S. Inglis, *Multiculturalism and National Identity*, Academy of the Social Sciences in Australia Annual Lecture, 1988, pp. 17–18.

23 Stefan Kamasz, 'Time to raise marketing tempo', *Weekend Australian* 24–25 June 1989, p. 43.
24 Wes Santina, 'Move to better administration', *Australian Soccer Weekly* 9 (342), 1988, p. 17.
25 Keith Gilmour, 'Franchise the Clubs!', *Australian Soccer Weekly* 9 (348), 1988, p. 3.
26 Jenkinson, p. 27.
27 Mossop; Ray Gatt, 'The faces are familiar but it's a whole new ball game', *Australian* 31 October 1989, p. 21; Frank Scicluna, 'Gold Cup euphoria must continue', *Australian Soccer Weekly* 9 (347), 1988, p. 18; Greg Blake, 'How to turn the decent fans away', *Australian Soccer Weekly* 9 (342), 1988, p. 2.
28 Quoted in Daizy Gedeon, 'Soccer needs "tough decisions" ', *Australian* 29 July 1988, p. 23.
29 Jeff Wells, 'Why Dr Bradley is doing a major disservice', *Australian* 23 May 1990, p. 36.
30 Ray Gatt, 'Those were the days—but now, only stagnation', *Australian* 5 July 1989, p. 35.
31 Ray Gatt, 'Segregation sickness reaches Australia', *Australian* 21 March 1990, p. 39. Also see Joe Taylor, 'Unity', *Australian Soccer Weekly* 9 (346), 1988, p. 22.
32 Stefan Kamasz, ' "Australianising" the NSL is imperative', *Weekend Australian* 1–2 April 1989, p. 42.
33 Geoff Stead, 'United goal for supremo', *Courier-Mail* 3 August 1988, p. 56.
34 Charles Price, 'Southern Europeans in Australia: problems of assimilation', *International Migration Review* 11 (3), 1968, p. 11.
35 Mario Etchart, 'Fifth Sydney Ethnic Soccer World Cup', *Australian Soccer Weekly* 9 (353), 1988, p. 24.
36 Tony Sims, 'Franchising', *Australian Soccer Weekly* 9 (350), 1988, p. 22.
37 Quoted in Laurie Schwab, 'Perkins' grand plan for soccer', *Age* 7 May 1988, p. 39.
38 Mike Cockerill, 'Australian soccer still rides the financial rollercoaster', *Sydney Morning Herald* 11 February 1989, p. 70.
39 Mary Kalantzis, 'The cultural construction of racism: education and multi-culturalism', in Marie de Lepervanche and Gillian Bottomley (eds), *The Cultural Construction of Race*, Sydney Studies in Society and Culture, No 4, Sydney, 1988, p. 90. Also see S. Castles et al., *Mistaken Identity: Multiculturalism and the Demise of Nationalism in Australia*, Pluto Press, Sydney, 1988, p. 13.
40 Andrew Jakubowicz, 'Speaking in tongues: multicultural media and the constitution of the socially homogeneous Australian', in Helen Wilson (ed.), *Australian Communications and the Public Sphere: Essays in Memory of Bill Bonney*, Macmillan, Melbourne, 1989, p. 107.
41 Andrew Jakubowicz, 'State and ethnicity: multiculturalism as ideology', *Australian and New Zealand Journal of Sociology* 17 (3), 1981, p. 8.
42 Geoffrey Blainey, 'Mr Hawke's other Bicentennial scandal', *IPA Review* 39 (3), 1985–86, p. 16.
43 Ken Baker, 'The nation devalued', *IPA Review* 42 (2), 1988, p. 35.
44 Stephen J. Rimmer, 'The politics of multicultural funding', *IPA Review* 42 (2), 1988, p. 33.

45 Ken Baker, 'The Bicentenary: celebration or apology?', *IPA Review* 38 (4), 1985, pp. 175–82.

46 Nancy Fraser, 'Rethinking the public sphere: a contribution to the critique of actually existing democracy', *Social Text* 8 (3)–9 (1), 1990, p. 69.

47 Brian Graetz and Ian McAllister, *Dimensions of Australian Society*, Macmillan, Melbourne, 1988, p. 27.

48 Gill Bottomley, 'Ethnicity and identity among Greek Australians', *Australian and New Zealand Journal of Sociology* 12 (2), 1976, p. 119.

49 R. W. Connell and T. H. Irving, *Class Structure in Australian History: Documents, Narrative and Argument*, Longman Cheshire, Melbourne, 1980, pp. 292–3.

50 Lois Foster and David Stockley, 'The rise and decline of Australian multiculturalism: 1973–1988', *Politics* 23 (2), 1988, p. 2.

51 Jakubowicz, 'Speaking in tongues', p. 106.

52 Victor J. Callan and Cynthia Gallois, 'Anglo-Australians' and immigrants' attitudes toward language and accent: a review of experimental and survey research', *International Migration Review* 21 (1), 1987, p. 49.

53 Jakubowicz, 'State and ethnicity', p. 7; and M. D. R. Evans, 'Immigrant women in Australia: resources, family and work,' *International Migration Review* 18 (4), 1984, p. 1068.

54 Marie de Lepervanche, 'Racism and sexism in Australian national life', in de Lepervanche and Bottomley, pp. 82–4.

55 Quoted in John Warhurst, 'The politics and management of Australia's Bicentenary year', *Politics* 22 (1), 1987, p. 9.

56 ABA, *Eighth Annual Report*, Sydney, 1988, p. 3.

57 ABA, *The Official Bicentennial Book*, n.place, n.d.

58 J. G. Starke, 'Current topics', *Australian Law Journal* 63 (3), 1989, pp. 153–5.

59 Baker, 'The Bicentenary', p. 177.

60 Quoted in Warhurst, p. 16.

61 John Carroll, 'The denigration of Australia's British links', *IPA Review* 40 (2), 1986, p. 29. Also see Hugh Morgan, 'The guilt industry', *IPA Review* 42 (3), 1988, pp. 17–20.

62 Robert Manne, 'Bicentennial guilt', *Quadrant* 34 (3), 1989, p. 72.

63 Blainey, p. 15.

64 Jim Kirk, 'Great work from BCCs', *Bicentenary '88* 8 (4), 1988, p. 2.

65 ABA, *Annual Report* vol. 1, Sydney, 1989, pp. 8–9.

66 ABA, *Eighth Annual Report*, p. 57.

67 'Brazil devalues the price of "gold" ', *Australian* 8 June 1988, p. 32. Also see Keith Gilmour, 'Brazil pledge quality', *Australian Soccer Weekly* 9 (341), 1988, p. 1.

68 Daizy Gedeon, 'Pelé confirmed for Gold Cup', *Australian* 18 May 1988, p. 33.

69 'Editor', *Australian Soccer Weekly* 9 (342), 1988, p. 17.

70 Australian Associated Press, 'Maradona's withdrawal leaves Cup without Gold', *Australian* 9 June 1988, p. 24.

71 Jan Edwards, Letter to Brian Emery, 17 December 1987, ABA file P50–2452.

72 SBS-TV, *Sport Report*, 15 June 1988.

73 Daizy Gedeon, 'Warren puts the shine back into the Gold Cup', *Australian* 16 June 1988, p. 22.

74 Octavio Pinto Guimaraes, 'Brazil throws out a challenge', *Australian Soccer Weekly* 9 (342), 1988, p. 12.

75 Quoted in Laurie Schwab, 'Argentina set for Bicentenary Cup battle', *Age* 28 June 1988, p. 40.

76 'Socceroos go oh so close', *Sport 88*, 5, 1988, p. 3 and Steve Warnock, 'Oz soccer gets the nod', *Sport 88*, 4, 1988, p. 1.

77 Daizy Gedeon, 'Argentina names strong Cup squad', *Australian* 21 June 1988, p. 21.

78 John Warren, '12 days of gold-plated football', *Australian Soccer Weekly* 9 (343), 1988, p. 11.

79 Greg Blake, 'Argentina tops—vouches Crino', *Australian Soccer Weekly* 9 (343), 1988, p. 3.

80 'Argentine's strongest possible squad', *Australian Soccer Weekly* 9 (342), 1988, p. 10.

81 'Winners', *Australian Soccer Weekly* 9 (344), 1988, p. 3.

82 Keith Gilmour, '$50 mill worth of players', *Australian Soccer Weekly* 9 (344), 1988, p. 24.

83 SBS-TV, *Sport Report*, 1 July 1988.

84 ABC-TV, *Sports Arena*, 2 July 1988.

85 ABA, *Sport 88*, pp. 2–3.

86 Steve Warnock, 'Big TV audience for Roos success?', in *Bicentennial Gold Cup*, Playbill, Sydney, 1988, p. 50.

87 ABA, *Eighth Annual Report*, p. 55.

88 John Brown, 'Foreword', in DSPRAT–ASC, p. v.

89 Graham Dempster, 'Challenges', in DSPRAT–ASC, p. 121.

90 John Warren, 'That was the week that was for the Socceroos', cited in *Australian Soccer Weekly* 9 (346), 1988, p. 11.

91 Adrienne Smith, Note for file on telephone conversation with Arthur George, 19 November 1985, ABA file P50–2452.

92 Arthur George, 'Bicentennial Gold Cup', in *Bicentennial Gold Cup*.

93 See, for instance, SBS-TV, *Sport Report*, 15 June and 1 July 1988.

94 Murray Hedgcock, 'Another false dawn?—Only time will tell', *Weekend Australian* 23–24 July 1988, p. 86.

95 Quoted in Ray Gatt, 'Arok bows out but withholds the bucket', *Australian* 9 March 1990, p. 23.

96 Les Murray, 'Brazil–Argentina rivalry ensures Gold Cup success', in *Bicentennial Gold Cup*, n.p.

97 Tom Anderson, 'Socceroos go down fighting in the mud', *Daily Telegraph* 8 July 1988, n.p.

98 Bruce Kapferer, 'Nationalist ideology and a comparative anthropology', *Ethnos* 54 (3–4), 1989, p. 187.

99 John Carroll, 'National identity', in John Carroll (ed.), *Intruders in the Bush: The Australian Quest for Identity*, Oxford University Press, Melbourne, 1982, pp. 209–17.

100 'National sporting bodies prepare for Bicentennial sporting feast next year', *Warwick Daily News* 9 October 1987, n.p.

101 Ray Gatt, 'Case of the missing fervour', *Australian* 12 April 1989, p. 33.

102 Philip Schlesinger, 'On national identity: some conceptions and misconceptions criticized', *Social Science Information* 26 (2), 1987, p. 219.

103 Ernest Gellner, 'Nationalism', *Theory and Society* 10 (6), 1981, p. 757.

104 Anthony D. Smith, 'The supersession of nationalism?', *International Journal of Comparative Sociology* 31 (1–2), 1990, pp. 9, 11.

## Chapter 7

This chapter was first published in article form in *Cultural Studies* 5 (1), 1991, where it was accompanied by a fuller set of notes and references. Some minor revisions have also been made in preparing the text for publication in this volume.

1   For a fuller discussion and exemplification of this connection, see Paul Greenhalgh, *Ephemeral Vistas: The Expositions Universelles, Great Exhibitions and World's Fairs, 1851–1939,* Manchester University Press, Manchester, 1988; and Robert Anderson and Eleanor Wachtel, *The Expo Story,* Harbour Publishing, Madeira Park, British Columbia, 1986.

2   For as good an example as any of the synchronisation of these different times, see Debora Silverman, 'The 1889 exhibition: the crisis of bourgeois individualism', *Oppositions: A Journal of Ideas and Criticism in Architecture* Spring 1977.

3   Although not dealing specifically with an official international exposition, Colin McArthur's discussion of the Glasgow Empire Exhibition offers a telling illustration of this point. See Colin McArthur, 'The dialectic of national identity: the Glasgow Empire Exhibition of 1938', in Tony Bennett et al. (eds), *Popular Culture and Social Relations,* Open University Press, Milton Keynes, 1986.

4   For a detailed discussion of the city politics associated with Chicago's World's Columbian Exhibition, see Badger R. Reid, *The Great American Fair,* Nelson Hall, Chicago, 1979.

5   Tony Fry and Anne-Marie Willis, 'Expo 88: backwoods into the future', *Cultural Studies* 2 (1), January 1988.

6   See Jennifer Craik, 'The Expo experience: the politics of expositions', *Australian-Canadian Studies* 7 (1–2), 1989.

7   Melbourne *Sun* 31 October 1988.

8   Umberto Eco, *Travels in Hyper-Reality*, Picador, London, 1987, p. 293.

9   Michel Foucault, *The Order of Things: An Archaeology of the Human Sciences,* Tavistock, London, 1970, p. 262.

10  Carol A. Breckenridge, 'The aesthetics and politics of colonial collecting: India at world fairs', *Comparative Studies in Society and History* 31, (2), p. 200.

11  For details, see Greenhalgh; and Robert W. Rydell, *All the World's a Fair: Visions of Empire at American International Expositions, 1876–1916,* University of Chicago Press, Chicago, 1984.

12  Michel Foucault, *Discipline and Punish: The Birth of the Prison,* Allen Lane, London, 1977, p. 161.

13  Foucault, *Discipline and Punish,* p. 162.

14  For other instances of the technology/progress connection, see Greenhalgh, pp. 23–4.

15  Eco, p. 296.

16  See Anderson and Wachtel.

17  For the fullest discussion of the display of people as living props for evolutionary rhetorics of progress, see Rydell.

18  For an account of the emergence and increasing significance of corporate pavilions, see Burton Benedict, 'The anthropology of world's fairs', in B. Benedict (ed.), *The Anthropology of World's Fairs: San Francisco's Panama Pacific International Exposition of 1915*, Scolar Press, New York, 1983, pp. 24–5.

19  For a discussion of a similar rhetoric in another context, see Tony Bennett, 'Hegemony, ideology, pleasure: Blackpool', in Tony Bennett et al. (eds), *Popular Culture and Social Relations*, Open University Press, Milton Keynes, 1986.

20  Fry and Willis, p. 132.

21  Fry and Willis, p. 137.

22  It's relevant, in this context, to note the contrast between Expo 88 which, as Fry and Willis rightly note, remained modernist in its governing conceptions, and the Australian Bicentennial Exhibition (ABE) in which the design principles, emerging largely from Sydney, were governed by postmodernist assumptions. For a discussion of this aspect of the ABE, see Peter Cochrane and David Goodman, 'The great Australian journey: cultural logic and nationalism in the postmodern era', in Susan Janson and Stuart MacIntyre (eds), *Making the Bicentenary, Australian Historical Studies* 23 (91), October, 1988.

23  For a detailed discussion of the role of the Great Exhibition in this regard, see Richard D. Altick, *The Shows of London*, Belknap Press of Harvard University Press, Cambridge, Mass. and London, 1978.

24  Warren Perry, *The Science Museum of Victoria. A History of its First Hundred Years*, Science Museum of Victoria, Melbourne, 1972.

25  These distinctions were, however, less sharp in the United States where museum ventures like P.T. Barnum's straddled the worlds of circus, zoo, freak show, cabinet of curiosities, theatre and museum. For further details, see Neil Harris, *Humbug: The Art of P.T. Barnum*, Little Brown and Co., Boston, 1973; and John R. Betts, 'Barnum and natural history', *Journal of the History of Ideas* 20, 1959.

26  David Goodman, 'Fear of circuses: founding the National Museum of Victoria', *Continuum* 3 (1), 1990.

27  I have, however, offered a fuller account elsewhere. See Tony Bennett, 'The museum, the fair, and the exposition', *Eyeline* 7, December 1988.

28  See Paul Greenhalgh, 'Education, entertainment and politics: lessons from the great international exhibitions', in Peter Vergo (ed.), *The New Museology*, Reaktion Books, London, 1989.

29  Cited in Edo McCullough, *World's Fair Midways: An Affectionate Account of American Amusement Areas*, Exposition Press, New York, 1966, p. 76.

30  Three amusement parks were established at Coney Island in the course of a decade: Sea Lion Park in 1895 (changed to Luna Park in 1903); Steeplechase Park in 1897; and Dreamland in 1904. For full accounts of these, see John F. Kasson, *Amusing the Millions: Coney Island at the Turn of the Century*, Hill and Wang, New York, 1978. For a discussion focusing specifically on the role of mechanical rides in modernising the culture of the fair, see Robert E. Snow and David E. Wright, 'Coney Island: a case study in popular culture and technical change', *Journal of Popular Culture* 9 (4), 1976.

31 See, for example, my discussion of the formation of Blackpool's Pleasure Beach: Tony Bennett, 'A thousand and one troubles', *Formations of Pleasure*, Routledge and Kegan Paul, London, 1983.
32 *Australian Post* 18 April 1988, p. 17.
33 Cited in Greenhalgh, *Ephemeral Vistas*, p. 31.
34 Cited in Kasson, p. 15.
35 See the section 'National culture and recreation: antidotes to vice', in Sir Henry Cole, *Fifty Years of Public Work of Sir Henry Cole, K.C.B., Accounted for in his Deeds, Speeches and Writings*, George Bell and Sons, London, 1884, vol. 2.
36 See, on this aspect of nineteenth-century public life, Richard Sennett, *The Fall of Public Man*, Vintage Books, New York, 1978.
37 This transformation in the symbolism of the fair is fully detailed in Hugh Cunningham, *Leisure in the Industrial Revolution*, Croom Helm, London, 1980.
38 Cited in Kasson, p. 95.
39 For a further discussion of these issues, especially in relation to the Great Exhibition, see Tony Bennett, 'The exhibitionary complex', *New Formations* 4, Spring 1988.
40 *Women's Weekly*, May 1988, p. 54.
41 Alec McHoul, 'Not going to Expo: a theory of impositions', *Meanjin* 48 (2), 1989, p. 219.

## Chapter 8

1 Cf. M. Hall, 'Expos 86 and 88: a comparison', paper given to Expo 88 Seminar, School of Management, Queensland Institute of Technology, Brisbane, 8 October 1988.
2 Cf. M. Hall, 'The politics of hallmark events', in G. Syme et al. (eds), *The Planning and Evaluation of Hallmark Events*, Avebury, Aldershot, 1989, pp. 227–8.
3 Australian Bicentennial Authority file P50–0260.
4 J.K. Stanley and M.J. Hayman-Danker, *Preliminary Report on a Possible International Exposition in Melbourne in 1988*, Department of the Premier and Public Works Department, Melbourne, 1979; ABA file P50–0248/1979.
5 Quoted by D. O'Brien, *The Bicentennial Affair. The Inside Story of Australia's 'Birthday Bash'*, Australian Broadcasting Corporation, Sydney, 1991, p. 237.
6 M. Fraser, 'Letter to J. Bjelke-Petersen, MLA, Premier of Queensland', 23 March 1982, Office of the Prime Minister, Canberra, ABA file P50–0260/292.
7 W. Worth, 'Memo re visit to Brisbane–27/1/83', 28 January 1983, ABA file P50–0260/6.
8 *Courier-Mail* 25 March 1988, p. 8.
9 J. O'Hara, 'The grand design of a world's fair', *Macleans* 99, 17 March 1986, pp. 18–19.
10 P. Carroll, *Managing Expo '88: Organisational Choice and Intergovernmental Relations*, Research Paper No 15, Centre for Australian Public Sector Management, Griffith University, Brisbane, 1990, p. 20.

11  O'Brien, p. 235; ABA file P50–0260/6.
12  J. Budd, 'Paying for the party', *Courier-Mail* 26 July 1989, p. 9; K. Donohue, 'Preliminary report. An economic and financial analysis of Expo 88', paper given to Expo 88 Seminar, School of Management, Queensland Institute of Technology, Brisbane, 8 October 1988; O'Brien, p. 237.
13  *Courier-Mail* 30 March 1989, p. 3; *Courier-Mail* 15 February 1990, p. 15.
14  Carroll, p. 23.
15  N. Chenoweth, 'Expo's financial merry-go-round', *Australian Business* 5 July 1989, p. 62; Budd, p. 9.
16  Chenoweth, p. 62.
17  *Courier-Mail* 18 November 1989, p. 2.
18  *Australian Financial Review* 3 September 1991, p. 53.
19  Australian Bicentennial Authority, 'International Exhibitions: history', ABA file P50–0260, ABA, Sydney, n.d.
20  P. Carroll, 'The origins of Expo 88', paper given at Australasian Political Studies Association Conference, University of New England, Armidale, August 1988, p. 22.
21  O'Brien, p. 235.
22  Stanley and Hayman-Danker, p. 9.
23  Queensland Tourist and Travel Corporation, *Expo 88 Impact*, prepared by the National Centre for Studies in Travel and Tourism, James Cook University, Brisbane, 1989, p. 15.
24  L. Zimmerman, 'The seven eras of world's fairs—1851–1976', *Progressive Architecture* 8, 1974, pp. 64–9.
25  B. Benedict, 'The anthropology of world's fairs', in B. Benedict (ed.), *The Anthropology of World's Fairs*, The Lowie Museum of Anthropology and Scolar Press, London and Berkeley, 1983, pp. 15–18, 43–5, 53.
26  A. Short, 'Workers under glass in 1851', *Victorian Studies* 10 (2), 1966, p. 199.
27  T. Kusamitsu, 'Great Exhibitions before 1851', *History Workshop Journal* 9, Spring 1980, pp. 75–6.
28  P. Mercer, 'The Tasmanian International Exhibition, 1894–5', *Tasmanian Historical Research Association* 28, March 1981, pp. 26–7.
29  N. Harris, 'Museums, merchandising and popular taste: the struggle for influence', in I. Quimby (ed.), *Material Culture and the Study of American Life*, W.W. Norton and Co., New York, 1978, p. 158.
30  D. Ley and K. Olds, 'Landscape as spectacle: world's fairs and the culture of consumption', *Environment and Planning D: Society and Space* 6, 1988, p. 200.
31  R. Kelly, 'The dollar-a-year man', in R. Anderson and E. Wachtel (eds), *The Expo Story*, Harbour Publishing, Madeira Park, BC, Canada, 1986, p. 155.
32  Quoted by Ley and Olds, p. 202.
33  G. Davison, 'Exhibitions', *Australian Cultural History* 2, 1982/3, p. 19.
34  G. Davison, 'Festivals of nationhood: the International Exhibitions', in S.L. Goldberg and F.B. Smith (eds), *Australian Cultural History*, Cambridge University Press, Cambridge, 1988, p. 173.
35  Davison, 'Festivals of nationhood', p. 158.
36  Davison, 'Festivals', p. 172.
37  Quoted by L. Young, 'History of the Sydney International Exhibition',

*Sydney International Exhibition 1879. An Exhibition Celebrating the Centenary of the Sydney International Exhibition* exhibition catalogue, Museum of Applied Arts and Sciences, Sydney, 1979, p. 21.

38  Young, p. 19.

39  Young, p. 15; L. Young, 'The Sydney International Exposition: 1879, Australia's first Expo', *Heritage*, Winter 1988, p. 28.

40  Mercer, p. 29.

41  Mercer, p. 34; Davison, 'Festivals of nationhood', pp. 170–1.

42  Young, 'History of the Sydney International Exhibition', p. 21.

43  Mercer, pp. 35–6.

44  J. Parris and A.F.L. Shaw, 'The Melbourne International Exhibition 1880–1881', *Victorian Historical Journal* 51, November 1980, p. 246.

45  Mercer, p. 36.

46  Mercer, p. 37.

47  Mercer, p. 20.

48  D. Boorstin, *The Image. A Guide to Pseudo-Events in America*, Atheneum, New York, 1973, p. 102.

49  M. Hall and H.J. Selwood, 'America's Cup lost: paradise regained? The dynamics of a hallmark event', in G. Syme et al. (eds) *The Planning and Evaluation of Hallmark Events*, Avebury, Aldershot 1989, p. 113.

50  D. Getz, 'Special events. Defining the product', *Tourism Management* June 1989, p. 126.

51  M. Sparrow, 'A tourism planning model for hallmark events', in G. Syme et al. (eds), *The Planning and Evaluation of Hallmark Events*, Avebury, Aldershot, 1989, pp. 251–2.

52  Quoted by M. Wyman, 'That's culture', in R. Anderson and E. Wachtel (eds), *The Expo Story*, Harbour Publishing, Madeira Park, BC, Canada, 1986, p. 215.

53  *Sunday Mail* 14 August 1988, p. 27.

54  Getz, pp. 130–1.

55  M. Hall, 'Hallmark events and the planning process', in G. Syme et al. (eds), *The Planning and Evaluation of Hallmark Events*, Avebury, Aldershot, 1989, p. 22.

56  Hall, 'The politics of hallmark events', pp. 226–7.

57  H. Molotch, 'The city as a growth machine: toward a political economy of place', *American Journal of Sociology* 82 (2), 1976, pp. 309–31; H. Molotch and J. Logan, 'Tensions in the growth machine: overcoming resistance to value-free development', *Social Problems* 31 (5), 1984, pp. 483–99; P. Canan and M. Hennessy, 'The growth machine, tourism and the selling of culture', *Sociological Perspectives* 32 (2), 1989, pp. 227–43; S. Zukin 'Gentrification: culture and capital in the urban core', *Annual Review of Sociology* 13, 1987, pp. 129–47.

58  R. Smith and M. Keller, ' "Managed growth" and the politics of uneven development in New Orleans', in N. Fainstein and S. Fainstein (eds), *Restructuring the City: The Political Economy of Urban Redevelopment*, Longman, New York 1983, pp. 143–4.

59  H. Hiller 'Impact and image: the convergence of urban factors in preparing for the 1988 Calgary Winter Olympics', in G. Syme et al. (eds), *The Planning and Evaluation of Hallmark Events*, Avebury, Aldershot, 1989, pp. 119–31; H. Hiller, 'The urban transformation of a landmark event. The

Calgary Winter Olympics', *Urban Affairs Quarterly* 26 (1), 1990, pp. 118–37.
60 P. Day (ed.), *The Big Party Syndrome*, Department of Social Work, University of Queensland, St Lucia, 1988.
61 Department of the Arts, Sport, the Environment, Tourism and Territories, 'Australian Pavilion Survey', Summary of Results, DASETT, Canberra 1989.
62 Day, p. 78.
63 QTTC, p. 58.
64 '7.30 Report' ABC Television, 5 July 1988.
65 J. Warnock, 'Politics in Lotusland', *Vancouver Newest Review* 12 (7), 1987, p. 11.
66 *Courier-Mail* 14 June 1988, p. 9.
67 QTTC, p. 19.
68 Bureau of Tourism Research, *Impacts on Tourism of the Disruption to Domestic Airline Services*, BTR Occasional Paper No 5, Bureau of Tourism Research, Canberra, 1989, p. 9.
69 Bureau of Tourism Research, *BTR Tourism Update* 2 (4) 1989, p. 2.
70 BTR, *Tourism Update* 3 (2), 1990, pp. 1–3.
71 BTR, *Tourism Update* 3 (4), 1990, p. 2.
72 J. Craik, 'The Expo experience: the politics of expositions', *Journal of Australian-Canadian Studies* 7 (1–2), 1989, pp. 95–111; J. Craik, *The Role of Government in Tourist Promotion: An Evaluation of the Queensland Tourist and Travel Corporation*, Research Paper No 20, Centre for Australian Public Sector Management, Griffith University, Brisbane 1991; S. Rodgers 'South Bank challenge of century', *Courier-Mail* 15 March 1989, p. 27; M. Franklin, ' "Firm" plans for former Expo site "by next month" ', *Courier-Mail* 16 February 1990, p. 17; Budd, p. 9.
73 'South Bank Corporation Area Approved Development Plan. Part A', *Queensland Government Gazette* 293, (111), 28 April 1990, p. 2225.
74 Planning Workshop, *An Assessment of the Social Aspects and Implications of the South Bank Corporation Area Draft Development Plan*, report prepared for the Brisbane City Council, Planning Workshop, Sydney, 1989, p. 20.
75 M. Dickinson, 'Should "Brisbanism" be encouraged?', *Bulletin* 24 April 1990, pp. 95, 97.
76 *Courier-Mail* 18 November 1989, p. 1.
77 J. Doughty, 'Govt, council split on Expo commerce quota', *Courier-Mail* 22 March 1990, p. 11.
78 J. Doughty, 'Expo plan changed in major shake-up', *Courier-Mail* 14 March 1990, p. 1.
79 Dickinson, p. 97.
80 O'Brien, p. 237.
81 *Courier-Mail* 3 March 1989, p. 28.

## Chapter 9

1 *Longreach Leader* 28 January 1977 p. 8. and 4 December 1981, p. 2.
2 *Longreach Leader* 30 May 1980, p. 2.

3 *Stockman's Hall of Fame* 9, p. 3 and *Longreach Leader* 13 November 1981, p. 1.
4 *Stockman's Hall of Fame* 9, p. 3.
5 'White family sets up $30 000 trust fund', *Stockman's Hall of Fame* 6, p. 9.
6 Letters to the Editor, *Stockman's Hall of Fame* 11, p. 14.
7 Letters to the Editor, *Stockman's Hall of Fame* 15, p. 15.
8 M. Durack, 'The Aboriginal contribution to outback settlement', *Stockman's Hall of Fame* 12, p. 6.
9 'The loneliest stock route of all', *Stockman's Hall of Fame* 3 p. 5.
10 'Saga of the Scobie family', *Stockman's Hall of Fame* 3, p. 5.
11 Letters to the Editor, *Stockman's Hall of Fame* 30, p. 14.
12 Letters to the Editor, *Stockman's Hall of Fame* 17, p. 14.
13 Russel Ward, *The Australian Legend*, Oxford University Press, Melbourne, 1962.
14 'Harry Redford, our greatest cattle duffer', *Stockman's Hall of Fame* 1, p. 3.
15 Quotations from *Stockman's Hall of Fame*: 'Design competition', 2, p 2; Letters to the Editor, 3, p. 7; 'Birdsville bushies get together', 7, p. 14.
16 'Sir Ninian does the honours', *Stockman's Hall of Fame* 16, p. 1.
17 J.B. Hirst, 'The pioneer legend' in J. Carroll (ed.), *Intruders in the Bush: The Australian Quest for Identity*, Oxford University Press, Melbourne, 1982, pp. 14–37.
18 Tom Nairn, *Breakup of Britain*, Verso, London, 1981, p. 348.
19 'Early days at Maroota', *Stockman's Hall of Fame* 21, p. 7.
20 'Two new directors elected', *Stockman's Hall of Fame* 4, p. 3.
21 'ABA to consider project', *Stockman's Hall of Fame* 7, p. 2.
22 'Tourism chiefs squelch doubts on project', *Stockman's Hall of Fame* 7, p. 3.
23 A.D. Smith, *Theories of Nationalism*, Gerald Duckworth, London, 1971, p. 140; *The Ethnic Origin of Nations*, Oxford University Press, Oxford, 1986, p. 191; *Nationalist Movements*, Macmillan, London, 1976, p. 17; and John Hutchinson, *Dynamics of Cultural Nationalism*, Allen & Unwin, London, 1987, pp. 16–21.
24 'Sydney book launch', *Stockman's Hall of Fame* 12, pp. 8, 9.
25 Patrick Wright, *On Living in an Old Country: The National Past in Contemporary Britain*, Verso, London, 1985, pp. 146–7.
26 'Come on, Aussie, C'mon C'mon', *Stockman's Hall of Fame* 22, p. 1.
27 Hall of Fame News Release, August 1989.
28 'Campaign for $5 million', *Stockman's Hall of Fame* 37, p. 1.

**Chapter 10**

1 Raymond Williams, *Towards 2000*, Penguin, Harmondsworth, 1983, p. 192; these paragraphs have also drawn on Paul James, 'The nation and its postmodern critics', *Arena* 69, 1984, pp. 159–74 and Boris Frankel, 'National chauvinism and abstract internationalism', *Arena 82*, 1988, pp. 136–44.

2　*Commonwealth Parliamentary Debates* (1979) House of Representatives, Vol. 113, 5 April, pp. 1625–6.

3　*Commonwealth Parliamentary Debates* p. 1626.

4　*'National Programme', Bicentenary '88 Special Issue* 1985, p. 1.

5　Tracey Aubin, 'Dawkins attacks re-enactment as "insensitive farce" ', *Sydney Morning Herald* 5 August 1987, p. 1

6　Malcolm Andrews, 'Bi-centenary group hopes to lock up the tourists', *Australian* 25 August 1980, p. 9.

7　It has been suggested to us that the theme of journeying is gendered male. If this is accepted, the journey's appeal to the designers of the Exhibition as a universal and inclusionary theme would have to be qualified.

8　The Exhibition was organised according to six major themes, one to each module. These were: Journeys, The Australian Identity, The Environment, Living with Each Other, Living Today, and Futures.

9　Press kit given out at Exhibition preview, Ballarat, December 1987: 'The 10 Most Asked Questions About the Exhibition'.

10　For discussion of responses to the Bicentenary on the left, see: Verity Burgmann 'Flogging the Bicentenary', *Arena* 82, 1988, pp. 6–13; Colin Mercer 'The nation be in it?, *Australian Left Review* 101, 1987, pp. 8–14; David Burchell, 'Flying the flag? Nationalism and 1988', *Australian Left Review* 104, 1988, pp. 10–15.

11　Geoffrey Blainey argues that the Aborigines 'not through their own fault, had sat on rich resources and been unable to use them', so that the taking of the land could be justified because 'the more efficient use of those soils which the Aboriginals neglected' would in the end feed more people and save 'tens of millions of lives' (quoted by Ken Baker, *IPA Review* 39, p. 181).

12　The Armstrong/Reid administration spoke of unity in cathartic and thera-peutic terms, and placed extraordinarily high expectations on the Bicente-nary as a social galvaniser: 'People are yearning for a national unifying experience', David Armstrong told the Brisbane *Courier Mail* in 1982, 'after the diversions of recent years' (*Courier Mail* 6 March 1982).

13　Since 1984, when the Hyde Park Barracks Museum opened in Sydney, with a room dedicated to 'the changing faces of Sydney', there have been no less than six Australian exhibitions or new museums in which the multicultural/immigration theme dominated or figured prominently: (1) the Museum of Migration and Settlement in Adelaide; (2) 'The Story of Victoria', at the Museum of Victoria; (3) the Social History Exhibition in Perth; (4) the 'Australian Communities' exhibition in Sydney; (5) the 'First State '88' exhibition in Sydney, and (6) the Maritime Museum, Sydney.

14　Leonie Kramer to Des Kennard, 12 May 1987. Copy of letter, supplied by Leonie Kramer, in authors' possession. The Reference Panel consisted of a group of distinguished advisers appointed by the Authority to advise on the Exhibition's planning and direction. Among other members, and in addition to Dame Leonie Kramer, were Robyn Williams, Gerald Walsh, and Peter Maund of BHP.

15　*Canberra Times* 7 December 1981.

16　John Carroll, 'The denigration of Australia's British links', *IPA Review* 40, 1986, p. 27.

17　Ken Baker, 'The Bicentenary: celebration or apology?', *IPA Review* 38, 1985, pp. 175–6.

18 Baker, p. 182.
19 'Howard attacks "focus on guilt" ', *Australian* 26 January 1986, p. 2.
20 Malcolm Andrews, 'Bicentenary group hopes to lock up tourists', *Australian* 25 August 1980, p. 9.
21 Peter Ellingsen, 'Australia's Greatest Event will be BYO', *Age* 24 July 1982, p. 1.
22 'A birthday party for all Australians?', *Australian* 16 July 1985, p. 9.
23 After the failure of the Exhibition in Adelaide to attract significant audiences, some press criticism, and questioning in federal parliament of its 'cultural worth', substantial labelling of the exhibits was undertaken in mid-tour, as well as other changes designed to 'improve the performance of the Exhibition' (*Sydney Morning Herald* 14 March 1988, p. 4).
24 William Gardner, letter to editor, *Age* 26 December 1987, p. 12.
25 Desmond Kennard, letter to the editor, *Age* 1 January 1988, p. 10.
26 'Information Sheet', Exhibition Press Kit, 11 December 1987.
27 Kate Halfpenny, 'Take a Captain Cook at the greatest show in Australia', *Herald* 17 December 1987, p. 1.
28 'A birthday party for all Australians?' *Australian* 16 July 1985, p. 9.
29 Australian Bicentennial Exhibition publicity sheet, 11 December 1987.
30 Christopher Lasch, *The Culture of Narcissism*, Warner, New York, p. 24.
31 Susan Sontag, 'Notes on Camp', in *Against Interpretation*, Delta, 1979, New York, 1978, p. 280.
32 Frederic Jameson, 'Postmodernism, or the cultural logic of late capitalism', *New Left Review* 146, 1984, p. 56.
33 *Australian Bicentennial Exhibition*, p. 14.
34 ibid., p. 70.
35 *Australian Bicentennial Exhibition: Exhibit Catalogue*, Sydney 1987, p. 11.
36 A. Stephanson, 'Regarding postmodernism—a conversation with Fredric Jameson', *Social Text* 17, p. 43.
37 This 'window' is a copy of Lucien Henry's stained glass window on the southern staircase of the Sydney Town Hall. See Graeme Davison, 'Centennial celebrations', in G. Davison, J. W. McCarty and A. McLeary (eds), *Australians 1888*, Fairfax, Syme and Weldon Sydney, p. 28.
38 'A birthday party for all Australians?', *Australian* 16 July 1985, p. 9.

## Chapter 11

1 This analysis of 'First State 88' draws on ideas first developed in a radio program made with Julie Browning, and broadcast on the 'History Show' on Sydney radio 2SER on 2 August 1988.
2 David Burchell, 'The Bicentennial dilemma', *Australian Society* 6, December 1987, (12), p. 22.
3 David Harvey, *The Condition of Postmodernity—An Enquiry into the Conditions of Cultural Change*, Blackwell, Oxford, 1989, p. 48.
4 Meaghan Morris, 'Panorama: the live, the dead and the living', in Paul Foss (ed.), *Island in the Stream*, Pluto Press, Sydney, 1988, p. 182.
5 *Commonwealth of Australia, Parliamentary Debates (Hansard)* 150, 22 August 1986, Canberra, p. 554.

6   *Commonwealth of Australia, Parliamentary Debates (Hansard)* 141, 17 April 1985, Canberra, p. 1277.
7   Australian Bicentennial Authority, *Ninth Annual Report*, ABA, Sydney, 1989, p. 202.
8   Harvey, passim.
9   Abe David and Ted Wheelwright, *The Third Wave—Australian and Asian Capitalism*, Left Book Club, Sydney, 1989, p. 178.
10  S. Castles, M. Kalantzis, B. Cope and M. Morrisey, *Mistaken Identity— Multiculturalism and the Decline of Nationalism in Australia*, Pluto Press, Sydney, 1988.
11  Russel Ward, *The Australian Legend*, Oxford University Press, Melbourne, 1966, pp. 1–2.
12  Richard White, *Inventing Australia*, Allen and Unwin, Sydney, 1981, p. viii.
13  John Rickard, *Australia—A Cultural History*, Longman, London, 1988, p. 264.
14  Castles et al., pp. 5, 13.
15  Castles et al., p. 13.
16  Castles et al., p. 116.
17  Castles et al., p. 148.
18  Committee to Review Australian Studies in Tertiary Education, *Windows onto Worlds—Studying Australia at Tertiary Level*, Australian Government Publishing Service, Canberra, 1987, p. 27.
19  *Windows*, pp. 16–18.
20  *Windows*, pp. 178–9.
21  Christine Jennett and Randal G. Stewart (eds), *Politics of the Future—The Role of Social Movements*, Macmillan, Melbourne, 1989, p. 1.
22  Paul James, 'The nation and its post-modern critics', *Arena* 69, 1984, p. 165.
23  James, p. 166.
24  G. Gill, 'The enchantment of openness', *Arena* 89, 1989, p. 5.
25  See Meaghan Morris, 'A small serve of spaghetti', *Meanjin* 49 (3), Spring 1990, p. 475.
26  John Murphy, 'Conscripting the past—the Bicentenary and everyday life', in *Australian Historical Studies* 23 (91), October 1988, p. 54; Morris, 'Panorama', p. 161.
27  Harvey, p. 353.
28  Harvey, p. 117.
29  J.J. Matthews, ' "A female of all things": women and the Bicentenary', *Australian Historical Studies* 23 (91), October 1988, p. 93; Kay Daniels, 'Slicing the past', *Australian Historical Studies* 23 (91), October 1988, p. 136.

# Index

For Product Safety Concerns and Information please contact our EU
representative GPSR@taylorandfrancis.com
Taylor & Francis Verlag GmbH, Kaufingerstraße 24, 80331 München, Germany